ON FAMILIAR
TERMS

Also by Donald Keene (in English)

BOOKS

The Battles of Coxinga

The Japanese Discovery of Europe: 1720–1830

Japanese Literature: An Introduction for Western Readers

Living Japan

Bunraku: The Art of the Japanese Puppet Theatre

Nō: The Classical Theatre of Japan

Landscapes and Portraits (Appreciations of Japanese Culture)

Some Japanese Portraits

Meeting with Japan

World Within Walls: Japanese Literature of the Pre-Modern Era, 1600–1867

Dawn to the West: Japanese Literature in the Modern Era, Volume One (Fiction); Volume Two (Poetry, Drama, Criticism)

The Pleasures of Japanese Literature

Travellers of a Hundred Ages: The Japanese as Revealed Through 1,000 Years of Diaries

Seeds in the Heart: Japanese Literature from Earliest Times to the Late Sixteenth Century

TRANSLATIONS

The Setting Sun (by Dazai Osamu)

No Longer Human (by Dazai Osamu)

Five Modern Nō Plays (by Mishima Yukio)

Major Plays of Chikamatsu

The Old Woman, the Wife, and the Archer (by Fukasawa Shichirō, Uno Chiyo, and Ishikawa Jun)

After the Banquet (by Mishima Yukio)

Essays in Idleness (by Yoshida Kenkō)

Chūshingura (by Takeda Izumo, Miyoshi Shōraku, and Namiki Sōsuke)

Madame de Sade (by Mishima Yukio)

Friends (by Abe Kōbō)

Twenty Plays of the Nō Theatre (editor and translator)

The Man Who Turned into a Stick (by Abe Kōbō)

Three Plays (by Abe Kōbō)

ANTHOLOGIES

Anthology of Japanese Literature

Modern Japanese Literature

ON FAMILIAR TERMS

✳✳✳✳✳

A JOURNEY
ACROSS CULTURES

DONALD KEENE

KODANSHA INTERNATIONAL
New York • Tokyo • London

Kodansha America, Inc.
114 Fifth Avenue, New York, New York 10011, U.S.A.

Kodansha International Ltd.
17-14 Otowa 1-chome, Bunkyo-ku, Tokyo 112, Japan

Published in 1994 by Kodansha America, Inc.

Printed in the United States of America

94 95 96 97 98 6 5 4 3 2 1

Portions of this book first appeared in somewhat different
form in Japan as columns in the following newspapers:
Tokyo Shimbun and *Asahi Shimbun* (in Japanese translation);
and the *Asahi Evening News.*

Grateful acknowledgment is made to the following for
allowing their photographs to appear:
Nikkei (page iv), New Directions (page 168),
Shinchōsha (page 224, page 230), and the
Donald Keene Center of Japanese Culture at
Columbia University (all others).

Library of Congress Cataloging-in-Publication Data

Keene, Donald.
On familiar terms: a journey across cultures / Donald Keene.
p. cm. Includes index.
ISBN 1-56836-006-1
1. Keene, Donald. 2. Critics—United States—Biography.
3. Translators—United States—Biography. 4. Japanologists—United States
—Biography. I. Title.
PL713.K43A3 1994
895.6'09—dc20
[B] 93-28224   CIP

Book design by The Sarabande Press
The text of the book was set in Garamond Number 3
Composed by Graphic Composition, Inc.
Athens, Georgia

The jacket was printed by
Phoenix Color Corporation

Printed and bound by Arcata Graphics,
Fairfield, Pennsylvania

To the memory of all my teachers

CONTENTS

A NOTE ON JAPANESE NAMES AND USAGE

Japanese names are presented in Japanese order, that is, surname first and given name second. The only exceptions to this are for Japanese who have emigrated and adopted the Western fashion.

Japanese words are italicized on their first, but not subsequent, usage (except for words generally familiar to the English-reading audience, which are not italicized at all). Macrons are used to denote long vowels, except in the case of well-known place-names.

CHAPTER ONE

*****

DIGGING TO JAPAN

While I was growing up in New York someone told me that if I dug a deep enough hole in the garden I would eventually reach China. Japan seemed even farther away. I certainly began to distinguish between the two countries in the early 1930s, when I was eleven or twelve. I still have the notebook I kept for the year 1933 in which I carefully pasted articles I had cut from the newspapers every day. This was a particularly fateful year: in America, Roosevelt became president; in Germany, Hitler seized power; and in China, the Japanese army occupied Shanghai. Probably the first time I ever seriously thought about Japan was in connection with the war in China. Japan seemed like a very frightening country. I am sure that if anyone had predicted at the time that when I grew up my life would be devoted to Japan, I would have been absolutely astonished.

The period of junior high school and high school was perhaps the saddest of my life. I have few of the happy memories of childhood authors commonly describe. It was the time of the Great Depression, and New York was especially hard hit. Men sold apples at the street corners, and I remember the lines of men waiting for food outside the charity centers. In my own house, too, the depression was ever present. As the result of business losses my father was forced to give up his office and conduct business in the basement of our house. At dinner the only subject of conversation was money. The depression seemed to be an unalterable fact of life. It is true that I listened with worshipful attention to the broadcasts of President Roosevelt, my idol, but even though I desperately wanted to believe his messages of hope, I was convinced in my heart that the depression would last forever.

Even during the worst of the depression I never suffered from hunger or cold, but I was so humiliated never to have any pocket money like the other children of the neighborhood that I resorted to the contemptible expedient of stealing postage stamps from my father's office and selling them back to the post office. The depression affected me indelibly: it convinced me I must never become a businessman like my father or take any other economic risks. Dreams of success and riches never tempted me, and I became so timid about money that even today I am repelled by even the most innocent forms of gambling.

In the midst of the general atmosphere of gloom pervading the times, two tragedies struck my household. My younger sister suddenly took ill and died, leaving me an only child. Soon afterward the discord between my parents, which I had not noticed before, became apparent, and after a long series of quarrels lasting for months my father finally left the house. I felt so deeply embarrassed that it was years before I could admit even to my closest friends that my father was not living with my mother and myself.

My refuge from the unpleasant realities surrounding me was in books, and I dreamed constantly of running away. It did not matter where I went as long as I could escape from New York. I am sure that the eagerness with which I later took up my studies of China and Japan largely stemmed from an imprecise desire to flee as far as I could from my house and, if possible, from myself.

At the time of the Sino-Japanese War, while I was in high school, my sympathies were entirely with the Chinese. I remember how indignant I was when I learned that the scrap metal obtained from tearing down the elevated railway in New York had been sold to Japan; I was sure it would be used to make munitions. My father was an ardent pacifist, and this was the one respect in which he influenced me most. I was so disgusted by the thought of war that for years I was afraid even to take from the shelf the volume of the encyclopedia with the letter *W* lest by chance I should open the book to the photographs of the World War. The war in China and the civil war in Spain both filled me with dismay. Unlike some of my friends, who dreamed of fighting with the loyalists in Spain, I had no desire to fight against anyone, not even the worst tyrant, but I was appalled by the possibility that Japan, Germany, and Italy might together conquer the world. I could not think of any way of preventing this except by military force, but this was the one possibility I could not accept. I waited for a miracle to solve the problems of the world and of my own life.

On my sixteenth birthday, in June 1938, I received a letter from Columbia University informing me that I had been granted a scholarship for four years. This scholarship would not only pay for all tuition expenses but provide money for my subsistence. I was elated. The longed-for miracle seemed to have occurred. I knew now that I could graduate from the university without worrying about money. In a sudden burst of independence I resolved that henceforth I would not accept any more money from my parents.

I entered Columbia in September of that year. This was just after the signing of the Munich agreement, and most of the students were bitter about the betrayal of Czechoslovakia by England and France, but to a pacifist like myself anything seemed preferable to war.

When I registered at Columbia I thought I knew exactly what I wanted to study. Under the influence of a high school teacher I had decided to become an expert in comparative literature, and to that end I proposed to study French, German, Latin, and Greek for four years, and if possible nothing else. Although Columbia was exceptionally liberal in its requirements, my adviser informed me that I would have to take the general education courses required of all students. Perhaps it was because I could not carry through my original plan that I never properly learned German or Latin, the two languages I sacrificed, but if I had studied nothing but four European languages I would not have known the teachers who exercised the greatest influence on my life.

I was lucky to have been at Columbia. The faculty at this time was unusually brilliant, and the university policy of restricting classes to thirty or fewer students resulted in an intimacy between teachers and students that was rare in American university education.

My favorite course in my first year was in reading English translations of the great books of Western literature from Homer to Goethe. The teacher, Mark Van Doren, was a poet as well as a scholar. Unlike most teachers, he lectured without notes, but what impressed me most was that he seemed to be thinking all the time. Whatever he said was at once simple and profound. He was able also, through his questions, to draw from the students their own reactions to the books we read, considering each opinion with the utmost seriousness. Nothing could have been more flattering to green freshmen than to have this great man treat our half-formed comments with respect, somehow extracting from even the most childish opinion a kernel of wisdom that illuminated the book we were discussing. I realize now that my own teaching, to the degree I could achieve it, was modeled on Professor Van Doren's. I did not use notes either, and I tried to think afresh through each literary problem I discussed rather than present the same information year after year. But I have never been able to engage the students in my discussions. He was a Socratic philosopher, but I am more like an actor, improvising my lines as I go.

Professor Van Doren's class was crucial in my life for another, totally unpredictable reason. We were seated in the classroom in alphabetical order, and it just so happened that Keene was next to Lee, a Chinese. He became my closest friend during my years at Columbia, and it was because of him that I began the study of Chinese and eventually of Japanese. It astonishes me now when I realize that if he had been seated five feet away my whole life would have been different. I had never before felt any special interest in the Far East, and even while listening to Professor Van Doren's lectures, seated a few inches away from a Chinese, it had never occurred to me that the Western books we were reading represented only a part of the heritage of mankind. But gradually, as the result of the friendship I felt for one Chinese, I began to read books about China, at first with some bewilderment because of the unfamiliar names and terms, but later with the most intense interest. These readings did not lead me to abandon my other studies, of course, but the excitement of discovery was intoxicating.

This discovery of Asia occurred at almost exactly the same

time as my discovery of opera, and these enthusiasms, so contrary in nature, have not only remained with me to this day, but seem, even to myself, to express the two sides of my personality.

Although I enjoyed my studies at Columbia and remember many professors with gratitude and affection, my life outside the classroom was isolated and lonely. For one thing, I was forced by my mother's insistence to live at home, and this involved spending an hour and a half traveling to and from the university on the subway. The time was too precious to waste, so I ruined my eyes studying in the badly lighted cars. Moreover, the necessity of returning home every day almost as soon as classes ended cut me off from the students living in the dormitories, and even in the classrooms I made few friends. I was two years younger than most other students, and although I could hold my own intellectually, I must have seemed like a child to these classmates who were so proud of their young manhood. I might have tried to look older by taking up cigarettes or even by cultivating the few hairs on my upper lip into a mustache, but everything in me rebelled against accommodating myself to tastes that were not my own. If the others would not accept me as I was, I would do without their company.

I regret now the self-centeredness implicit in this attitude, but I really felt almost no connection between myself and the other students. Some irritated me by their attempts to behave exactly like the college students depicted in Hollywood movies, excitedly discussing the prospects of the Columbia football team or boasting of their successes with girls. I was no more attracted by their enemies, the politically active students, eternally circulating petitions and inventing new and malicious gossip about the doddering old president of the university. I suppose that my political sympathies were with these left-wing students, but they annoyed me with their arrogant insistence that they knew the truth about everything. I was delighted when the Soviet invasion of Finland upset their conviction that only capitalist countries would ever commit acts of aggression, and caused some of them to desert their cause. With the right-wing students, few in numbers, I felt no ideological sympathy, but their affectations of aristocratic disdain for the masses were amusing.

Being thus cut off from most other students by my own lack of sociability, I turned for companionship to other lonely people, especially to my Chinese friend. Unlike myself, Lee was gregarious and enjoyed the company of even the most stupid athlete, but being in a foreign country he too was lonely at times, especially during the vacations. During the summer after our first year at Columbia, 1939, the New York World's Fair was held. We went together four or five times, delighting in the fanciful architecture and the vision (as we supposed) into the world of the future. When we reached the Japanese Pavilion I was curious and wanted to go in, but Lee refused. I finally went in alone, feeling rather guilty toward my friend, whose hatred of Japan was intense. I remember nothing about the display, but the young guides and salespeople seemed so unlike the ferocious soldiers whose activities were reported in the press that I wondered how one country could produce such different kinds of people.

That summer Lee and I went swimming fairly often at a nearby beach. I enjoyed his company, but we had very little in common. He was planning to become an engineer and had no interest in the literature courses he was obliged to take as part of the general education requirements. At a loss for other conversational topics, I asked Lee to teach me Chinese characters. He drew characters in the sand and I imitated them. He would explain: "One is one horizontal stroke, two is two strokes, three is three strokes, and four is a box with a mustache in it." By the end of the summer I had learned about one hundred characters. Lee bought me a brush and Chinese ink, and I practiced writing characters enthusiastically.

When we returned to the university that autumn we agreed to meet every day for lunch at a nearby Chinese restaurant. After we had finished lunch Lee would teach me a little Chinese. The textbook was a novel written in Cantonese, full of strange words. Lee made no attempt to explain the grammar, and he was reluctant to teach me the Cantonese pronunciations. I retained very little of the vocabulary lists I painstakingly compiled each day, but learning Chinese became an obsession. This was the autumn that war broke out in Europe. Hitler had sent his armies into Poland, and England and France were threatened. The outlook was bleak, and I threw myself into this fantastically difficult study as a refuge from the newspapers.

In the autumn of 1940, after the fall of France and while the Battle of Britain was raging, I formally began the study of Chinese at Columbia. On the strength of my lessons in the Chinese restaurant I was admitted as a second-year student. The four others in the class were all women at least twenty years older than myself. The teacher, Professor Goodrich, was an American who had been born in China. He looked Chinese, despite his Western features, and suggested the traditional Confucian scholar devoted to the lore of the Chinese past. The pace of instruction was leisurely, and the texts we read dealt mainly with little boys who showed unusual filial devotion to their parents.

When my friends discovered I was studying Chinese most of them thought I must be deranged. Some even challenged me, demanding how I could be so foolhardy as to study a remote civilization when I was still so ignorant about my own. But at the end of the autumn term I dropped both French and Greek literature to concentrate on Chinese studies. I had no idea where these studies might lead me, and I was extremely afraid (being a child of the depression) that after graduation I would not find a job, but I was resolved to go on with my Chinese.

One day in the spring of 1941 a stranger came up to me in the East Asiatic Library. He said he had noticed me at the Chinese restaurant and suggested we might have dinner together that night. I agreed, though even the slightest unexpected expense inevitably upset my carefully planned budget. At dinner my new friend, George Kerr, told me about himself. He had lived for some years in Japan and Taiwan but had never learned Japanese properly. He had decided to hire a Japanese tutor that summer and study at his house in the mountains. He was afraid, however, that unless he had companions in his study he might lack the willpower to study when the weather and scenery tempted him outdoors. He asked if I would join him and another friend.

I hesitated at first. I had never considered studying Japanese before, if only because I was afraid of what my Chinese friend would think. But the chance to leave New York during the summer was too good to reject. I finally agreed, and thus another unforeseen circumstance determined my life's work.

*****

My friend's house was in the mountains of North Carolina, a place so remote (at least at that time) that the natives still spoke a kind of eighteenth-century English. The day I arrived my friend and the Japanese tutor were picking cherries in the orchard. I asked the Japanese, "What is this fruit called in Japanese?" That is how it happened that *sakurambo* was my first word of Japanese.

The textbook we used was the usual one for elementary schools, beginning with "See how the cherry blossoms have bloomed!" The tutor, a young man named Inomata, was completely inexperienced and unable to explain anything, but he was full of goodwill. At the end of the summer I had not made much progress in Japanese, but the teaching at Columbia itself was still so primitive that on the basis of my two months in the mountains I was put in the second-year Japanese class.

There were only four students in the class: a rich woman who had spent some time in Japan, a girl who was partly Japanese, a man who was learning Japanese in order to read Japanese commentaries on the Chinese classics, and myself. The teacher, Harold Henderson, had originally received a degree in chemical engineering but for some reason had gone to Japan and become an enthusiast for Japanese art and poetry. I got to know him much better after the war and found that he was a kind and generous man. He also wrote a useful book on haiku poetry and made many elegant translations of haiku, but he was not a good teacher.

Beginning that autumn a new textbook had been introduced for Americans learning Japanese. It was edited by Professors Serge Elisséeff and Edwin Reischauer of Harvard University. The purpose of the textbook was to teach people (preferably people who already knew Chinese characters) to read (but not speak) Japanese. Each lesson, as I recall, had dozens of new words of vocabulary to learn, but few of these words were repeated in subsequent lessons. It was immensely difficult for students who attempted to absorb all the new words and grammatical constructions in each lesson. It seems to have been almost equally difficult for the teacher. Again and again I caught him riffling through his dictionary to look up words that occurred in the next sentence.

Of more importance to me than these classes in Japanese language was the course on the history of Japanese thought offered by Ryūsaku Tsunoda, the man who, more than any other, I think of as my *sensei* (teacher) in the old-fashioned sense of the term. When I went to Tsunoda-sensei's office to ask permission to take a graduate course even though I was an undergraduate, he readily agreed. Soon afterward, I discovered that I was the only person who planned to take the course. The steadily deteriorating relations between Japan and the United States seemed to have diminished the interest of Columbia students in Japan. I went to see Tsunoda-sensei again and offered to drop the course, to spare him the necessity of teaching it for the benefit of only one student. He answered, "One is enough."

For the first couple of sessions I was in fact the only student present, but Tsunoda-sensei was always in the classroom before I arrived, and the blackboard would be covered with passages of classical Chinese (of the kind written by Japanese philosophers) which, at this stage in my career as a student of East Asia, I definitely could not decipher. He also brought a stack of books, so that if by chance I asked a question that required confirmation in an original text he could look up the passage at once. Naturally, I was completely incapable of asking any such questions: it was all I could do to copy into my notebook the many quotations on the blackboard. Later, three other students joined the class, and I felt somewhat less obliged each day to prove myself worthy of Tsunoda-sensei's elaborate preparations for the class.

Tsunoda-sensei had lived in America for more than twenty years, but he spoke with a strong Japanese accent. His vocabulary, however, was rich, and (most important for me) there was no mistaking his passionate interest in the matters he discussed. He communicated his enthusiasm to every student, and he was so beloved by his students, who refused to let him retire, that he was still teaching after the war at the age of eighty. I know that I shall never fully repay the indebtedness I owe him as a scholar.

Perhaps my greatest indebtedness to Tsunoda-sensei's scholarship came from the special attention he devoted to Japanese independent thinkers. This attention probably stemmed from the need he felt to believe that the traditional intellectual life of the Japanese was not monolithic but allowed the possibility of dissent. My book *The Japanese Discovery of Europe* was inspired by Tsunoda-sensei's lectures on Honda Toshiaki, one of the independent thinkers of the Tokugawa period.

The most unforgettable class was one at which Tsunoda-sensei was not present. The day after the war between Japan and the United States broke out in December 1941 I went as usual to the classroom where Tsunoda-sensei was to lecture on Japanese thought. I had felt the shock of the outbreak of war particularly because I was a pacifist by conviction and could not accept the idea of killing people, for whatever reason it might be. But I knew that for Tsunoda-sensei the problem was more complex. He loved his own country, Japan, but he also loved the United States. He did not wish either of the two countries to lose the war. He hated the Japanese militarists, but he realized that those who would suffer most in the war would be the ordinary people, not the militarists, and this kept him from hoping for an American victory. He did not appear in the classroom that day because he had been detained by the American authorities after someone had reported to the police that he frequently took long walks without a dog!

I had heard the news of the Japanese attack on Pearl Harbor

the day before. December 7, 1941, was a Sunday, and Tadashi Inomata and I took the ferryboat to Staten Island, where we spent the day hiking. When we returned that evening the *Enquirer,* the only newspaper published on Sunday nights, had a huge headline: JAPANESE ATTACK PEARL HARBOR. I laughed at this, and told Inomata about other sensational headlines in the same unreliable newspaper, such as FLOODS TO WIPE OUT NEW YORK. When I got back home, however, I discovered that for once the *Enquirer* had told the truth.

My first thought was for Tadashi Inomata. I decided I must find him and reassure him. I took the subway into the city. The faces of the other passengers looked just as bored and apathetic as always. It seemed inconceivable there should be no excitement, no reaction to the outbreak of war. Everything had the clarity and unreality of a dream.

Inomata was not in his room. I searched everywhere in the neighborhood for him, without success. I later learned that, fearful of American reaction against the Japanese, he had gone into an all-night cinema and hidden himself until the next day. As I made my way back home, dejected, I dully thought that although the war I had long dreaded had begun, and many thousands of people would surely die, my only concern was for the safety of one friend.

The day after the Japanese attack I went to Columbia University as usual. Students stood in little clusters in the halls, exchanging rumors about the number of American warships that had actually been sunk. During the first class of the morning (in nineteenth-century English poetry), Professor Lionel Trilling remarked with sardonic humor that students who were conscripted would not be required to submit term papers; however, if Trilling himself was also conscripted and sent to the same camp, he would expect papers as usual. At lunch in the Chinese restaurant I heard President Roosevelt's voice on the radio as he declared war on Japan and Germany.

Not long afterward, I heard about the Navy Japanese Language School at the University of California in Berkeley. As a pacifist, I had no desire to go to war, but I envied students who, as the result of joining the Navy, could devote their full energies to learning Japanese. Soon after the outbreak of war I heard a radio broadcast to the effect that only fifty Americans knew Japanese. This was absurd: there were hundreds of thousands of Japanese-Americans who knew Japanese. But I believed the broadcast, and I wondered if, with my scanty knowledge of Japanese, I qualified as one of the fifty. I wrote a letter to the Navy Department expressing interest in attending the Navy Japanese Language School.

In January 1942 I received a letter from Washington and went there for an interview with the administrator of the language program. I don't remember anything of the interview, but a few weeks later I received a letter telling me to report to the Language School in Berkeley. I had never traveled in the United States before, so I took a circuitous route across the continent that took five full days on the train. I had always supposed that the outbreak of war would be the most calamitous event that could befall me, but in fact I felt mainly a sense of liberation. I had succeeded at last in escaping from New York, and I was about to devote myself completely to the studies I most enjoyed.

When I left New York it had been snowing, but as I traveled south to New Orleans the landscape became green. The sunshine and the clarity of the air in the deserts of Arizona made me wonder why anyone lived in New York. In Berkeley the fruit trees were already blossoming.

I had made almost no friends at the university and had sadly concluded that it was simply not in my nature to get along successfully with other people. But within a few days of my arrival in Berkeley I made many of the friends closest to me today. The students at the Language School consisted of two groups: the sons of missionaries and others who had lived as children in Japan, and students with no experience of Japan but who had compiled outstanding academic records. At first I had little to do with the missionary group, but the latter were the most interesting and varied people I had ever met.

Classes met six days a week for four hours each day. There were two hours of reading, one of conversation, and one of dictation. The textbooks used were originally prepared for American naval and diplomatic personnel studying in Japan. The teachers were mainly *kibei;* that is, Americans of Japanese ancestry who had been sent to Japan for their education and had returned to America, but there were also first-generation Japanese and two or three missionaries. Classes were never larger than six people. With few exceptions, the teachers had never taught before. Most were too polite ever to correct a mispronunciation. But the few professionals guided the others, and instruction was generally very good.

The most difficult part of our studies was dictation. There is a great difference between a passive recognition of *kanji* (Chinese characters) and an ability to write the same kanji at dictation speed. In those days, moreover, one was not taught the abbreviated characters in use today, and we learned the old-fashioned spellings of the words rather than the phonetic spellings used today.

Perhaps the most important element in our rapid progress was that of rivalry. With the exception of the missionary children who had learned their Japanese in Japan, the students were exceptionally bright young men, eager to demonstrate their skill in learning a difficult language. There was no advantage to be gained by excelling in one's studies; but a natural spirit of rivalry made us work harder than absolutely necessary. When we entered the school it was often said that no Western person could really learn Japanese, or that it took a minimum of ten years of study in Japan before a Western person could learn Japanese, but in eleven months we completed the course, and were able to read, speak, and write Japanese. We had even had a taste of classical Japanese and of *sōsho* ("grass writing," a fluid, cursive style). Of course, we were still a long way from being fluent, but the groundwork had been successfully laid.

At the Navy Language School most of the students came into contact with Japanese people for the first time in their lives. I myself could easily count on the fingers of one hand all the Japanese I had previously met, though one of them—Tsunoda-sensei—was to exercise great influence over my life. There were about thirty Japanese or Japanese-American teachers at the school. For some of them it must have been difficult to reconcile the purpose of the school—training Americans in the Japanese language in order to enable them to gather information from captured Japanese documents and prisoners of war—with their natural attachment to Japan, where all of them (including the Japanese-Americans) had spent most of their lives. One teacher was in fact dismissed after it was discovered he had been teaching us to write such Japanese war slogans as "Asia for the Asiatics!" But the teachers, virtually without exception, threw themselves wholeheartedly into the task of enabling Americans to speak, read, and write their language.

The relations between the teachers and students were unusually close. The students quite naturally felt affection for teachers who were so patiently guiding them along the difficult byways of the Japanese language, and this affection sometimes revealed itself in unconscious imitation of the teachers' mannerisms. At the time, when two Japanese passed each other in a corridor, it was normal for each to draw in his breath; presumably indicating, as a mark of respect, that neither was breathing on the other. This habit sometimes elicited amused comments from non-Japanese, who described the Japanese "hissing" at one other. But at the school some students adopted this practice and, without a trace of parody, "hissed" as their teachers did. Bowing the head as a form of salutation was also quite common. Without realizing it, we were learning from our teachers more than elements of grammar and pronunciation.

We were also invited from time to time to the teachers' houses where we ate Japanese food, many students for the first time in their lives. I have heard that there are now at least three hundred Japanese restaurants in New York, but at that time there was only one, and in the rest of the United States—with the exception of such cities as Los Angeles and Honolulu where there were large Japanese populations—there were no Japanese restaurants at all. (On the other hand, there were innumerable Chinese restaurants all over the country.) For most students the first taste of sashimi, like a first cigarette, would be remembered for the rest of their lives as a step into the unknown. I never heard of anyone who did not like sashimi after trying it, but there was generally an element of resistance to the idea of eating raw fish.

After dinner on such occasions the teachers sometimes taught us the elements of such games as *gomoku-narabe, shōgi,* and *hana-fuda.* We did not realize it at the time, but every crumb of knowledge we acquired about Japan, whether a card game, or a nursery song, or the name of a dish of food, was an essential element of our understanding of Japanese culture as a whole. Sometimes such information helped in unexpected ways. For example, a year or two after I had graduated from the Language School, someone came into the office in Pearl Harbor where Japanese documents were translated and showed me a mysterious new "code." I recognized from one look at the "code" that it was in fact *shakuhachi* music, written with katakana notations. I knew this because one night after dinner a teacher had played the shakuhachi for us and I remembered the appearance of the music.

During all the time we were at the school we had absolutely no instruction in navigation or any other aspect of naval training. At some point, before we entered, the naval authorities had wisely decided that it would be counterproductive if our attention were divided between learning Japanese and learning about warships. We accordingly did not wear uniforms and we were not even subjected to any physical tests. (When an especially nearsighted member of our group was asked to remove his glasses and read an eye chart, he asked after removing the glasses, "Where is the chart?") Surely there have never been less martial-looking officers in any navy.

On one occasion, when a student formally requested that we be given some naval indoctrination, the captain (who had a sense of humor) solemnly read aloud all the offenses that were punishable by death, such as deliberately running one's ship aground on a reef. That was the sum total of my knowledge of the Navy. Later on, when I was actually on a battleship, I at first did not know which was the front and which the rear of the ship, and I also innocently strolled along a part of the deck reserved for the captain, but I managed somehow to survive without being reprimanded.

On graduation day from the Language School we put on uniforms for the first time. As I examined myself in the mirror, I was impressed by the reflected gold buttons and the single gold stripe around the sleeve. But I could not take myself seriously as a naval officer. When I was in junior high school I had taken part in school dramatics and had at various times dressed myself as a bullfighter or as the Dauphin, the unfortunate son of Louis XVI and Marie Antoinette. The naval uniform at first seemed like just another exotic costume, only for me to realize suddenly that wearing this uniform meant that I was really participating in a war, despite my childhood fear and hatred of war.

At the graduation ceremonies I delivered the valedictory address in Japanese. I do not remember now what I said. Probably I did little more than express, on behalf of the entire class, our gratitude to our teachers. But the fact that I was delivering the talk in Japanese, a language in which I could not have uttered a simple sentence a year earlier, meant that a milestone in my life (and in my becoming a scholar of Japan) had been passed.

After the ceremonies we each received orders from the Navy informing us of our destination. Some of us were to go to Washington, perhaps to engage in high-level work on naval policy with respect to Japan, but most of us were bound for Pearl Harbor, a name familiar since the Japanese attack a little more than a year before. I felt not the least particle of envy of those who were destined to spend the war in the safety of Washington; on the contrary, my heart leapt at the thought of Hawaii, and beyond Hawaii, Japan. I certainly did not see myself in the role of a hero, whether leading a charge or going down with my ship. I in fact never was obliged during the course of my war service to fire a gun, and even when it was appropriate for me to give commands to subordinates (as when I took part in the Okinawa campaign) I was never able to say anything more heroic than, "Who would like to go to the front lines with me?" I was not cut out to be a naval officer or to command people, and the triumphs I would have during the war were restricted to my battles with the Japanese language.

CHAPTER TWO

*****

A PACIFIC WAR

I was one of a group of Japanese-language officers who sailed in January 1943 from San Francisco for Pearl Harbor. The ship, an old passenger liner, was without doubt the dirtiest and most disagreeable I encountered during all my military service. The weather was stormy and for the first few days none of us was interested in eating the food that was prepared for real sailors (as opposed to language officers like myself.) It was with immense relief that we sighted Hawaii on the horizon.

We reported first to an office in Pearl Harbor where Japanese documents were translated. We were welcomed by a lieutenant in the regular Navy (a graduate of the Naval Academy in Annapolis), who informed us that the work we were about to do was highly secret, and that any betrayal of this secret would unquestionably lead to the death penalty. He continued, "And I personally will see to it that you are hanged." This officer never changed his low opinion of us. He refused even to acknowledge that we too were officers, invariably referring to us as "you language students." His smiles were rare and always sardonic. I later had the occasion to reflect on the paradox that he and I were officially on the same side in the war, but the Japanese prisoners, whom I liked, were enemies.

With the lieutenant's friendly words in mind we set about our first translations, the work for which we had been prepared for eleven months. Unfortunately, the material, almost without exception, was extremely boring and without any conceivable military value. There were detailed reports on the health of Japanese army units that had ceased to exist, charts of equipment down to the last nail and bottle of ink, and long lists of the names of soldiers in a battalion. At first we worked with great seriousness, wanting to believe that our translations were of the highest importance, but gradually the dullness of the material dampened our initial enthusiasm. To make life more interesting we tried translating the documents into eighteenth-century English or into a lush poetic style that hardly accorded with the contents. Everything we did exasperated the lieutenant, and almost every day he denounced us individually and collectively.

Once a translation had been completed we were expected to request another document. One day as I went to receive my next assignment, I was hoping that I might be given something slightly more absorbing than a manual or a list of hospital equipment or an old bankbook. I noticed then, for the first time, a box filled with malodorous little books. I asked the most experienced of the translators what they were and was informed that these were diaries taken from the bodies of dead Japanese soldiers and sailors. The odor was caused by the dried blood with which many of the diaries were stained. I naturally felt disinclined even to touch these books, but I was so bored by the usual documents that I was eager for a change. I gingerly selected a diary without any noticeable bloodstains, and began to read.

The handwriting made the diary far more difficult to read than printed or mimeographed materials. We had received some training at the language school in reading the *sōsho* cursive style, but what confronted me now was not the artistry of a master of calligraphy but the scrawl of a soldier writing in a foxhole in the jungles, or perhaps in some isolated salient where he could expect only death. Despite the difficulties in deciphering the script, I persisted, and eventually reading captured diaries came to be my special field of competence. (At the end of the war I actually received a decoration from the Navy for my ability to read such documents!)

These diaries had been captured on Guadalcanal. Probably even the name of this island is unknown to most people under fifty, but it was the scene in August 1942 of the first counterattack of the American forces against the Japanese, who until this time had been victorious everywhere. For almost six months possession of the island was contested in some of the most bitter fighting of the war. The diaries I read were written toward the end of the struggle for Guadalcanal, when the Japanese troops were combating not only the Americans but malaria and starvation. In some of the diaries the name Guadalcanal, rendered *Gatō* in Japanese, was written with characters meaning "Starvation Island." As I read the diaries of men who were suffering such hardships, it was impossible not to be moved.

By contrast, the letters of the American sailors I had to censor once a week revealed no ideals, and certainly no suffering, but only their reiterated desire to return to their former lives. Throughout the war this contrast haunted me—the consecration of the Japanese to their cause and the total indifference of most Americans to anything except returning home. Although I did not in the least accept the ideals of the Japanese militarists,

I could not help but feel admiration for the ordinary Japanese soldiers, and in the end I came to believe that the Japanese really deserved to win the war.

One day a week I was free from my usual duties, and I invariably went into Honolulu. The city was picturesquely ramshackle, looking like a scene from a novel by Maugham. (Honolulu is today a totally different city that retains almost nothing of its former appearance.) The first sight of Honolulu coming in from Pearl Harbor was of the row of brothels along the river, and the fat Hawaiian women sitting on the sidewalks in front selling pineapples and weaving flower leis. The shops along Hotel Street were small, dark, and mysterious. One could find almost anything in them if one searched long enough, whether recordings of "*Shina no Yoru*" ("China Night") or autographed volumes of the poetry of T. S. Eliot. But the chief attraction of the city for me was to be surrounded by Asians, for the first time in my life. For reasons which I could not analyze, I felt happier among these Japanese, Chinese, and Koreans than among Americans or Europeans. In New York I was completely indifferent to strangers on a bus or to shopkeepers or to small children in the streets, but in Honolulu even the most casual conversation or smile from a child gave me pleasure. Unlike the sailors whose letters I read, I had absolutely no desire to return home.

*****

In March 1943 I was informed with great secrecy that I was to take part in an operation. I later discovered that I had been chosen by Otis Cary (now a professor at Dōshisha University) as his "partner"; we were to constitute a team, Cary (whose spoken

Japanese was indistinguishable from that of a Japanese) would interrogate, and I would translate documents. It was anticipated, however, that sometimes Cary would translate and I interrogate, and for this reason I was taken to the Marine brig, where the prisoners were confined, to give me practice in speaking Japanese. I do not remember much about this first encounter with Japanese prisoners, but I was amused to read years later the account written by the novelist Toyoda Jō, who was one of the prisoners; he described me as having been too shy even to emerge from behind Cary, who was able so easily to chat with the Japanese. No doubt I still did not possess much confidence in my ability to express myself in Japanese.

Cary and I left Hawaii for San Francisco on a flying boat, probably a relic of the first trans-Pacific flights, and from San Francisco proceeded to San Diego, where we reported for duty. We still had no idea where the operation in which we were to participate would be fought, but occasionally hints were dropped that we would need our summer uniforms. Before boarding ship for our destination I bought another lightweight uniform. But once the ship set sail the wind became not warmer but considerably colder, and we realized that we had been deliberately misinformed; we were heading north to the frigid Aleutian islands.

I had been in the Navy for well over a year, but until I boarded the old battleship *Pennsylvania* on my way to the North Pacific I had never set foot on a warship. The novelty of the experience made it interesting for the first few days, but the pleasure did not last long. There was little to occupy my time, and the small cabin (formerly the captain's pantry) was filled with eight or nine junior officers with bunks in tiers, like an old-fashioned third-class sleeper. The thought seldom crossed my mind that I was approaching a dangerous area and that I would likely see war, which I had dreaded since childhood; like most people of my age, I was convinced that I was immortal and I saw myself as a witness to the warfare rather than as a participant.

At a place called Cold Bay in Alaska, Cary and I were transferred to an Army transport. The ship was carrying the Seventh Division to the island of Attu. We were told that prior to boarding ship the division had been trained in desert warfare, an example of the conspicuous lack of coordination that typified military operations. On the ship were Army interpreters—nisei from California and elsewhere. Our teachers at the Navy Language School had included many nisei, but they were not in uniform, and nothing suggested that they might be experiencing conflicts of loyalty between their Japanese ancestry (and, often, their education in Japan) and their duties as American citizens; but seeing the nisei on the transport in Army uniforms and realizing that they might be called upon to kill Japanese during the ensuing operation, I wondered if they might not feel some internal conflicts. I must say, however, that neither at this time nor at any time later did I detect the slightest ambivalence.

They might well have felt considerable resentment. The Navy absolutely refused to admit even one Japanese-American to its ranks; that was one reason why the Navy had spent such large sums of money in teaching Japanese to me and the others. It is true that there were many nisei in the Army, including soldiers who distinguished themselves in the fighting in Italy, and others who served as interpreters and translators in the Pacific area; but, regardless of their education, none of them was a commissioned officer. This injustice undoubtedly rankled, and the knowledge that they were not the only ones discriminated against—there were virtually no other Asians or blacks in the Navy except as cooks and attendants—could not have brought much solace. It must be difficult for Americans who have served in more recent

wars to imagine that such discrimination ever existed. I sometimes feel a sentimental longing for the past (like everyone else)
and contrast the harsh realities of the present with romanticized memories of the more civilized way of life that prevailed
in my childhood and youth, but with respect to racial discrimination the situation in the world has unquestionably improved.

The nisei interpreters had been informed that the Navy interpreters and translators were all incompetent, and Cary and I, in
our different ways, felt obliged to prove that this was not true.
But as I became more friendly with these Japanese-Americans I
had many occasions to ponder, probably for the first time in my
life, what it meant to be a Japanese or an American.

The landing on Attu, the westernmost of the Aleutian Islands,
was effected in an almost impenetrable fog. As we moved toward
shore, we heard terrible screams from nearby. Later, we learned
that the ramp of a landing barge had mistakenly been lowered
and the soldiers aboard were dropped into the sea. The water is
so cold in the northern Pacific that it can kill a man in minutes
if not seconds. This was my first taste of war.

Cary and I were still wearing our thin summer uniforms; because of the usual stupid rivalry or even hostility between Army
and Navy, we (unlike the soldiers) could not obtain warm clothes
aboard ship, and we shivered as we made our way along the
beach. Then I saw, lying in the sand, a dead Japanese soldier. He
was the first dead person I had ever seen. When I was a child I
was taken to a waxwork museum and had been terrified by the
unblinking eyes and motionless hands of the people so realisti-
cally portrayed. Now, before my eyes, was no waxwork effigy but
a human being who, perhaps up to a few minutes earlier, had

been patrolling the beach or firing his gun. I stared in horror as I absorbed the reality of my second taste of war.

My recollections of the campaign on Attu are confused. I recall first of all the tundra that released icy water when one stepped on it, and became liquid mud if one penetrated the surface. I recall, too, trying to translate captured documents even as my nose kept running maddeningly. But most of all, I recall the fate of the Japanese garrison on the island: of the some two thousand men, at least half committed suicide. This was the *gyokusai* ("breaking of the jewel") reported proudly in the Japanese press as a paradigm of how Japanese soldiers should behave. Although Japanese had become prisoners of war in the Russo-Japanese War without incurring lifetime disgrace, those who fought the Pacific War were indoctrinated with the belief that Japanese soldiers were never taken alive. A soldier who was left with only one hand grenade did not throw it at the enemy but pressed it against his chest, rather than become a prisoner.

I could not accept such motivation, but the gyokusai on Attu profoundly impressed people, not only in Japan but in regions of Southeast Asia which the Japanese army had occupied. Chairil Anwar, perhaps the outstanding Indonesian poet of this century, wrote to his beloved Ida about Colonel Yamasaki, the commander of the Attu garrison, who had committed suicide along with his troops: "Colonel Jamasaki, Ida! A brave warrior from Attu! Ah, be in harmony with this noble spirit. The personification of the ideal! Observe, my darling, the service given to his Homeland, ever more fervently, by Tennō Heika [the emperor], the sentiments reaching higher and higher—and I think most of them must be included in that life energy which flares up fantastically, until it is concluded in death." (Translation by Burton Raffel)

My inability to share the fascination with death of the many

Japanese soldiers who had killed themselves on Attu probably represented a first setback in my attempt to understand the Japanese. I thought at the time that the suicides were a manifestation of fanaticism. I no longer think that, and when I read the love-suicide plays of Chikamatsu Monzaemon, I sympathize with the men and women who choose to die rather than live in a hostile world. But suicide has robbed me of some precious Japanese friends, and despite my attempts to empathize, I have never really experienced the appeal of the god of death.

Although the official Japanese reports on the campaign on Attu proclaimed that the garrison had died to the last man (the word *gyokusai* came into common usage from this time), there was in fact a handful of Japanese prisoners, both military and civil employees of the army. These men were in no way remarkable except in the sense that they were the sole survivors of the two thousand Japanese who were on Attu. The Americans continued to meet the same intense resistance throughout subsequent campaigns—so much so that at times I wondered if, when the war was over, the only Japanese survivors might not be the few prisoners we had taken.

The next campaign in which I participated was the attack on Kiska, another island in the Aleutian chain which had been occupied by the Japanese in 1942. For weeks prior to the actual landing on the island we had been informed by the photographic interpreters that they could detect no sign of movement on the island, but the aviators continued to report that they were encountering antiaircraft fire, and their testimony, although deluded, was believed. Preparations for the attack were accordingly made with the assumption that the Japanese garrison was still there and that the resistance would be as severe as on Attu.

When we landed we discovered, to our great relief, that the aviators were wrong: there was not a single Japanese on the island. It was a mystery how they had managed to escape despite the American naval blockade, and this mystery would not be solved until, a year or so later, I read the diary of a Japanese naval officer who had taken part in the evacuation of the island. This discovery was, I think, my greatest contribution to the war effort.

Even when it became absolutely clear there were no Japanese on the island, the American and Canadian troops landed in exactly the same manner as if in the teeth of desperate resistance. Some soldiers were actually killed when one group of Americans fired on another, taking them for Japanese.

It occurred to one of the high-ranking officers, deprived of the satisfaction of a fight for Kiska, that there might be Japanese soldiers on the nearby island of Little Kiska, and it was decided to send a boat to investigate. I went along as the interpreter. The fog was so thick that we had hardly left Kiska when it was blotted from sight. An Army officer was navigating the boat with a compass, when he suddenly noticed the Navy insignia on my cap and insisted I take command. I was too embarrassed to admit that, despite being in the Navy, I knew nothing of navigation. I was much more likely to direct the boat to the North Pole than to Little Kiska. Fortunately, even as we politely argued about who should be in command, Little Kiska appeared through the fog. I was saved again.

The Japanese military had of course anticipated that Kiska would be occupied by the Americans, and they left behind messages such as one I remember seeing on a blackboard at an underground headquarters, "Americans! You are dancing under foolish orders of Roosevelt!" I remember also an inscription in Japanese on a signboard. The least competent of the American translators of Japanese brought me the signboard saying, "Of course I get the general meaning, but I am not sure *exactly* what

This picture was taken in Adak in the Aleutian Islands, shortly before the attack on Kiska in the summer of 1943. I am standing at left holding a carbine (which I never fired) in one hand and a Kenkyusha Japanese-English dictionary in the other. Otis Cary is standing at right.

it means." The inscription was perfectly clear: BUBONIC PLAGUE VICTIMS GATHERING POINT. I don't know if there were actually any Japanese victims of bubonic plague, or if the signboard was intended for our benefit alone, but a hasty appeal for serum was sent to San Francisco, and for days afterward we searched our bodies for telltale spots.

Once the Kiska campaign was officially over, we were sent back to Hawaii aboard an ammunition ship. This ship traveled by itself because if it exploded while in a convoy it would blow up all the other ships. We sat on sixteen-inch shells in the ship's hold to see nightly movies. There were only two films: one was *Casablanca,* and I have forgotten the other. I saw *Casablanca* about fifteen times in the course of the voyage, and even now remember some of the dialogue.

The high point of the voyage was sighting Hawaii. I know how unlikely it is, but I distinctly recall that as we approached the islands we could smell their fragrance. But perhaps this was no more than pleasure at seeing such lovely islands after the bleakness of the Aleutians.

*****

For the next year and a half—from September 1943 to March 1945—I was stationed in Honolulu. I worked in a joint Army-Navy translation office that had been established on Kapiolani Boulevard in what was then a rather forlorn section of the city. The primary purpose of this office was the translation of handwritten documents. The reason why it was a joint office was that the Navy correctly believed the Army nisei translators would be better able to decipher difficult handwriting than the Navy translators. However, the Navy refused to allow nisei, even men in American Army uniforms, onto the naval base at Pearl Harbor, and the joint office was therefore set up in Honolulu. It was not difficult for me to imagine how the nisei felt about such discrimination, but everybody was happy to be living and working in Honolulu, rather than at some military base.

Our office was in a two-story building disguised by a sign proclaiming that this was the STATE HOME FURNISHINGS store. There was even a display of furniture in a window facing the street, together with a small sign saying the place was temporarily closed. Perhaps a few people were deceived, but it was not possible to maintain secrecy in the eyes of our neighbors when they could see thirty nisei soldiers, many of them from Hawaii, and four or five young naval officers entering the building each morning. Next to our building was a factory where the young women who made cushions soon entered into friendly relations with the soldiers. Across the street was a restaurant where we often ate lunch, and the waitresses were equally friendly. They may not have known that we were translating captured documents, but it did not take a genius to guess that we were engaged in some sort of intelligence operation.

I lived in Honolulu in a big house shared by six intelligence officers. We were entitled to one day off each week, and I arranged to divide this day into two mornings that I spent at the University of Hawaii studying Japanese literature. A few of the Navy translators joined me in the class. During the first term we read modern novels, one a week, and then wrote book reports in Japanese. I had never before read anything in Japanese as long as a novel, and it was exhilarating to discover I could do it. This experience emboldened me to ask the professor to teach us *The Tale of Genji*. Needless to say, I had no idea how difficult it was!

Life in Honolulu was pleasant for most of us. Those who had wives or children naturally missed them, but we all knew how much luckier we were than soldiers in foxholes or sailors on destroyers. But there was something unreal about our lives. We would spend most days translating diaries, letters, notebooks, and the like, but it was difficult to imagine that what we were doing was of any conceivable use to anybody. And there was the irritation of being under a commanding officer whom we disliked. This reserve officer was absolutely cold toward us, supposing that he was maintaining discipline, and so meticulous in his speech that one could practically hear the commas and semicolons. But when depressed I could look out of the windows of the former State Home Furnishings and see water buffaloes plodding in the nearby fields, and the Oahu mountains crisscrossed with rainbows.

The most vivid memories of my life in Hawaii during the war years are of the prisoners I interrogated. Some officers (like Otis Cary) were primarily engaged in interrogation, but the rest of us were sent to the prisoner-of-war stockade only occasionally, to keep us from forgetting our conversational Japanese. I looked forward to these sessions, and I was greatly helped by Cary, who saw to it that I was given intellectual prisoners to interrogate.

At first, however, most of the prisoners were not Japanese but Koreans. They had been conscripted into "patriotic labor corps" by the Japanese army, but extremely few of them entertained patriotic sentiments toward Japan. Unlike the Japanese, they saw no reason to die in combat, and, when they could, they became prisoners. They possessed very little military information, and the interrogation sessions usually drifted into conversations about the prisoner's family or work. Many were of the same age as I, and it was easy to become friends. I felt so enthusiastic about them that I started taking Korean lessons from a priest in Honolulu. Whenever I went to the stockade I brought them kimchi and other Korean food.

I could not think of these Koreans as enemies. Were they not victims of the Japanese? Sometimes I would go to the stockade in the evening just for the pleasure of talking with them. I did have one shock, however. The Korean prisoners had requested permission to drill in military style, facing right or about-facing in the usual way. One day I was talking with a prisoner while the rest were busily engaged in their drill. He said, looking out at the others, "When I see them drilling that way, it makes me think of a book I once read, a book that inspired me." I asked him what it was. He answered, "*Wa ga Tōsō.*" At first the Japanese words did not mean anything to me, but suddenly I realized that they were a translation of *Mein Kampf.* I was appalled that anyone should have been inspired by Hitler and said so. "But we all read it and believed it," he said. I realized this must be so, and I could not really blame a man who was not well educated for having been taken in by propaganda; but all the same, I felt a stab of pain as I thought of all that separated me from this friend.

There were far fewer Japanese prisoners. Most of them had been taken prisoner involuntarily, when they were stunned by an explosion or had fallen ill. Some had hidden in the jungle until they all but starved. I remember Takahashi Yoshiki, a Dō-mei news agency reporter who was captured on Guam. When I first saw him he was so emaciated that when he smiled the skin of his face sagged instead of curving upward. After the war he published under the pseudonym Horiuchi Tan accounts of my interrogation. He wrote that when I asked him if he knew of executed American prisoners and he denied any knowledge, I had given a sinister smile that showed I *knew* he actually had seen a prisoner executed. My smile was not sinister; I am sure that I believed him and I smiled because I was relieved he knew nothing about this terrible incident.

The most memorable experience I had with the Japanese prisoners of war occurred the night I took a phonograph to the stockade. A prisoner with whom I had become especially friendly, a young naval officer who had been captured on Saipan while unconscious from an explosion, had told me how much he missed hearing classical music. It was easy for me to imagine what a deprivation this would be, and I decided to let him and the others hear some music. He said that his favorite piece was Beethoven's *Eroica* symphony, and that was what I chose.

The phonograph was an inexpensive portable, and the sound was poor, but I arranged to hold the "concert" in the shower room where the sound would echo and be amplified. I assembled the prisoners and told them I would play first some Japanese music, and then the Beethoven symphony. I had bought the Japanese records at a shop in Honolulu without any knowledge of which songs were likely to please the prisoners. It occurred to me only much later that it might be a painful rather than an enjoyable experience for these Japanese to hear music that would surely remind them of home and the people they loved. My first consideration was the Beethoven, and the popular songs were intended to keep prisoners who did not like classical music from feeling they had been ignored.

I played four or five popular records, then explained that the next piece would be long, and suggested that those who did not like classical music should leave, though hardly anyone did. Of course, these were short-play records, so the symphony was on five records. Nobody said a word during the performance or while I changed records. I had never been so moved by that symphony before, and even today, if someone asks me which is my favorite symphony I say the *Eroica,* remembering that experience. At first I was somewhat self-consciously aware that I was sharing music with enemy prisoners, but when I looked at their faces, I realized that it did not make sense under such circumstances to speak of enemies. After a while I could think only of the music, and when the symphony ended I knew that I had had an experience I would never forget.

When the music was over some of the prisoners crowded around me to ask questions. Who was the conductor? What kind of needle had I used? Was this the same orchestra that had appeared in the film *Orchestra Girl?* Nobody said he was glad to have heard the music, but I did not need words to understand this.

It was too late by this time for a bus back to Honolulu, so I stood by the side of the road and hitchhiked. I was picked up by a naval officer who asked what I was doing with the phonograph. Foolishly, I told him. He was enraged. He demanded, "Do you think the Japanese play music to our prisoners?" I did not try to explain but sat in silence until we reached the city.

Some years later my friend Takahashi wrote an article on the same concert. He too was puzzled about why I had played music to the prisoners. Was I trying to catch them off guard when they listened to music? Or had I chosen this particular symphony by Beethoven because I wanted to indocrinate them with his ideals? But at the end of his article he admitted that while I was listening to the music I seemed to be thinking of nothing else.

I was only twenty-one when I first interrogated prisoners of war. I had had virtually no experience of the world except for what I had learned from books. I had no clear political convictions beyond a general dislike for any form of coercion or fanaticism. I had never visited Japan, and my knowledge of the Japanese way of life was confined to its survival among Japanese-Americans, especially my teachers at the Navy Japanese Language School. I was capable of speaking Japanese fairly well, but subtleties of expression (such as the proper level of politeness to use when talking with prisoners) were quite beyond my ability. And yet I was obliged again and again to guide and encourage men who were my seniors in every respect.

When I interrogated intellectual prisoners and found that we shared tastes in literature and music, it was easy to assume that they also deplored the actions of the Japanese militarists that had led to the war, and it came as a shock to discover that some prisoners were convinced that the Japanese aims had been misunderstood and that the Japanese desired not domination of Asia but the liberation of Asia from the colonial powers. Sometimes too the prisoners would ask me questions that I found hard to answer, such as the causes of race riots in Detroit, a subject that had been carefully reported in the Japanese press.

I was out of my depth when it came to discussing politics, but I felt sure of one thing, that these prisoners must someday play an important part in postwar Japan, and I wanted to help them. When one man insisted that becoming a prisoner was such a terrible disgrace that he could never return to Japan, I searched in the library of the University of Hawaii until I found a book that described how Japanese who had been captured during the Russo-Japanese War of 1904–1905 had in fact returned to Japan. (There was even an account of how Japanese officers had complained that they were not being shown proper respect and insisting that they should be given vodka and allowed to skate on the ice.) When a prisoner seemed absolutely convinced of the sanctity of the imperial family, I borrowed from the library works of Japanese proletarian literature for his edification.

I see now that, instead of comforting them, I may have been making it even more difficult for them to adjust to the limbo of the prisoner-of-war camp.

*****

The sessions I had with Japanese prisoners were by far the most interesting part of my work in Hawaii. Most of my time was spent, however, making translations of captured documents. In the meantime, battles were being fought on different islands in the Pacific, slowly getting nearer to Japan. A few members of my office would be sent out as interpreters for each operation, and when they came back with sunburned faces we would listen to their accounts of the fighting with something close to envy. One day was much like another at the office in Honolulu, but these people had confronted death. Although I had absolutely no desire to kill or be killed, I kept thinking that unless I experienced war at first hand I would not really know the nature of the most important event of my life.

It was therefore with excitement, rather than fear, that one day in March 1945 I reported to CINCPAC, the headquarters of the commander of the Pacific Fleet. I knew this meant I would be sent out on an operation somewhere. A group of us translators and interpreters were ushered into a room at the headquarters building near Pearl Harbor and were briefed by an officer. The next objective, we were informed, was Okinawa. I could hear a gasp go through the group at this news. The American forces had been "island hopping" ever since the battle for Guadalcanal, but Japan still seemed very remote, and nothing had shaken my basic conviction that the war would probably last forever. But Okinawa was part of Japan—the war might actually end!

My next thought was of the Okinawan civilians. Up to that

point the war in the Pacific had been fought over islands with small civilian populations (or, in the case of Attu, no civilians at all), but on Okinawa there would be hundreds of thousands of people in addition to the military, and many surely would be killed. By chance, most of the Japanese-American friends I had made in Hawaii were of Okinawan descent, and I felt a special warmth for them. I wanted to tell them about my destination, but of course this was something I absolutely could not reveal.

That day we were also given a general description of Okinawa. I remember especially a talk by a doctor on the poisonous snakes. (During the fighting he was the one American to be bitten by a snake!) I left the briefing session with feelings of excitement and, I confess, fear. It was evident even to me that the Okinawa operation would involve great danger not only from the Japanese army garrison but from planes and ships sent from Japan itself.

The only preparation I made for going to Okinawa was to visit an oculist in Honolulu to ask if there were not some way of strengthening my shortsighted eyes. I was afraid that I might lose my eyeglasses in combat. The doctor prescribed eye exercises that I practiced constantly, but without noticeable results. I also hid some captured diaries written by Japanese soldiers and sailors in which the writers, realizing that they would be killed, asked the American who found the diaries to return them to their families after the war. We were supposed to forward captured documents to Washington, but I put these aside, intending to send them to the writers' families as requested. But while I was on Okinawa someone went through my belongings and removed the diaries. I wonder where they are now.

I could not say good-bye to my friends but took off one day in secret, with a group of interpreters, for Samar in the Philippines. The plane stopped again and again at American island bases. Wherever we stopped (since we were flying westward) it was always breakfast time, and there being nothing else to do, we would go to the dining hall and eat another stack of pancakes with nauseating syrup as at the previous island. It seemed like a grim foretaste of the world after the war.

Samar was my first experience of the tropics—not the pleasant warmth of Hawaii but the killing heat of a merciless sun. The streets of the village were liquid mud after a shower, and the houses tilted precariously in every direction. Naked children with stomachs distended by malnutrition wandered through the streets. I supposed that these dismal conditions were the result of intensive fighting, but I learned that there had been no fighting at all in this village; the misery was the normal state of affairs. I had never before realized the irony that in the tropics, where plants and trees overflow in wild abundance, nature is so stingy with edible matter.

We went by launch from Samar to Leyte, following the incredibly green coast. The fighting on Leyte had ended only a few months before, but already there was in Tacloban, the main town of Leyte, a large building of woven palm fronds that served as the officers' club. The place did not interest me, and I decided to go to the stockade of the Japanese prisoners of war, where I was sure of finding someone agreeable with whom to talk. I had no car, so I hitchhiked. The Filipinos who picked me up spoke old-fashioned, very polite English that was welcome after the usual military language. When I told them that I wanted to go to the prisoner-of-war camp, they seemed surprised. I learned that it had been difficult to restrain Filipinos from killing whatever Japanese they discovered in the jungles. "Yes," said the driver of the truck in which I was riding, "the prisoners in the camp should be considered the lucky ones."

The prisoner-of-war stockade on Leyte was far bigger than I expected. Evidently many Japanese soldiers had surrendered here, though this had not been reported in the press. The prisoners with whom I spoke seemed more disconsolate than those I had known in Hawaii, perhaps because they had not yet had sufficient time to become accustomed to being alive and in enemy hands. Oddly enough, I still hear occasionally from one of the prisoners I met at that time.

I forget now how long I spent on Leyte. Needless to say, I did not keep a diary or make any other kind of notations that might help me now to recall how I spent my days there. It was a transitional period with nothing special to do except wait for the order to board ship for Okinawa. No doubt I was bored most of the time. Finally, the order came. I had been assigned to the command ship of a convoy of transports. By this time the attacks of the kamikaze planes had succeeded in sinking a fair number of American ships, and I felt more nervous about this danger than when I had headed for the Aleutian islands. Fortunately, I still believed in my own immortality, and I was excited rather than frightened at the prospect of treading Japanese soil for the first time.

My only recollections of the ship are that it was extremely hot all the time. I had hated the Aleutians because of the unremitting cold, but I now decided that it was appropriate that poets always described hell as being hot. Quite apart from the tension (both conscious and unconscious) of being aware that the ship was advancing into a dangerous area, the heat made it difficult to sleep. Very early one morning, unable to sleep, I went out on deck where it was cooler. I could see the other ships of the convoy moving in parallel courses. Suddenly I noticed that a distant dark point in the sky was approaching. I realized that it must be a kamikaze plane. The speck grew larger, and soon it was apparent that it was headed for the ship I was on, by far the largest of the convoy. I stared at it in fascination, unable to think of anything. There was nowhere I could run to, no escape. The plane began to descend, aiming all the while at my ship. It was perfectly clear that the pilot intended to crash against it with a bomb or torpedo. I was incapable of movement or even of crying out. Then, the incredible happened: the descending plane struck the top of the mast of the adjacent ship and plunged into the sea. All this happened in the space of seconds. I later heard that the pilot had been rescued.

I suppose that this was the closest encounter with death I have ever experienced. I have been frightened at times when the plane in which I am traveling has dumped its fuel in the ocean and returned to a distant airport. On several occasions during the fighting on Okinawa I felt a stab of fear, wondering if the next cannon barrage might not hit the shelter where I cowered. And no doubt I have been in danger of my life more than once when recklessly crossing a street in New York or Tokyo. But this was the only time I saw death headed in my direction, as clearly as if I had been standing before a firing squad. The experience seems to have cured me of the romantic dreams, dating back to boyhood days, of reveling in dangerous adventures.

The landing on Okinawa on April 1 was unexpectedly easy, but hardly was I on shore than I was faced with a situation for which I was unprepared. A woman about thirty, with a baby in her arms and a small child by her side, was wandering over the beach. I ran up to her and told her that it was dangerous, and that she should follow me to a safe place. She paid no attention to my words but kept repeating something that I could not understand. Unable to communicate with her, I became frantic, and finally picked up the child and ran with it to a medical unit. The woman ran after me, still repeating again and again the same words. I have no idea what she was saying, but I realized later that many Okinawans, especially women, did not speak Japanese at this time. Later on in the day I acquired an interpreter, a boy of nine or ten who had been to school and could speak Japanese. I went around with him from cave to cave, wherever the Okinawan civilians might be hiding, persuading them to come out. It is bad enough in warfare when the combatants are all military personnel, but when old people, women, and children, some of them with no idea what is happening to them, are caught up in the fighting, the madness of war becomes excruciatingly evident.

On the same day two prisoners were taken, an army lieutenant and a navy ensign. They were kept inside a stockade, a hastily built enclosure near the beach surrounded by barbed wire, until a more suitable place could be found to keep them. The army officer seemed cheerful and even joked with the Americans, but the navy officer was obviously tormented by the thought that he had committed a crime, or at least an unpardonable error, in having allowed himself to be taken prisoner.

Some days later, when that part of Okinawa had been secured, I went to see him again. He asked me if I would talk with him not as an enemy officer but as a fellow "student soldier." Of course, I agreed. He asked me what point there was for him to go on living. I had been asked similar questions by the prisoners I knew in Hawaii, but here we were but a short distance from the front lines where many people were being killed every day. It would seem that if one wished to die, nothing could be easier, but because this man was a prisoner, he was not free to die; in fact, every effort would be made to keep him from killing himself. He could perhaps, in the ancient manner, have bitten off his tongue and bled to death. Or he might have done something to make a trigger-happy guard fire. But I tried, using language that was now familiar to me, to persuade him to live. Perhaps I convinced him, or perhaps he simply never had an opportunity to kill himself.

A few years after the war ended I had a letter from the army officer in which he happily styled himself "Prisoner Number One" and told me about the business he had founded in Nagoya after being discharged from the military. I hoped for some communication from the navy officer, anything at all that would indicate that he was glad he had not died on Okinawa, but nothing ever came. Five or six years ago I was asked by a weekly magazine in Tokyo which carries a column devoted to requests by readers for things they are searching for if I was not looking for some book or scholarly reference, or perhaps a person I had not seen in many years. I remembered the navy officer from Okinawa and asked in the column about his whereabouts, using the pseudonym he had used when captured so as not to embarrass him. I had an answer, not from the man himself but from a friend, who told me that the man was teaching high school in Tokyo. The friend asked me if I wished him to arrange a meeting with the navy officer. "Only if he wants to meet me," I replied. That was the last I heard of him.

Perhaps the officer had still not forgiven himself for having become a prisoner, despite all the changes that had occurred in Japanese society and in Japanese interpretations of history. Or perhaps he quite reasonably decided that even if we met we would not have much in common. Certainly, there was nothing in the bleak prisoner-of-war stockade or the sounds of distant gunfire to make either of us feel nostalgic. His request that we talk as fellow students rather than as enemies, which so profoundly moved me at the time, may have been no more than a

45

momentary impulse that soon passed. But forty-five years after our first meeting, when I have forgotten so much of what I experienced, I still remember clearly that attempt to transcend the battle raging around us and talk, one student to another.

*****

On Okinawa I was at first attached to the headquarters of an Army corps. The Navy had little need for most of its interpreters and was generally willing to lend them to the Army. Corps headquarters was a relatively peaceful place, far from the battle lines, but there were occasional bombardments and air raids. I remember sharing a pup tent with another officer who was terrified of being killed in a raid. He literally shook with fear, the first time I ever saw anyone in the grip of such fright, and he kept murmuring his wife's name. I was surprised to discover that I was not afraid, although I am surely one of the least heroic people in the world. I was still convinced, in the face of all the contrary evidence around me, that I would not die, and I felt something like amusement as I watched my friend tremble.

But death was a constant presence. Even if only one man at the corps headquarters was killed as the result of a bombardment, it was likely to be someone I knew. One victim was a sergeant whom I had envied because he could speak fluent Persian. Another was a man with a rather overpowering sense of humor who was constantly telling jokes. Why, I wondered, was one man killed and another spared? It was like some strange lottery which awarded death to people who held the lucky numbers.

During the raids the safest places were the Okinawan tombs built into the hillsides. These imposing stone edifices were regarded with suspicion by the Americans as possible hideouts for

Japanese military, but nobody seemed afraid to disturb the ghosts that might be haunting them. Inside the tombs were large, brightly colored ceramic vessels that held the remains of people who had died under quieter circumstances than those that threatened us every day.

The hills were riddled with caves as well as tombs. The American soldiers would use bullhorns to call to anyone who might be hiding inside. "*Dete koi!*" they shouted, "Get out!" These were their only words of Japanese. If nobody emerged, they sometimes built fires at the mouth of a cave to "smoke out" anyone who might be hiding. On one occasion I was present when some civilians who had been inside a cave were forced out by the smoke. There were only old people and children. It would be hard to imagine a more pitiful group of victims of the war. When the soldiers moved on to the next cave, I stopped them from building a fire, saying that I would go in myself and persuade the people to come out. I went in confidently, only to see to my astonishment a Japanese soldier sitting behind a gun. I have no idea why he did not fire on me. I leaped out of the way of his gun and never again attempted such heroics.

On another occasion I went into a cave where someone had discovered Japanese documents. The cave, which slanted down a long shaft, had evidently been used to store valuables. In one chest I found medals and decorations, in another handfuls of documents. But when I used my flashlight to examine one I found that it was twenty years old. It was obvious that there was absolutely nothing of military significance in these papers. I climbed back to the mouth of the cave where I saw another interpreter. He said, "I didn't know you were down there. They were just about to seal off the cave." If I had lingered a little longer over the documents I might never have emerged alive. I had a sudden vision of beating against walls of stone with my fists. In retrospect it is clear that I had every reason to be just as frightened as my friend.

But even during the worst of the fighting there were occasional moments of humor. The wedding of Lieutenant Kimura and his Okinawan bride ranks high among such moments. Kimura and his lady friend had surrendered together, probably the first time during the war that a Japanese officer had surrendered with a woman. Some American intelligence expert decided that this couple might make a good source of information about the Japanese military, and it was arranged to have interpreters eavesdrop twenty-four hours a day on the room where the couple were detained. What could be more absurd than to suppose that a man and woman in bed would chat about military secrets? Nevertheless, the plan went through and several nisei interpreters spent their days listening to whatever sounds emerged from the room.

At this point the commanding officer, a moral man, expressed shock that a man and woman were living together even though they were not married. It was decided therefore to hold a wedding. As far as I know, Kimura and the lady raised no objections, but they probably had not had a wedding in mind when they surrendered to the Americans. The wedding was conducted by a Protestant minister in the same way as in a church, but a torii, the kind of arch found at Shinto shrines, had hastily been erected to give an authentic Japanese touch. Somebody played on an accordion the strains of the "Wedding March" from *Lohengrin,* but unfortunately, no one had taken the precaution of briefing Kimura on the conduct of a Christian wedding. When he was given a ring, instead of placing it on the third finger of his bride's left hand, he put it in his pocket, and, to the disappointment of everybody, he failed to kiss his bride at the end. Photographs of the wedding ceremony later appeared in various American magazines, and some readers expressed anger over the excessive kindness we had shown to an enemy prisoner. I wonder what happened to Mr. and Mrs. Kimura afterward.

It was about this time that word came that the 96th Infantry Division needed a language officer. I volunteered, testing myself as usual, to see if I had the courage to leave the safety of the corps headquarters for an Army division which was actively engaged in the fighting. From the first night spent at the 96th Division I was made aware of the difference in the danger. The headquarters was subjected to artillery bombardment every night. At first I could not sleep at all, partly because of the noise, partly because of fear, but after a few days I became capable of sleeping through anything. One night I was shaken from sleep by another officer, who urged me to go to a safer place. I went with him. He kept muttering, "During the time I woke you up I could have been killed." Some years later I met him again. He was at that time the timpanist of the Metropolitan Opera Orchestra. I reminded him of what he had said that evening, but his remarks had obviously been less memorable for him than for me.

Our favorite place in Okinawa was Futemma, where we found a large concrete pigpen that we cleaned out and transformed into an air raid shelter where we could sleep undisturbed even during a bombardment. Twenty-five years later when I again visited Okinawa, I searched for the pigpen, but naturally it had disappeared along with the town of Futemma itself, which at that time was covered with the housing of American military personnel.

While on duty with the 96th Division I had, for the first time in my life, a group of men in my command. The group consisted of nisei interpreters and translators. At the time, there were no nisei language officers, and because Army officers who had been trained in Japanese were still insufficient in numbers, even a Navy officer was welcomed. Most of the ten or so Japanese-Americans in my command were from Hawaii, but a few were from California. At first I was obliged to demonstrate (as usual) that I really could read and speak Japanese, but it did not take long to become friends.

Among my "men" the most interesting was a young soldier from Hawaii we all called Jirō. He had been born in Hawaii but, as a child of three, had been taken by his family to Okinawa, where he had grown up and been educated. At the age of eighteen he returned to Hawaii, hardly capable of speaking English. Soon afterward he had signed up for military service. He quickly picked up a knowledge of the fifty or sixty English phrases most commonly used by American soldiers, mainly clichés or profanities, and could rattle them off so authentically that most of the other soldiers thought he spoke perfect English.

I imagined that it must be a traumatic experience for Jirō to see the island where he had spent most of his life caught up in terrible warfare—people killed, houses burned, camps of terrified prisoners—but I never detected the slightest trace of sentimentality or even of compassion in his attitude. He was now an American soldier and he acted in every way exactly like other American soldiers. He was rather like a *shōgi* (Japanese chess) piece that had been turned in the opposite direction, and now was pointed against his former friends. If he saw the corpse of a Japanese soldier who had been killed in some curious posture, he would laugh or imitate the final gesture of the dead man. This at first horrified me, but gradually I came to realize that this was a "normal" attitude for soldiers. It was not mine, but if

I am pictured with some of the men in my command in Okinawa, while fighting was still going on.

wars had always been fought by people like me, there would have been fewer heroes in history.

One day Jirō suggested to me that we have lunch at his aunt's house. He had already gone to visit her, and the family was delighted to see Jirō again, even if he was in American uniform. Now that I think back on it, it was most peculiar and even dangerous for an American to go for lunch at a Japanese house while the fighting was still at its height, but I felt not the slightest anxiety. I felt exactly as I did when I was invited to the house of Okinawan friends in Hawaii, and it did not even occur to me that the family might put poison in the food of an enemy officer. When we arrived at the aunt's house we were politely, even effusively welcomed. I was at first hesitant to eat the food that was put before me, not because I feared poison but because the civilians on Okinawa had so little to eat. I ate, all the same, and everything went well until the final soup. I have no idea what was in that soup, but it was the worst-tasting thing I had ever imbibed. Fearing to wound the feelings of kind people who were sharing their meager food with me, I somehow got the soup down, not without great effort, only to be offered a second helping.

*****

For the first time during the Pacific War, many Japanese soldiers became prisoners. I can remember a long line of prisoners passing my tent on the way to a camp somewhere. I have the July 20, 1945, issue of the American Army newspaper *Yank,* published in Saipan. One photograph shows hundreds of Japanese prisoners in a camp, another shows me interrogating a prisoner. I am squatting down on the ground, apparently sitting on my left foot. The prisoner, who looks much better fed and happier

From Yank (Saipan edition, July 20, 1945)

than I, seems to be sitting on a rock, and looks down over me as I write his answers to my questions. To tell the truth, I have no recollection of where or when the photograph was taken, but it typifies my days on Okinawa.

In earlier campaigns most of the prisoners had been taken against their will. Some were stunned by an explosion, others too badly wounded to move, still others were picked up at sea as they fought off sharks. But on Okinawa many soldiers raised the white flag of surrender. I remember, for example, one Japanese soldier who explained that he was half Ainu and for this reason had been badly treated by the Japanese military. He offered to lead us to a cave where his buddies were still holding out. He said he was sure he could persuade them to come out. I went with him to the mouth of the cave. He called on them to surrender, saying that the Americans would not mistreat them, and told them (what they knew already) that resistance was useless. But nobody came out. Finally, he flew into a rage and urged us to seal off the cave and kill all the stupid soldiers inside. I think, as a matter of fact, that they had all slipped out of the cave while he was surrendering and that nobody heard his words.

One other prisoner I remember because of the interesting conversations we had, even in the midst of the fighting. Years later I met him in Tokyo. At the time, he told me, he was working for the International Ocean Exposition Okinawa 1975. Having regained a second life on Okinawa, where he thought that he would certainly die, he felt obliged to offer this second life to the service of Okinawa.

Other prisoners were Okinawans who had been drafted into the *bōeitai,* a defense unit. Most of them had had no military training, and some were bitter about the treatment they had received from the Japanese from Naichi (the four main islands of Japan). But there were so many prisoners, in contrast to earlier operations, that I had very little time to spend with each. When I left Okinawa for Hawaii in the middle of July it was on a ship with a thousand prisoners, Japanese military, Okinawan bōeitai, and many Korean laborers.

When the ship called at Saipan somebody made a mistake and introduced sea water into the hold. We were obliged to spend about two weeks waiting for repairs to be completed. One night at the officers' club on Saipan I heard an aviator betting anyone that the war would be over in a month. Naturally, I did not believe this was possible. I had learned never to trust anything an aviator said, but as a matter of fact his base was on the nearby island of Tinian, and he knew a secret that the people of Hiroshima and the rest of the world would learn about in a matter of weeks.

We arrived in Hawaii during the first week of August 1945. It was pleasant to see my friends and to be able to listen again to the music I liked. I was also happy to think that I was eligible to return home on leave, having served two and a half years overseas. The house in Honolulu that I shared with five other officers looked reassuringly the same, but the first night I slept there after my return I had a strange dream. It was of a newsboy shouting that something extraordinary had happened. There were no such newsboys in wartime Honolulu, so it must have been a dream, but early in the morning I turned on the radio to see if anything unusual had actually happened. It was then that I learned of the dropping of the atomic bomb on Hiroshima.

That morning I went to headquarters in Pearl Harbor to report my return. The commanding officer informed me that I was entitled to a leave, but asked if I would prefer to go to Japan instead. The news of the atomic bomb had convinced him that the war would soon end. I did not answer at once, but asked for a little time to make my decision.

I went out to the prisoner-of-war camp that same day. The prisoners had also learned about the atomic bomb. Some of them congratulated me. I did not know how to respond. Even supposing that they were completely disillusioned about the sacred mission of Japan, the impending defeat of their country must surely have been painful. They probably also wanted to be alone at such a time. One or two at a time they went out, and finally there was just one prisoner left in the room with me. I did not know him, but he introduced himself. He told me that, unlike many prisoners who had been unconscious or ill when they were captured, he had deliberately surrendered. He said, "I surrendered, thinking I might be the only one, but determined that there be at least one." He was eager to return to Japan to help rebuild it as a better country, and said that the defeat would make this possible. He asked, "Won't you help, you who understand us?"

"No," I answered, "I am returning home. It is not for me to help you. It is your country."

"But in the meantime, during the occupation at least . . ."

And that is how it happened that I left Hawaii the same night for Guam, my first stop (I thought) on the way to Japan. It was while on Guam that I heard the broadcast of the emperor on August 15. We had learned that there was to be an important broadcast and guessed that it might be an announcement of the end of the war. I went with two or three prisoners to the headquarters tent and listened with them to the broadcast. Reception was poor, and I really could not understand what the high-pitched, disembodied voice was saying, but when I saw the tears on the faces of the Japanese by my side I could infer the content of the message. Years later one of the prisoners, later a professor at a university in Kyushu, visited me in Tokyo. To tell the truth, I did not remember him. He was disappointed, unable to believe that I had forgotten someone with whom I had shared so momentous an occasion, but I had been so intent on trying to understand the emperor's words that nothing else had really registered. Until I heard the broadcast I had unconsciously assumed that the war would never end, that I would spend the rest of my life in uniform, but now a new life was to begin.

*****

I remember very little of what happened during the weeks between the emperor's broadcast and my departure for China. The one event that affected me most was a disagreement with a superior officer. I forget precisely what was involved, but my recollections of this particular man are all bad. He was partly Japanese, but in order to prove that he was 100 percent American he was always disagreeably anti-Japanese. Probably that was the cause of our tense relations. I tried to keep out of his way, but he no doubt sensed my dislike, and (a condition of military service) a superior officer was always in a position to annoy and even to humiliate a junior officer. He knew that I badly wanted to go to Japan. During the weeks after the end of the war most of the other interpreters were in fact sent to Japan, and before long we received word of their activities. I remained on Guam, impatiently waiting my turn, only to be informed by my superior that I was being sent to China instead.

It was not exactly a disappointment to be sent to China. I still retained the interest in the country that had inspired my first steps in what would be my life work, the study of East Asia; but after having spent almost four years thinking about Japan, that was where I wanted to go. It was obviously impossible to question the decision of my superior officer, and I resigned myself to a second-best destination.

I was assigned to the Sixth Marine Division. The Army had not objected to my wearing Navy insignia when I was serving with the Army in the Aleutians or on Okinawa, but the Marine Corps insisted that I wear a Marine uniform and insignia. I did not object, but it seemed to me ludicrous that a short, thin, nearsighted language officer like myself should be posing as a Marine.

It was not until the end of September 1945 that I finally left for China. The transport I boarded sailed in a convoy, as usual.

The lights of the other ships, reflected in the ocean, seemed strange after the years of blackout. Somewhere along the way (I forget where) the intelligence section of division headquarters was transferred to a destroyer. We were to serve as an advance party. The night before the ship reached Tsingtao, the port toward which we were headed, there was a storm at sea. The destroyer rocked in the waves and, one after the other, the officers began to look greenish and left for their bunks. The chief of the intelligence section, to show his superiority to the elements, ostentatiously lit a cigar. It was my great pleasure to see him, moments later, abruptly put down his cigar and rush off somewhere, no doubt to some spot where he could vomit without being seen. I also felt queasy, but managed to get to my bunk without any disasters.

That night the waves struck at the ship with a sound like metal clanging against metal. I had to clutch at the railings on the sides in order to avoid being thrown from my bunk. When my watch showed that it was at last seven in the morning I got up and dressed. The storm had abated, and I went out on deck. In the distance I could see the silhouettes of mountains. China! I stared at the shore, unable to believe that my dream of many years had been realized.

In stunning contrast to the stormy weather at sea the night before, the harbor of Tsingtao was so calm and radiant in the sunlight as to seem unreal, like a huge picture postcard. As the ship moved closer to the dock, we could distinguish people waving to us. This was certainly unlike any landing during the war. Indeed, every sight seemed to be confirming the truth that the war was really over, that what awaited us was not danger but the normal excitement of a city visited for the first time, a city populated by people who wanted to be our friends. The Marines, being Marines, made their usual landing over the side of the ship, armed to the teeth, shovels bouncing from their hips, presumably for entrenching themselves in the city streets. But I had had enough of the pretense of being a military man, and I went ashore peacefully as I had when I visited Europe as a child.

Several of us walked to the end of the pier where we could see a cluster of Chinese military men. I tried to remember how to ask questions in Chinese, but after almost four years of studying Japanese I could scarcely frame the simplest sentence in Chinese, let alone ask for useful information. I approached a Chinese officer who addressed me before I could say a word. He asked, "Captain, could you tell us how to get to the International Club?" I have often had the experience of being asked directions ten minutes after I arrived in some foreign city for the first time, but never have I been less prepared to answer than I was at that moment.

Eventually the Chinese officer and I found the International Club, where members of the advance party were to stay. We were not, however, the first Americans there. Upstairs, in a kind of dormitory room to which I was led, there were three or four aviators who had been in Tsingtao for a week or more. They profited by their advantage as "old hands" to give me advice on how to get along in China. First of all, they were convinced that the Chinese were basically stupid. "Otherwise, how do you account for the fact that they're always standing around outside any store we go into, with nothing better to do?" asked one of the old hands. Another warned me against the dishonesty of the Chinese: "At home I throw my dirty clothes in a bag and never even count what I give in laundry. But here I don't trust them one minute. I can't stand that slimy grin of theirs." And so on. It was useless for me to disagree; they were sure, on the basis of their profound research into the Chinese character, that they spoke the ultimate truth.

After depositing my belongings on one of the cots, I left the room. The others were still giving fresh proofs of their contentions. When I reached the stairs, I heard a man down below shouting in English to a Chinese upstairs, "You come down at once, or I'll kick you down myself." Appalled by the savagery of the expression, I recalled stories I had heard from Chinese friends of signs in the public parks: DOGS AND CHINESE KEEP OUT. I don't know whether or not such signs actually existed, but the peremptory tone of the man downstairs inescapably brought to mind the worst of a century of cruel discrimination. I later learned that the shouting man downstairs, the manager of the International Club, was an Australian who had only recently been released from the Japanese internment camp at Wei-hsien. Perhaps abusing the servant was his way of "getting even" for the humiliation he himself had suffered, but I was not in a mood to forgive him.

I left the International Club with feelings of disgust that the war had done nothing to change old prejudices. The club building itself, a relic of the German occupation of Tsingtao before the First World War, had stained-glass windows showing the arms of the great cities of Germany, and the architecture itself was in the oppressive manner of the late nineteenth century. But I was uninterested in this or any other relic of Europe—I had eyes only for China, for my first sight of a country that had been so much in my mind since I was sixteen.

I did not know where to go. The information we had been given on Tsingtao certainly did not indicate the tourist attractions, if any. After I had walked only a few steps I was surrounded by rickshas and men clamoring to take me aboard. On an impulse I got into one and motioned "straight ahead!" But all of my prejudices and convictions of many years made it impossible for me to sit quietly and enjoy the landscape unfolding around me. I tried sitting forward, imagining this might make it easier for the ricksha man (in fact, the opposite is true), and in my embarrassment over being pulled in this way by another human being, I dug my nails into the armrests. In the meanwhile, I had become an object of interest to people in the streets. Bicyclists almost fell from their bicycles in the effort to get a better look at me, and children ran after the ricksha shouting all the while. A group of actors, some wearing the traditional wispy false beards of the Chinese stage, saluted as I went by, and a work party of Japanese soldiers by the roadside also saluted. The whole experience was so unreal, so unlike the life I had led in the military during the past three years, that it seemed more like a dream than reality, and I felt a wonderful exhilaration, the counterpart to my depression at the International Club.

After a while I got down from the ricksha and went walking through the streets. I was the object of great attention, but I felt no fear or even a sense of being in an alien place. A young Chinese officer who spoke some English joined me and offered to take me shopping. I had heard from friends who had been sent to Tokyo that the shops were so empty and necessities so scarce that one could trade a package of cigarettes for a work of art; but here in Tsingtao there was sprawling abundance along the streets—food of every kind being sliced and weighed, boxes of tea, cigarettes, clothing, brushes, inkstones, pottery. With my friend's help I bought a jade ring, a Chinese robe, and Chinese shoes. "Everything Chinese now except the face!" he said laughing.

The next day I paid my first visit to Japanese Military Headquarters. My dealings with the Japanese military up until this point had been clearly defined: we were enemies, and they were prisoners of war. Of course, this had not prevented me from feeling friendship for them, and I believe this was reciprocated, but individual sentiments had not altered the basic relationship. Here in Tsingtao, however, the situation was different. The Japanese army had not surrendered, still possessed its weapons, and still occupied buildings both within the city and in the surroundings. Japanese soldiers were in fact still guarding Tsingtao and the railroad line connecting the inland cities with the coast.

As soon as I set foot inside the Japanese headquarters I was startled by a corporal bellowing at some privates: "*Kei-rei!*" ("Salute!") I addressed them in Japanese, only to get a shaking of the head to indicate they didn't speak English. Eventually, I met a Japanese officer of about my own age with whom I struck up a pleasant conversation about recent Japanese literature. As I was leaving he asked, "How about getting together and having a drink, now that the war is over?"

*****

Tsingtao seemed during the first few days an enchanting city, the embodiment of my old dreams about China, but as time passed it began to lose its charm. I enjoyed associating with Japanese army and navy personnel, this time not as a captor dealing with prisoners but as colleagues attempting to terminate as smoothly as possible the long Japanese occupation of the city. Our relations were friendly, and on several occasions we even got drunk together. But an unexpected development not only clouded these relations but made my stay in Tsingtao painful.

One day, while talking with a Korean accused of acts of intimidation after the end of the war, I mentioned a certain Japanese naval officer with whom I was on particularly friendly terms. The Korean said with an ironic smile, "Yes, he's a nice man who can eat human liver and boast of it." Astonished, I asked what he meant. The grisly details he related led me to investigate the sordid crimes committed by certain Japanese naval personnel against Chinese accused of anti-Japanese activity. These Chinese were used for bayonet practice to harden the fighting spirit of the Japanese sailors, and then their livers were torn from their bodies and consumed as a medicine.

I had absolutely no training as a criminal investigator, and the work depressed me intensely, but I felt I had no choice but to find out what had happened. Word soon spread of my activities, and some Japanese with minor crimes of their own to conceal imagined that by denouncing other people they themselves would be enabled to escape punishment. Every morning several would-be informers waited outside my office.

The investigation of war crimes was so distasteful that for the first time I really wanted to go home. When I requested that my "points" be calculated to determine whether or not I was eligible to apply for a discharge, the commanding officer promised me a week in Peking if I would remain in Tsingtao another month or so. This was a temptation. Peking for years had attracted me more than any other city, the way Venice attracts some people and Paris others, and I was willing to do anything to go there, except to conduct war crimes investigations. But that was the condition—I could go to Peking only if I continued my work. After much hesitation, I repeated my request to be sent home as soon as possible.

When I think back on the decision now, I regret it. Peking in the late autumn of 1945 would not have been at its best, but it certainly would have looked more like the Peking of my dreams than it did when I finally visited the city six or seven years ago. Friends of mine who knew the city before 1945 and have seen it in recent years are unanimous in the belief that the charm of the old city has been destroyed. There is still much to see, of course, and I am glad I was able to get there at last, but I was dismayed by the wide avenues that had been brutally driven through the old city, and the drabness of the remaining houses.

In any case, once I had made my decision I was eager to leave as soon as possible. Even things that had pleased me in Tsingtao had now been corrupted by the obtrusive presence of American sailors and Marines, and every investigation I made led inevitably to the discovery of weaknesses and often evil in human beings that profoundly depressed me, inexperienced as I was. Among my colleagues too there was an officer who systematically visited the houses of Japanese who were reputed to own objects of art, promising to help them get repatriated in return for treasures that, in any case, they could not take back to Japan. The other language officers were shocked and we refused even to speak to him, but in this way he founded an impressive collection. There must have been something in the air of Tsingtao— perhaps its colonial past—that favored corruption of the human spirit.

I was not sorry to leave Tsingtao when I received authorization to return to America for discharge. I flew from Tsingtao to Shanghai, where I spent a few days waiting for a plane. I had been prepared to detest Shanghai as an excrescence on the face of China, but I was fascinated by this incredible city where one could see every variety of architecture and every variety of life.

Like all naval officers I traveled under orders, and I expected that they would entitle me to accommodations in Shanghai, but the orders were ambiguously worded, and I was refused at the various hotels where I requested a room. If the Americans won't take care of me, perhaps the Japanese will, I said to myself, and headed for Japanese naval headquarters. There I asked for a room, much to their surprise, and after much telephoning they persuaded the proprietress of a Japanese restaurant to let me spend the night. No doubt she was apprehensive about what I, as a member of the American armed forces, might demand, but I did my best to reassure her. It now seems almost unbelievable that, scarcely four months after the end of a bitter war, I should have turned to my former enemies, the Japanese, rather than to my compatriots, for help when I needed it. My enmity obviously had not been deep-seated. Or it might be more accurate to say that a friendship, begun with *The Tale of Genji* and interrupted by the war, had officially been resumed.

Two Japanese naval officers had been delegated to keep me company at the restaurant. The senior of the two, Lieutenant Yamada, had worked for one of the giant *zaibatsu* conglomerates before joining the navy, and he soon made it clear that he did not welcome the rumored dissolution of the zaibatsu by order of the American occupation. I had often had the impression when talking with prisoners of war about their hopes for Japan when the war had ended that they told me what they supposed I wanted to hear. If so, this was entirely understandable in terms of their own uncertainty about whether or not they could even return to their country, let alone improve it. But Yamada had no such doubts. He had accepted the end of the war as a fact, and he had no reason to attempt to ingratiate himself with me.

For this reason our conversation that night was particularly memorable for me. Instead of receiving the usual "That's right, I'm sure" or "I hadn't realized that was true" in response to my criticisms of Japanese militarism, Yamada disagreed with me and sometimes made me feel that my understanding had been faulty. For example, when the subject of the banzai attack (as the charge of Japanese soldiers into certain death was called by the

Americans) came up, I questioned whether it represented true bravery because of the lower value placed on human life by the Japanese than by the Americans. Up until now, when such a subject had come up in conversation with Japanese prisoners, they had uniformly agreed with me, but Yamada did not.

He replied, "No people clings to life more than the Japanese. The Japanese is passionately desirous of remaining alive, no matter what the circumstances of his life may be. But the Japanese have learned to cultivate that part of man which is human as opposed to animal. If a man responded at once to hunger, desire, or the instinct for self-preservation by seeking immediate satisfaction of these cravings, he would be purely animal. The Japanese, in common to a certain degree with other peoples who believe in Buddhism, have sought to deny this animal incentive in order to show that they have been liberated from primitive, unreasoning drives. There is nothing more painful for a Japanese than to give up his life, but he will make even this sacrifice because he is superior to the animal which knows nothing higher."

I was so unaccustomed to this kind of defense of Japanese wartime actions that I could not think of an answer. Or it might be more correct to say that I was so struck by Yamada's words that in a sense I wanted to believe them, though I had always assumed that the impetus for the banzai charge was fanaticism— quite the contrary of any Buddhist belief in the importance of denying unreasoning instincts.

Later, when Yamada had left, I talked with Ensign Sakurai, who had taken little part in the conversation. He volunteered, "I agree with you, not Yamada. The Japanese soldier knows nothing of those high principles, but acts instead as part of a mass. If the mass goes on a suicide attack at the command of an officer, the individual soldier becomes intoxicated with the spirit and goes along. There are no abstract principles involved."

I didn't know whether to feel glad or sad over these words, but I did learn a lesson that would serve me in good stead in later years: never accept at face value the opinions of anyone who professes to speak for an entire people.

That night I spent several hours talking with Ensign Sakurai. Although the only thing we had in common was that we had both studied French literature as undergraduates, we spoke like old friends, perhaps because we were more or less the same age. I was particularly intrigued by his account of student life in Tokyo only six or seven months earlier. He might have been talking about events of a whole generation before.

He told me about the term in the spring of 1945. "It was very strange. We never talked about women or politics or other things that young men discuss, but only food and how to get enough of it so that we wouldn't feel hungry all the time. It seems ridiculous now, but we were all confident that Japan would win the war somehow. The feeling ran contrary to reason and certainly to our empty stomachs, but it was inconceivable that Japan would be defeated. One night there was a terrible firebombing of Tokyo, and the flames came right up to our school. We fought the fire until four in the morning, went to bed for two or three hours, and then had crew races on the river as scheduled. It never occurred to us to despair."

There was something very appealing in his story, which bespoke the confidence and energy of youth even under the most adverse conditions. At the same time, it was eerie to think that but for a development over which neither of us had any control—the end of the war a few months earlier—this young man and I, who were talking like old friends, would have vowed to spare no efforts to kill each other. I had had such thoughts before, of course, especially when talking with prisoners of my own age, but as Sakurai and I chatted in the room of a Japanese restaurant in Shanghai it was as though the war had never happened, and the occasional recollections of how much had separated us seemed like actions in a fading nightmare, almost devoid of reality.

Yamada came to see me again the next day. I had told him the previous evening of my intention of stopping over in Tokyo on the way back to Hawaii, even though my orders made no mention of a stop in Japan. He had brought a sheaf of papers he wished me to deliver to his mother in Tokyo. He had fallen in love with a Japanese girl in Shanghai and wanted his mother to know about her before the marriage. I gladly agreed to serve as his courier, it not being possible at the time for Japanese to send mail abroad.

A day or so later I was on a plane bound for Tokyo. My orders read simply, "You will return to your original command," without specifying where that might be. I made up my mind that when I arrived in Japan I would inform the American military that my "original command" was now at the naval base in Yokosuka, reasoning that they would not be too suspicious now that the war was over.

As the plane neared Japan I strained for a first glimpse of the country that had been in my thoughts virtually every minute for the last four years. Suddenly we were over Japan, I don't know where. My first impression was of the greenness of the country. In China virtually the only trees were those planted around the Japanese shrines, but here the mountains were covered with trees, and where there were no trees there were carefully cultivated fields.

When the plane landed at Atsugi I was so excited at the thought of being in Japan that I stammered when asked to show my orders and explain my presence. But, obviously, nobody was interested in me, and soon afterward I was on a military bus bound for Tokyo. Japan at last!

As the bus moved toward the center of Tokyo I had the opposite of the usual impression one receives on entering a city: buildings became fewer, not more numerous, and eventually we were passing through areas without a single building left standing. In other places there were only isolated storehouses, their earthen walls having resisted the fires better than the traditional wooden Japanese houses. Near what I took to be the center of the city there were some brick or concrete buildings that seemed to be whole, but on closer inspection they sometimes proved to be no more than burned-out shells.

Not having proper orders, there was nowhere in the city where I could legitimately stay. Fortunately, I remembered from a letter where most of the Japanese-language translators were lodged and I somehow made my way to the building, which was near the Yūraku-chō station. It had originally been a business building, but now one floor was given over to rows of cots where the translators slept. I was glad to see some old friends. They told me that the legal occupant of one of the beds was in Nagoya, and without hesitation I took possession.

There were many things I might have wanted to do during my first days in Japan, but what I wanted most of all was to inform the families of the prisoners and of the Japanese I had met in Tsingtao that they were still alive. For some I had fairly detailed addresses, for others only general notations. I found the grandfather of the wife of my closest friend among the Japanese in Tsingtao, a tea master living in Yotsuya in the basement of a house that had been destroyed during the bombing. I was not so lucky in my next venture. I went to Kugenuma in Kanagawa prefecture in search of the family of a prisoner with whom I had been friendly in Hawaii. I thought that the town would be so small somebody would surely have heard of the prisoner even though I did not have his address. Unfortunately, however, his name was Satō, and even in Kugenuma there were a great many people with that name. I walked from police-box to police-box, asking at each if they knew about someone named Satō who had gone off to war, but without success. In the meanwhile, children of the town, attracted by the foreigner who spoke Japanese, began to follow me around in my peregrinations, and eventually I had a whole train of children trailing me, rather in the manner of the Pied Piper of Hamelin. But to the end I never found the Satō I was looking for.

My most memorable search, however, was successful. I had been asked, again by my friend in Tsingtao, to inform the president of his company that he and his family were safe. The president's house was in Kamakura. I went there one evening with a friend, another translator who was stationed in Yokosuka. It was only about six o'clock, but it was already dark. I rang the bell and presently a girl came to the door. She took one look at the two American naval officers and let out a shriek. The people inside the house, who could see us through the opened door, did not shriek, but they might well have, at the thought that we had come to requisition the house. Later, when I had explained my errand, we were cordially received, and the girl who had shrieked played the piano.

We left the house about eight. As I recall, the streets were not illuminated, but the moon was bright, and at my friend's suggestion we walked along the railway tracks toward the Great Statue of Buddha, the Daibutsu. Suddenly the statue was before us, serene in the moonlight. For the first time I felt that I was truly in Japan.

I made one other call on the family of a Japanese I had known abroad. As Lieutenant Yamada had requested, I took to his mother, who lived in Kichijōji, the documents of his fiancée in Shanghai.

Mrs. Yamada was startled when I appeared at the door, but when I had explained my mission she was most hospitable. I had intended merely to deliver the documents, but she insisted that I have tea with her. At the time, as I was aware, sugar was extremely scarce and expensive, but Mrs. Yamada put spoon after spoon of sugar into my tea. It was much too sweet for my taste, but I drank it anyway, appreciating the generosity that had impelled her to part with the precious commodity. No doubt she was eager to look through the various documents I had brought with me, but she politely refrained until I had left from even a glance.

Instead, she talked to me about her son: "My boy was always so much interested in America. He studied English and neglected everything else. What a terrible thing that war should have come between two countries he loved!" Her words surprised me. Nothing in the course of our conversation in Shanghai had suggested that Yamada was particularly devoted to America. I had supposed instead that he was one of the Japanese who had not questioned the wartime ideology, but perhaps he had spoken in such terms in order to distinguish himself from the many Japanese who were now declaring, "It was a blessing that we were defeated."

Mrs. Yamada also asked about my wartime experiences. "Were you really on Okinawa? What a frightful place that must have been. They said that everyone was killed, even the women and children, but now it says in the newspapers that there were prisoners. I suppose the prisoners will be coming home soon.

Once that would have been considered very disgraceful, but now it doesn't matter. It couldn't be helped."

*****

The only sightseeing I did during my week in Japan was to go to Nikkō. When I was learning Japanese it had said in the textbook, "Don't say anything is wonderful before you've seen Nikkō." I thought I should see so extraordinary a place, and when I heard that a few of my friends from the office in Honolulu planned to go there, I asked to be taken along. We went by jeep. There were almost no cars on the road, and there were so few signposts that we stopped again and again to make sure we were on the right road. When the jeep passed through a village the children lining the roads waved their hands and shouted greetings, as if welcoming us.

The inn in Nikkō was deserted, and the innkeeper seemed glad to accommodate us. We had brought rice with us from Tokyo. That night a miracle occurred: our polished rice, when it appeared on the table, was transformed into unpolished rice, a veritable prodigy. That night it was very cold, and when I awoke in the morning there was snow on the tatami mat near my pillow. My friends, for whatever reason, were not interested in the shrine, and I went there alone. A boy in middle-school uniform became my guide. There was not another tourist in the whole place. Snow lay on the brightly colored buildings. I have since twice visited Nikkō without being much impressed by the elaborately carved pillars, but perhaps the snow helped on the first visit. As I gazed entranced at the splendid white and gold gate of the Tōshōgū, my young guide turned to me. "Before the war a wealthy American offered a great deal of money—a million dollars I think—for this gate, but it was a national treasure and not for sale. I suppose it will go to America now anyway, won't it?"

I finally became apprehensive lest the Navy discover that I was playing truant in Japan, and one day I reported to an office in Yokosuka that I had been mistaken: my original command, after all, was in Honolulu and not in Japan. I suppose that it sometimes happened that officers were genuinely mistaken about where their original commands had moved after the war, and my story was believed. In any case, nobody seemed surprised, and I began to wish that I had not revealed my mistake so soon. I might have been able to spend more time sightseeing!

During my week I had seen very little of Japan. I had not seen Kyoto, Nara, or even any of the famous temples of Kamakura. The only sight of Tokyo I could remember having noticed was General MacArthur's headquarters facing Hibiya Park. I had not met a single Japanese scholar or, for that matter, visited a university. I had not even asked whether or not the museums were open. As I recall, when I expressed interest in seeing a performance of Kabuki, I was told that it was off limits to American military personnel. But in the course of my wanderings in search of the families of my friends I had again and again encountered remarkable kindness. When I stopped at a house to ask directions I was sometimes invited in and offered tea with perhaps a segment of sweet potato as a substitute for cake. I certainly did not wish to deprive these people of food, so scarce at the time, but it was hard to resist their hospitality. And I marveled always that this kindness came after American planes had destroyed not only military installations but the little wooden houses where people totally unconnected with the war had lived and died.

The day before I left I visited a bookshop in Yokosuka, looking for something to take the prisoners who were still in Hawaii. I heard two old women talking. One was telling the other, "My daughter lived in Yokosuka, right next to the navy yard. When the first American planes started to bomb Japan, my son-in-law decided that it was dangerous in Yokosuka, and he moved the family to Kōfu in the mountains. There aren't any military installations there, so we thought she would be quite safe. But they bombed Kōfu often, almost every week, and her house was burned down, while they didn't bomb Yokosuka at all!" I remembered then having asked a B-29 navigator why Kōfu was bombed so often when there wasn't anything there of great military importance. He answered with a laugh, "Well, for one thing it's easy to find, right on the direct route to Tokyo. For another, there isn't much antiaircraft fire there."

The next morning, before dawn, I was awakened and told that I was to board a ship for Kisarazu, on the other side of Tokyo Bay. As usual, after having been hurried to the pier in the cold darkness, I was obliged to wait interminably before the ship left. At last the ship pulled out into the still dark bay. I was standing on the deck looking out for some sign of the dawn when suddenly Mount Fuji loomed up before me, pink in the light of the rising sun. This was almost too perfect a farewell to Japan. Because of the widespread destruction in Tokyo almost nothing obstructed my view of the mountain. It seemed amazingly big, and as close as it appears in the early nineteenth-century prints of the city. I gazed at the mountain as it gradually changed color, all but moved to tears by the sight. Someone had told me that if one sees Fuji just before one leaves Japan it means that one will visit Japan again. I wanted very much to believe this, and thought perhaps it might be true. But it was to be almost eight years before I saw Japan again.

CHAPTER THREE

*****

LIVING
TRADITION

I returned to Hawaii shortly before Christmas, 1945. I visited the offices where I had translated Japanese documents for over two years, but they were all but totally deserted, and I did not recognize the clerical personnel who now presided over the empty spaces where the Japanese-language translators had worked. When I requested discharge from the Navy and the necessary forms, I rather expected that someone would try to persuade me to remain in the Navy a while longer; but it was evident that I had been forgotten during the four months since the end of the war, and nobody cared whether I remained in the Navy for the rest of my life or resigned the same day.

The only people who seemed glad to see me again were the prisoners of war. Of course, they had been reading the newspapers and had a general idea of conditions in Japan since the end of the war, but they were eager for details. I told them what I could and gave them magazines I had happened to buy during my short stay in Japan. I tried to answer their questions, but it was not in my power to answer the one question uppermost in their minds: would they be able to return to Japan?

I supposed that I would be sent back to New York immediately, but (as usual) paperwork took time. I have absolutely no recollection of Christmas that year. After having led a life that was prescribed by the exigencies of war, and having performed each day the duties expected of me, days with nothing to do, no responsibilities, seemed so unreal that it would not have surprised me much if I had awakened one morning and discovered that the war was still and eternally being fought.

One day word finally came ordering me to report to the aircraft carrier *Saratoga* for transportation to the West Coast of the United States. The *Saratoga* was fated to be blown up by a hydrogen bomb at Bikini, but it was certainly the pleasantest ship I traveled on during my military service, and I was sorry to learn of its demise.

From California I once again took a train across the country to New York. Again, I have no recollections of the journey, not even a general impression of comfort or discomfort. The only memory of my return to New York is of struggling on the subway with a seabag (a large canvas bag traditionally used by Navy personnel) and a suitcase. When I reached my stop, a woman with her son, a boy of twelve or thirteen, took pity on the returning hero, and directed the son to help me with my baggage. He started to carry the suitcase, but his mother, whose primary concern was naturally for her child rather than for the hero, at once decided it was too heavy for him. It is strange that this should be the only memory I retain of my imminent return to civilian life after four years in uniform. Perhaps, I tell myself now, it indicates my disappointment that there was to be no symphonic resolution to the absurdity of someone like myself having posed for so long as a military man.

When I saw my mother again and displayed the souvenirs I had brought her—embroidery from China, a doll someone had given me in Japan, a fan—I felt like a tourist returning from exotic travels abroad. But when I took out my prize, a sword that a Japanese general in Tsingtao had given me, my mother let out a shriek and declared she would not have anything so terrifying in her house. I put the sword away, remembering then how desperately most American military (including myself) had craved a Japanese sword. The war had definitely ended.

Strange to say, during all the time when my thoughts were dominated by the hope that I would soon be released from military service, I had never given much serious thought to precisely what I would do when once I was free to determine my own life. Most of the other officers who learned Japanese at the same time as myself had already begun preparing for their lives as lawyers, politicians, diplomats, or whatever before the outbreak of war, and when they were discharged resumed their interrupted careers. A few attempted to keep up with their Japanese, but a knowledge of Japanese was not considered to be much of an asset in 1946. It was the common assumption that it would take at least fifty years for Japan to recuperate from the war and resume the position it had formerly occupied. Some who had learned Japanese and had become genuinely interested in East Asia shifted their attention to China, mainly because they believed that China was the source of Japanese civilization, but also because it seemed likely that China would replace Japan as the leading power in East Asia. A few whom I met in later years told me, with a touch of pride, that they had forgotten every word of Japanese they ever knew.

My case was rather different. During my undergraduate years I had been tormented by the thought that there was really nothing I wanted to do to earn a living, and my studies were certainly not focused on any career. The study of Chinese and later Japanese had opened up a possibility of a fruitful occupation. I had enjoyed the study of Japanese, especially the oddities of the language. Every time I discovered the pronunciation of an unfamiliar place-name or personal name, it was a little triumph. I remember one wartime translation especially. I was retranslating a document that someone else had previously translated in an inadequate manner. It contained the word *kōhyōteki*, rendered by the earlier translator as "prime targets," a more or less literal translation of the term. But "prime targets" did not make much sense in context, a description of the Japanese attack on Pearl Harbor, and I tried to think of a better word. Suddenly the words *midget submarine* flashed into my head. I tried this translation at every point in the text where *kōhyōteki* occurred, and I was elated to discover that it worked. Obviously, *kōhyōteki* had been used as a code word. My success with this term and similar though less spectacular successes with others persuaded me that this was what I could do best, that I was made to do battle with the complexities of the Japanese language. Regardless of what my friends might do, I had no intention of abandoning the one gift the war had bestowed on me, a knowledge of Japanese.

But what, specifically, was I to do with my Japanese? At the time there was virtually no demand for instruction in the Japanese language, much less Japanese culture, at American universities. I later discovered, when I attempted to get to Japan as an interpreter for a business concern, American companies thought of interpretation as menial labor and paid for it accordingly; it was far cheaper to hire a Japanese on the scene than send someone like myself to Japan. I might well have been deterred from continuing my study of Japan if I could have thought of some other occupation I liked, but I couldn't. I was, in the great poet

Bashō's words, *"Tsui ni munō mugei ni shite tada kono hitosuji ni tsu-nagaru"*—In the end, incapable and untalented though I was, bound to this one course for life.

People sometimes congratulate me on my remarkable pre-science in having realized even in 1946 that an economic miracle would occur in Japan twenty-five years later. Of course, I had absolutely no idea that there would be anything resembling an economic miracle. My decision in 1946 to continue my study of Japan, even though all but a handful of those who had learned Japanese during the war had lost their interest in the language, was based mainly on a vague awareness that I was temperamen-tally suited to this study. Years ago, when I applied for a visa at the Japanese Consulate General in New York a young vice-consul said to me, "You were clever to have studied Japanese. You would never have become famous in anything more compet-itive." It naturally did not please me to be told this in so many words, but he may have been right. Perhaps the study of Japan was the *only* occupation for which I was suited.

It was not clear to me, however, where I should pursue my studies. I decided to get some advice before I made any firm decision, and went to Washington to consult with an officer of the American Council of Learned Societies. He was both patient and well informed, but the conclusion he reached, and which I accepted without much enthusiasm, was that the best place for me was Columbia.

Although the prospect of studying once again with Tsunoda-sensei was appealing, I had never attended any university other than Columbia, and I thought my return to academic life would be more exciting if it took place at an unfamiliar institution. I now believe that I made the right decision, but at the time I felt a twinge of regret that I would not be studying at one of the ancient universities of Europe or amid the sylvan surroundings of an American university situated far from New York.

I, like others who had served in the war, was fortunate in that I needed not worry about the cost of study. Under the G.I. Bill of Rights, an act of Congress passed in 1944, the government paid all tuition expenses plus the cost of books and sixty-five dollars a month (a meaningful sum in those days) for living expenses to veterans who enrolled at a university. I shall never forget the excitement of attending classes again after four years in the military. Nowadays, when students of mine fail to appear for class I am tempted to tell them what a privilege and a joy it should be to study what one likes. But each person must make that discovery for himself.

I too made a discovery about myself at this time. I had always hoped to follow in Arthur Waley's footsteps and be a scholar of both Chinese and Japanese, and for this reason I divided my study as a graduate student between the two languages. I discovered, however, that when I attended the lectures given by Professor J. J. L. Duyvendak, a great authority on Chinese language and history, I did not derive any pleasure from spending an hour reading a single sentence and determining the exact meaning of each particle. I wanted to read quickly and widely. Professor Duyvendak must have noticed my lack of enthusiasm. He asked me after class one day if anything was troubling me. I told him frankly that although I knew how important the old Chinese texts were, I enjoyed reading Japanese much more. He answered, "Then, why don't you concentrate on Japanese? We need good scholars of Japan." And that was how it happened I gave up my dream of becoming the second Waley and decided to become only half of him, a scholar of Japan.

*****

After having spent four years in the Navy, the freedom I enjoyed as a graduate student to do what I pleased was exhilarating, though I realized that there were restrictions even on the freedom of a graduate student. One had to prepare assignments, write papers, take examinations. And there was an inescapable feeling that what I was doing was of less importance than my wartime activities. During the war I had often felt frustration when I thought how unlikely it was a document I had translated would be of use in ending the war even a fraction of a second earlier, but at times, especially when talking with Japanese prisoners and persuading them it was worthwhile to go on living, I had felt joy over helping another human being. I no doubt exaggerated the importance of my conversations with the prisoners, who certainly must have been guided by other factors than my immature wisdom. I was also mistaken in my underestimation of the value of the graduate instruction.

Among the courses I took that spring, for example, was a survey of Asian art. I felt dissatisfied with the manner of presentation—an endless series of slides—and with the evident ignorance of Japanese on the part of the professor, who (for example) pronounced *nyorai* (a person who has attained Buddahood) as "nigh-oh-rye." But years later, when I visited Iran and India, I felt grateful for the acquaintance with the art of those countries I had obtained.

Another course I took, for the pleasure of attending lectures by Mark Van Doren, was on the long poem. After spending most of my time for four years thinking and reading about Japan, it was good to renew my acquaintance with Dante, Spenser, Milton, and other poets, and I benefited from Professor Van Doren's unpretentious but truly enlightening interpretations. I was, however, aware of being an outsider in a class composed of graduate students in English literature. My term paper was a comparative study of the *Divine Comedy* and *Ōjō Yōshū* (Essentials of Salvation) by the tenth-century priest Genshin. The *Divine Comedy* was obviously far superior as a work of literature, but I realized that nobody else in the class—not even Professor Van Doren—had ever even heard of *Ōjō Yōshū,* and it seemed that the study of such a work, unknown in the West, was more suited to my abilities than a new interpretation of the *Divine Comedy.*

By far the most important courses, however, were those I took with Tsunoda-sensei. When I had taken his course on the history of Japanese thought during the three months before the outbreak of the war I had been unable to do much more than copy into a notebook the content of his lectures, but now I could understand some of the quotations he wrote on the blackboard, and I was even tempted into reading secondary materials in Japanese on the thinkers whom Tsunoda-sensei discussed. I had gained confidence in my ability to read Japanese, thanks to the many military documents I had translated, but it was quite another matter reading old texts. I often despaired of ever being able to do more than decipher.

One day, while in the stacks of the East Asian Library, I was prey to particularly masochistic feelings. Gloomily surveying the many volumes, I tried an experiment. I took a book from a shelf at random, and opened it, convinced I would be unable to read it. To my astonishment, I could actually understand what it said. It was a volume from the works of Hirata Atsutane, a nineteenth-century Shinto thinker. I felt a surge of joy that swept away my masochism. I told myself that, despite everything, some day I *would* be able to read Japanese. How lucky I was that my hand fell on a volume of Hirata, who is easy to read, than on one by a Buddhist theologian!

Among the Japanese thinkers with whose works I became acquainted as the result of attending Tsunoda-sensei's lectures, I was most attracted to those who stood outside the mainstream of Tokugawa intellectual history. I recognized the significance of the views put forth by the different schools of Confucianism, but they did not engage me very deeply. I could only conclude (what I now know to be true) that my interests are essentially literary rather than philosophical; I was attracted less to the opinions of the Tokugawa thinkers about the proper way for people to conduct their lives than to the thinkers themselves as individuals living and writing in the Japanese society of their time.

I was particularly attracted to Honda Toshiaki (1744–1821), a man who was in a sense my opposite number. Six years later I was to publish *The Japanese Discovery of Europe* in which I described how a small group of Japanese in the eighteenth century devoted themselves to learning about the West, despite the closure of the country and despite the immense difficulty of learning a European language. This group of men, usually called *rangakusha,* or scholars of Dutch learning, were aware that Japan had fallen behind the nations of Europe in scientific progress, and attempted, with immense efforts, to acquire this vital knowledge. The only Europeans permitted to reside in Japan were a handful of Dutch merchants who were confined to a trading station on Deshima, an artificially created island in Nagasaki Bay, and it was from these men that the rangakusha sought the books and scientific instruments they needed.

The rangakusha were interested primarily in medicine, astronomy, mathematics, and other sciences that were of obvious benefit to a country, but some also investigated European painting, engraving and other arts. Honda Toshiaki favored the adoption of the practical European alphabet in place of the cumbersome combination of Chinese characters and Japanese kana normally used in writing Japanese. He praised the realism of Dutch paintings, which lent themselves to pedagogic purposes, unlike the typical Japanese (or Chinese) renderings of vague or mist-covered scenes that existed only in the painter's imagination. His test was always whether or not a given practice was of use to the nation, not whether or not it conformed with tradition or was ethically desirable.

Unlike Honda Toshiaki, I had turned to Japan—not for the sake of my country or for technical knowledge that might benefit my countrymen, but for the pleasure of new knowledge. It was difficult to learn the many characters used in writing Japanese, and there were always problems in guessing the correct pronunciations of the names of people and places, but this was part of the appeal of Japanese. Of course, I was exasperated from time to time. How often I cursed the author of a book I was reading for not having had the courtesy to provide an index! I was once so infuriated by the unhelpfulness of a dictionary of Genroku-period Japanese that I threw it from the seventh-floor window of the dormitory where I was living. (It fortunately did not hit anyone.) I often compared the problems I daily encountered in my battles with the Japanese language with the ease with which I could have acquired another European language. It was only by comparing my problems with those Honda Toshiaki and the other scholars of Dutch learning had faced at a time when there were no dictionaries or grammars to help them that I was able to see myself in a somewhat better perspective. I too, like Honda Toshiaki and the rangakusha, wanted to discover another civilization.

It now seems strange to me that my first sustained piece of academic work, the master's essay I wrote on Honda Toshiaki, was in the field of intellectual history rather than of literature. No doubt this was because I was much under the influence of Tsunoda-sensei. He read literature widely and loved it, but he did not think of it as a subject of academic research. During the twenty and more years he had spent at Columbia he had built up an excellent collection of books on Japanese religion, philosophy, and traditional history, but I discovered to my disappointment, now that I was at last capable of reading books in Japanese, that there were hardly any on literature. Some years later, at Cambridge University, I made a similar discovery—undergraduates at my college were not permitted to study English literature because it was insufficiently difficult.

In any case, I am very glad now that I was influenced by Tsunoda-sensei. Sometimes I catch myself exerting what might be considered to be excessive influence over my own students, but I tell myself that someday they will be grateful I pushed them into a subject that especially interested me. I hope this is true.

I was influenced in many other ways by Tsunoda-sensei and felt particularly close to him at this time. His country had been defeated in war and he felt extremely depressed, as I could tell every so often. I think that he probably would have been equally depressed if Japan had won the war. He clearly had no sympathy for Japanese militarism, and had elected to remain in America rather than be repatriated. His was the tragedy of anyone who loves two countries. As long as the two countries are at peace, it is a great privilege to be able to enjoy two traditions, but if the countries become enemies, one is inevitably faced with painful choices.

In the hopes of cheering Tsunoda-sensei, a few of us invited him occasionally to the theater or to the ballet. I remember how happy he looked after a wonderful performance of *Giselle* with the Cuban ballerina Alicia Alonso. But I suppose that the way we cheered him most was by the enthusiasm with which we pursued our studies of his country. In the autumn of 1946 we asked him to give courses on Heian literature, Genroku literature, and Buddhist literature. He also taught his regular course on the history of Japanese thought. Seldom has any teacher been so overworked, but probably that was the best thing that could have happened to him under the circumstances—he was too frantically busy to brood over the defeat.

In the course on Heian literature we read sections of *The Tale of Genji* and *The Pillow-Book of Sei Shōnagon.* In the Genroku course we read the whole of Saikaku's *Five Women Who Loved Love,* plus *Oku no Hosomichi (The Narrow Road of Oku)* by Bashō, and an act of Chikamatsu's play *Kokusenya Kassen (The Battles of Coxinga).* In the Buddhist class we read *Tsurezuregusa (Essays in Idleness)* and two Nō plays, *Sotoba Komachi* and *Matsukaze.* It now seems to me incredible that we could have read so much in one year. My readings at this time anticipated my work in later years: two years later *Kokusenya Kassen* would become the subject of my Ph.D. thesis, *The Battles of Coxinga,* and in 1967 I would translate *Tsurezuregusa* under the title *Essays in Idleness.* The Nō plays I read at that time are still my favorites and formed my taste for the art. I sometimes think that all that I have done since as a scholar was anticipated by my work under Tsunoda-sensei during that year and a half at Columbia, and it pains me to think how little known he is in his own country.

Although I enjoyed my classes at Columbia, I really wanted to go to Japan to study, but there seemed to be no possibility of persuading the occupation to let me into the country. I thought then of going to China, and began in the spring of 1947 to study Chinese conversation at an evening school. I continued this course at Yale during the summer of the same year, and eventually became fairly proficient at speaking Chinese. I am often asked by Japanese acquaintances how many languages I can speak. They seem to believe that if one once learns to speak a language one never forgets it. Alas, this is not true in my case. I am now totally unable to speak Chinese and during two short visits to China of the past ten years I did not regain any of my old fluency. But I know as a fact that in the summer of 1947 I was capable of conversing in Chinese.

I did not go to China. It was just at this time that the Communist revolution was making its full strength felt, and it did not seem like a propitious time to study there. But I was restless and wanted to go somewhere. I suppose that my uncertainty over my future—whether I would ever learn Japanese well enough to be a scholar of Japanese literature, whether I would get a job, even if I succeeded in becoming a scholar—made me want to escape. But to where? I could go neither to Japan nor to China, and these were the two foreign countries where I wanted most to study. I eventually thought of somewhere to go. Like many students at other universities at the time, I thought of Harvard with awe. It was the oldest and richest university in America and its faculty was extremely distinguished. It is true that not all the Harvard graduates at the Navy Japanese Language School had impressed me with their scholarly ability, but I had made several close friends among them and I thought it would be agreeable to study alongside them in unfamiliar surroundings.

But how to tell Tsunoda-sensei that I was going to study under another teacher? I thought he might be upset, but I misjudged him. When I finally plucked up the courage to tell him of my plan, he answered that it was the practice among Buddhist monks to travel from one center of learning to another. The Japanese name for this practice, he told me, is *henzan*.

With Tsunoda-sensei's blessings, then, I went to Harvard in the autumn of 1947. The professor of Japanese Literature was Serge Elisséeff, a legendary figure much beloved by Harvard students. He had studied in St. Petersburg and Berlin, and then (after the Russo-Japanese War) entered Tokyo Imperial University, from which he obtained a degree. He had known Natsume Sōseki, who wrote a haiku about the young Russian scholar. Before going to Harvard he had taught in Paris. He was without doubt the best-known scholar of Japan in America at the time.

*****

While at Harvard I began the translation of Chikamatsu's play *The Battles of Coxinga.* Professor Elisséeff graciously allowed me to take what was called a "double course" with him, meaning I had private instruction for two hours a week. I also attended his survey course on Japanese literature. He was always friendly to me and he had a great repertory of anecdotes, especially about life in Russia before the Revolution but, to tell the truth, I was disappointed in his teaching. His lectures for the survey course were all written out, and he read his notes in a monotonous voice. Although he was a master of at least four other languages, his English was poor, and irreverent students would imitate him: "What are the author of this book we are not knowing. . . ." Accustomed as I was to Tsunoda-sensei's lectures, a teacher thinking before his students, these lectures seemed dry and dead.

My disappointment with Professor Elisséeff was not confined to the survey class in Japanese literature. He rarely prepared for the two-hour sessions of private instruction he gave me on the play by Chikamatsu I was translating, relying on his remarkable fluency in Japanese to overcome the difficulties in the text we were reading together. An early eighteenth-century puppet drama, however, has a special vocabulary and it contains expressions that cannot be explained without adequate preparation. At

times when the text eluded him, he would favor me with anecdotes about life in old Russia. Sometimes too, he would give me
bits of information based on his long residence in Japan that
would have been difficult to find elsewhere. I remember his explaining the difference between the way a Japanese woman and
a European woman sew (though I forget his explanation now).

My greatest dissatisfaction with Professor Elisséeff, however,
arose for a quite different reason. One day, when I happened to
mention Tsunoda-sensei in some connection, he said, "How can
a university have such a man?" His tone indicated utter contempt. I wanted to retort, "He knows ten times as much as you
will ever know," but I was a student and he was a great professor,
so I kept silent. He did not elaborate on this opinion, but I received the impression then, and later, that although he thought
of the Japanese as delightful friends, he believed that scholarship
was something that had been invented in Europe and existed
only in Europe (and in America, to the degree that Europeans
had crossed the ocean and brought enlightenment).

I admit that I may be exaggerating his attitude, but this was
definitely my impression at the time, and I found this attitude
repugnant. I was all the more astonished when one day he attacked one of his colleagues, Dr. William Hung, with whom I
was at the time taking a course devoted to the poetry of Tu Fu.
I forget precisely why he spoke ill of Dr. Hung, but this too
offended me. The course on Tu Fu was one of the most memorable experiences I have had in a classroom. Dr. Hung could not
have been better prepared to give this course. He had read everything written about Tu Fu in English, German, and Japanese, in
addition to (of course) Chinese. He knew most of the poems by
heart. One day he recited one of the long poems, not in standard
Chinese but in the Fukien dialect, which was his own. I can still
see him, leaning back, his eyes shut, reciting words that were a

part of his body and soul. The rhymes that have disappeared from standard Chinese can still be heard when recited in Fukien dialect, with the crack of the final consonants. At the end I saw the tears in his eyes. This, I thought, was the kind of scholarship I wanted to practice. When I took the final examination in his course, the last written examination I was ever to take, I felt that this examination, the only one I have ever enjoyed, marked a fitting conclusion to my life as a student.

I suppose that in a sense I was much influenced by Professor Elisséeff. When I came to teach a survey course of Japanese literature at Columbia, I decided I would do the opposite of everything he had done. I went to class with nothing in my hands, and talked about what had moved me in the works under consideration. Naturally, I did not remember the years of, say, the first woodblock edition of each work discussed, or the number of variant texts, but I knew in which books this information could be found, and I told students who were interested. Insofar as I have been successful as a teacher, I owe much to this negative influence.

I cannot conclude my discussion of the year I spent at Harvard without mentioning the person with whom I had the most lasting relationship, Professor Edwin Reischauer. At the time he was not nearly so famous as he became within a few years. The only publication of his that I knew was the textbook of Japanese that he and Professor Elisséeff had compiled in 1941. I believe that this was the first textbook of Japanese produced in America and intended for adults. It was certainly superior to the textbooks with which I had begun my study of Japanese—the ones intended for Japanese six-year-olds—but it had a special purpose that made it difficult to use. It was intended for people who wished to acquire a reading knowledge of Japanese, and no effort was made to introduce the patterns of the spoken language. At

At Harvard

the time, scholars of Chinese had become aware that Japanese research in sinology could not be ignored, and a textbook of this kind exactly met their needs. But, as I had discovered to my exasperation at Columbia, each lesson contained up to sixty or seventy new items of vocabulary and many new kanji, and no attempt was made to repeat grammatical points that had been covered in a previous lesson.

On the basis of this textbook, which I had studied for one semester immediately before entering the Navy Japanese Language School, I supposed that Professor Reischauer must be an elderly grammarian who saw no point in coddling students who were about to study a difficult language. I could not have been more mistaken. Not only was he young, but he had an almost boyish youthfulness about him. I attended one course which he shared with Professor Elisséeff in reading classical texts. As I recall, the two texts Professor Reischauer taught were *Konjaku Monogatari* and *Hōgen Monogatari*. In the classroom he had the authority of a scholar who was thoroughly familiar with the materials he was teaching, but his self-confidence was never overbearing. Indeed, when (as it happened very rarely) a student disagreed with an interpretation, Professor Reischauer considered the student's opinion with the utmost seriousness, and sometimes he would accept it, not reluctantly but with the pleasure a real scholar feels over a discovery, whoever's discovery it may be.

One of his former students was a close friend of mine, and the three of us would have lunch together from time to time. His interests extended to every aspect of Japanese civilization, and again and again I would be surprised by some remark which, though diffidently spoken, revealed his unquestionable understanding of Japan. No doubt many of the "discoveries" I have made had their origins in these lunchtime conversations.

In 1955 Professor Reischauer published the two volumes of his study of the ninth-century Japanese priest Ennin. One volume consists of a translation of the diary Ennin kept while he was in China from 838 to 847. *Ennin's Diary* is a superb work of scholarship. The text is in a difficult mixture of classical and colloquial Chinese, and at the time the translation was made there was hardly anything in the way of commentaries and very few studies of the contents of the diary. The translation is elucidated by close to 1,600 explanatory footnotes, each one the product of hours of research. But Professor Reischauer made a crucial decision when he prepared the second volume, *Ennin's Travels in T'ang China*. He wrote in the Preface, "I have written this book not only for those with a specific interest in the Far East, but also for those with a more general interest in the broad record of human history."

Professor Reischauer's decision to write a book for the educated general public rather than for specialists was probably not an easy one to make. In 1951 he and Professor Joseph Yamagiwa had published a volume of translations of classical Japanese literature. The translations are of immaculate scholarly accuracy, with no concessions made to readers who might simply want to read and enjoy *Izayoi Nikki* or whatever the work. This tendency was strong in the academic world of the day. In extreme cases some scholars put words like *the* or *is* in square brackets, to show that these words were not in the original. But Professor Reischauer must have sensed that publishing scholarly works for the benefit of the handful of readers who could appreciate them was not enough. He by no means abandoned scholarship, but from this time on he was increasingly concerned with communicating his ideas about Japan to the widest possible public.

Professor Reischauer was the son of a missionary, and he himself retained some of the characteristics of a true missionary. But his chief object was to proselytize in America, not in Japan. Painfully aware of the immense ignorance of Japan in the United States and other countries of the West, he began to write books that would be both accurate and readable, in the hopes of enlightening people who would make the effort to learn. His work of enlightenment was not confined to books. He was the moving force behind a television series of Japanese films, the most popular program ever shown on American public television, and he actively promoted the preparation of a series of films on Japanese culture that could be shown at colleges throughout the country, especially at institutions that lacked teachers of Japanese. I remember, too, one of his own appearances on television when he discussed modern Japan. After a young Japanese woman had played part of a Bach violin sonata, Professor Reischauer commented with typical humor, "I suppose some Americans may find it strange that a Japanese should play an American composer like Bach."

These activities of Professor Reischauer influenced me considerably. I had thought at one time that I wanted nothing more than to be a "pure" scholar, the kind of person who would spend months investigating a subject and then publish a two- or three-page article that was pure gold in a learned journal. But I gradually came to realize that there was something of the missionary in me too, and if my work is remembered at all it will probably be because of the books addressed to the general public, not my attempts at "pure" scholarship.

The years that Professor Reischauer spent as the American ambassador to Japan were no doubt the climax of his career. It was not an easy assignment. He took up his post just the year after the massive demonstrations against the U.S.-Japan Security Treaty of 1960, which tied Japanese security to American power. Those who participated in the demonstrations were not necessarily anti-American, but there was certainly an anti-American strain to the slogans and pronouncements. This strain continued to be sounded in publications aimed at intellectuals even after Ambassador Reischauer arrived on the scene, with repeated denunciations being made of the "Kennedy-Reischauer offensive." This was the only time in my years of residence in Japan that I have been invited to the embassy for an informal meal, and on several occasions I heard the ambassador discuss Japanese public opinion. He was never discouraged, never pessimistic. The friendship and understanding of the two countries he loved was too important to him to be affected even by serious clashes of opinion. He was the best exemplar I have known of a scholarly ideal, belonging to more than one country.

*****

About halfway through my year at Harvard I made the unpleasant discovery that I would soon exhaust my benefits under the G.I. Bill of Rights. I decided to look for a job teaching somewhere, but the only opening I heard of, at a college in Maine, was to teach "the history of all civilizations" and I did not feel up to this task. When I went to see a professor at Columbia who had always seemed interested in my career and asked his opinion, he examined my undergraduate record carefully and then, on the basis of my marks, suggested that I look for a job teaching Greek. This was hardly a welcome suggestion. I had not looked at a Greek text for seven years and I had no intention of abandoning Japanese. But, obviously, there were absolutely no jobs in Japanese studies. What to do?

At this point someone at Harvard told me about the Henry Fellowships that were awarded to Americans for study in England and to Englishmen for study in America. Preference was given to applicants who wished to study subjects that were not so well taught in their own country as in the host country. I knew nothing about the state of teaching Japanese in England, but I thought it would probably be a mistake to ask to study Japanese there. So I boldly opted for Arabic and Persian, without knowing much about this either, but assuming (because of the long-standing British relations with the Middle East) that the teaching of these languages in England was superior to that in America. I wrote the usual kind of proposal, pointing out the rarity of persons whose knowledge of Asia extended from one end to the other, and implying that learning two more difficult languages was well within my capacities.

Did I really mean what I wrote? There is no way for me now to recall whether I was sincere or merely opportunistic, but I believe that if, when I eventually arrived in England, I had been encouraged to study Arabic and Persian, that is exactly what I should have done. Fortunately, I was discouraged, but neither I nor the board of examiners before whom I appeared foresaw this. I eventually had word that I had been awarded a fellowship. My financial crisis had been solved for at least a year, and I was excited by the prospect of studying in Cambridge, even though I could not help feeling a little uncertain about the desirability of shifting my interests to Arabic and Persian.

Soon after I had decided to accept the fellowship I had a letter from an organization that called itself something like American Students in Cambridge, offering me friendly advice about what I should bring with me. I still remember the great emphasis given to the importance of peanut butter as a supplement to the meager fare provided in the rations. Peanut butter had not been a favorite dish even when I was a small boy, and I had not acquired a taste for it since, but I meekly followed the suggestion and asked family and friends who wished to provide me with nourishment to concentrate on peanut butter. It took me a *very* long time to dispose of all the peanut butter that followed me to England, and I never again heard from the American Students in Cambridge.

I sailed for England in September 1948 aboard an American ship that had recently served as a troop transport. When my mother came to see me off she burst into tears at the sight of the quarters I was to occupy, quite unlike those in which my father was accustomed to travel to Europe. But I was too excited to think of such things as physical comforts. I was on my way to Europe!

I was to begin my studies at Cambridge in the autumn of 1948, but before going to England I spent time in France, Belgium, and Holland. I had loved France ever since I was a child. In 1931, when I was nine, my father had taken me with him on a business trip to Europe, most of the time in France, an experience that had left an indelible impression. Unlike the other pupils in my school, who could not imagine why they had to learn a foreign language when so much of the world spoke English, I knew from my unsuccessful attempts to communicate with French children of my own age that English was not enough, and when we returned to America I begged my father to hire a tutor who would teach me French. This request coincided with one of the financial disasters that struck the family at this time, and I naturally did not get my tutor. I had to wait until I entered junior high school to begin my study of French, but from then on, until I took up Chinese and Japanese, I continued my study of the language and literature.

France in the autumn of 1948 was still recovering from the effects of the war. Every few months there was a change of cabinets, a situation accepted with cynical good humor by the French. I remember that when, in the course of a newsreel that showed Henri Queuille taking office as premier, the commentator said that he had succeeded in forming a stable government, there was a roar of laughter from the audience. The previous cabinet (of Robert Schuman) had lasted exactly one week. A huge poster in the subway stations (I forget what it was advertising) showed a procession of four figures of Marianne, representing the first, second, third, and fourth republics, and an anxious-looking fifth Marianne peering around a corner, waiting to be invited to join the procession.

A friend in New York had told me about an inexpensive hotel in Paris off the Place Monge, and that was where I headed. Most of the other guests in the hotel were White Russians, who still abounded in Paris. Living conditions seemed rather primitive even to me, but the atmosphere was friendly and I was seldom in my room except to sleep. Every morning I would set out walking, sometimes with a specific objective in mind but usually just for the pleasure of seeing the street life wherever my feet happened to take me. This was the first time I had ever fallen in love with a city, and the experience would not be repeated often later in life. Being in a city where I knew almost no one might under other circumstances have made me feel lonely, but during that week or two when I wandered through the streets of Paris, captivated by its charm (even though it was not at its best in 1948), there was never any danger of feeling lonely.

I knew a French girl who had been in my Japanese literature class at Harvard. No doubt because of the difficulty her parents experienced in sending money abroad, she lived very frugally, and others in the class, when we had lunch with her, would chip in so that she might eat something more appetizing than the cheapest dishes. Soon after my arrival in Paris I went to see her. I took with me a parcel of American cigarettes, tea, and other items then available only on the black market. I left the Métro at the indicated station and was surprised to see embassies and legations on both sides. My friend's apartment house stood on a corner facing the Bois de Boulogne. As I went up in the elevator to her floor I felt more and more ashamed of my parcel. A butler came to the door and showed me into a room with Gobelin tapestries on the walls. Later I saw the rest of the apartment, some twenty rooms, each sumptuously furnished.

The worst ordeal was at lunch. I felt extremely nervous in the unfamiliar elegance of the surroundings. A napkin was set on the plate before me, folded in the shape of a cone. I picked it up and, to my horror, a piece of bread concealed in the napkin flew over my head, striking the wall behind me. Next came the first course. Demoralized by my first fiasco, I was determined not to make any mistakes in eating. I imitated the man opposite me and used a fork, only for the liquid in the dish to run through. The butler came up and, in a voice loud enough for everyone to hear, announced, "You will have more success with a spoon." The man opposite me evidently was eating something different.

The lunch that day was typical of many I would have with French people in years to come. No attention was paid to me as a guest. The conversation dealt almost exclusively with relatives or about recent happenings in Paris of which I was unaware. Not one word was addressed to me even by my friend. I finished the meal in uncomfortable silence.

I went to the theater or opera almost every night. In those days tickets were inexpensive and not difficult to obtain, no doubt because more urgent matters than the classics occupied people's minds. I had always prided myself on my ability to speak and understand French, so it was a chastening experience to discover when I went to the Comédie Française that I had to listen with the utmost attention in order to understand even half of what the actors performing Corneille or Racine so beautifully spoke; and when I went to see a work of modern theater, I was baffled by the slang and the allusions to contemporary life. It made me aware how much more there is to learning a language than merely acquiring competence, a lesson I was to learn many times over when I finally got to Japan.

*****

After an unforgettable week or two in Paris (I cannot remember now how long I stayed, though the experiences themselves are still vivid), I went to Belgium. One of the major events of my year at Harvard had been the series of lectures I attended on early Flemish painting given by Professor Erwin Panofsky. I had never been particularly interested in painting of this period, but his lectures were superb and aroused in me an enthusiasm for Flemish painting that I have never lost. I could hardly wait to get to Ghent to see the great altarpiece painted by Jan van Eyck about which Panofsky had lectured so illuminatingly. Having this focus for my visit to Belgium made my visit memorable.

From Belgium I went on to Holland. Nowadays one is scarcely aware when one crosses a border in Europe, but at the time passengers had to leave the train with their baggage and submit to examination first by the customs officials of the country one was leaving, next by the officials of the country one entered. It made travel somewhat more of an adventure than it is today, and my old passport (unlike the present one) is filled with visas and official stamps that indicate exactly when I crossed just which border.

My special interest in Holland did not stem from my love of Dutch painting, though if I were asked now to name the greatest painter I would surely answer either Rembrandt or Vermeer, but from my interest in *rangaku,* the "Dutch learning" that flourished in Japan during the eighteenth and early nineteenth centuries. I had begun to study Dutch with a friend while in America and was able to carry on a simple conversation with him, but I was certainly not equipped to converse on any higher level. Fortunately, I discovered, everyone I met in Holland spoke at least three foreign languages—English, French, and German.

In the following years I would visit Holland fairly often, and I spent most of one summer in Leiden when I was working on *The Japanese Discovery of Europe,* the revised version of the master's essay on Honda Toshiaki I had written as a graduate student at Columbia.

I took the boat at the Hook of Holland for England. I felt not only anticipation, as I had before arriving in France, but also a certain tension at the thought that I would not simply be visiting but living in England for a whole year. (As a matter of fact, I was to spend five years there.) I did not know a single person in the whole country, and I had absolutely no idea of what it would be like to study (as I planned) Arabic and Persian. Reports I had read about "austerity," the discipline the British had imposed on themselves to surmount the economic crisis of the postwar years, made me wonder if I might even have to go hungry. And almost every account of postwar Britain suggested that, contrary to prewar days when the sun never set on the British empire, it now rained constantly.

My arrival in Cambridge initially confirmed my worst fears. I had been accepted by Corpus Christi College, and when I presented myself, a "gyp" (a college servant) led me to my rooms, remarking, "Coldest rooms in Cambridge, sir." My rooms consisted of a large sitting room and an almost-as-large bedroom with a window that it was impossible to shut. That afternoon the gyp brought me my daily ration of milk, about one inch of milk in a jug. And that night dinner consisted of whitefish with a white sauce and white potatoes and white cabbage on a white plate. I had never realized before how important color is to food. The thought of a year of austerity filled me with foreboding.

*****

I had feared that the traditional reserve of the English might keep me from making friends, but within a day or two I had developed at least a nodding acquaintance with several members of my college, and some of these eventually became friends. Although I already had an M.A. and was now twenty-six, the college, reluctant to give credit for degrees obtained elsewhere, considered me still to be an undergraduate. This did not upset me, but I found myself, for the first time in my life, the oldest in any group.

Shortly after my arrival, I was sent to a member of the Faculty of Oriental Languages to discuss my plans for studying Arabic and Persian. He asked, "How many years will you be here?" When I told him that my fellowship was for just one year, he smiled. "Do you think you can learn Arabic in one year?" he asked. "And Persian too," was my cheerful response. This, I think, was too much for him—as it would be for anyone who knew anything about those languages. He made it clear that there was no point in bothering the professor of Arabic with so presumptuous a plan.

What to do? As had become usual with me in times of crisis, I fell back on the Japanese. What this meant now was that I went to see the Lecturer in Japanese, Eric Ceadel. He advised me to study classical Chinese with Professor Gustav Haloun, and suggested that I might also help in the teaching of Japanese. Both suggestions were immediately accepted and I was grateful for them. Although I had found the pace of studying the Chinese classics at Columbia much too slow for me immediately after my wartime experiences, I seemed to have matured somewhat, and I came to enjoy the late-afternoon sessions of reading Chuang Tzu with Professor Haloun and four or five other students. We gathered not in a classroom but in the professor's living room, where we were diverted by a cat named Pluto and an asthmatic grandfather clock that struck the hours only after a long protracted wheeze.

I did the first teaching of my life at Cambridge that autumn. Once a week I held a session of Japanese conversation with three undergraduates. I had not spoken Japanese for almost three years, and no doubt my Japanese had become rather rusty, but there was not a single real Japanese in Cambridge. Only one of the three students had ever actually spoken Japanese at whatever level; the other two had begun their Japanese, as was then the practice in Cambridge (though this practice has long since been discontinued), with the Preface to the tenth-century collection of poetry *Kokinshū*. In terms of the traditional British education in the classics, it was normal to study a language like Latin or Greek that one would not attempt to speak. Beginning instruction in Japanese with the Preface to the *Kokinshū* was entirely in keeping with that tradition. The vocabulary of the Preface is restricted, very few kanji are used, and the grammar is absolutely regular. Only after the student had obtained a firm grasp of classical Japanese was he introduced (in his second year) to the modern language.

This system was logical in terms of pedagogy, but it made for the most peculiar conversation hours. The students mingled Heian period phrases with colloquialisms picked up from me or elsewhere, rather as if a Japanese had learned his English conversation from a combination of *Beowulf* and Ernest Hemingway. I was not a great success as a teacher, but in spite of me two of my three students went on to have distinguished academic careers, and toward the end of the year Professor Haloun asked me if I would not consider remaining in Cambridge as a member of the faculty.

I remember the day very well. It was a sunny day of a kind one rarely encounters in February. Aconites and snowdrops were in bloom here and there, proclaiming the coming of spring. I went for a walk to clear my thoughts. I had already accepted a position as an assistant professor at an American university, a job far more elevated than the assistant lectureship that was the most I could expect at Cambridge. The salary offered by the American institution was also about five times as much as assistant lecturers were paid. In material terms there was no comparison between the two positions. But I felt extremely reluctant to leave Cambridge.

Cambridge had brought my first acquaintance with living traditions. At first it seemed strange, for example, to wear an academic gown in the manner of students of long ago, and I remember my irritation when I was denied entry to the university library because I was not wearing a gown. But gradually this costume, worn in America only at graduation ceremonies, became a part of my life. I enjoyed seeing undergraduates in gowns (sometimes tattered) on their way to chapel or dinner and hearing the crunch of their footsteps on the gravel path outside my window. It gave me a sense of tradition, too, when I saw at night two officers of the university patrolling the streets on the lookout for undergraduates who were not wearing gowns. These men carried with them, as the source of their authority, a copy of university regulations framed a century earlier. Nothing dreadful would happen to an undergraduate caught not wearing a gown. Wearing a gown was in fact a privilege rather than a duty, and not wearing one a pleasantly dangerous activity. A body of legends had grown up about "night climbers"—undergraduates who had boldly defied regulations and returned to their rooms in college late at night without gowns or permission by scaling walls and spiked fences.

I enjoyed also eating in "hall," as the college dining room is called. The food was terrible. Whale meat was, I think, the worst thing served, but there were other, nearly as unpalatable dishes, all of which were listed on the menu with elegant French names. There was extremely little variety. One week, as I noted at the time, of twenty-one meals eaten in hall during the course of a week, fourteen had herring as their chief ingredient. (Years later, when in Kyoto for the first time, I blanched when invited to eat *nishin soba,* soba noodles with herring.) But hall itself was a splendid building, ornamented by the portraits of long ago masters of the college. I enjoyed, too, hearing grace said before meals each night in Latin by members of the high table, the dons of the college.

In short, I had developed such a strong attachment to Cambridge, even during this period of drab austerity, that I was not much tempted by California sunshine. As I walked along that day in February the college buildings had never seemed more splendid. I went into the library of Trinity College and examined the mementos of what seemed to be half the great men of England. I thought, I can't leave this place. The thought became a firm conviction as I walked back to my rooms in college, and that night I wrote a letter to the American university asking to be released from my promise to teach there. I had made a decision that would directly affect the next five years of my life, the years spent in Cambridge.

*****

My remembrances of my first year in Cambridge are mainly of my pleasure in the architecture and atmosphere. I enjoyed even the nights in November when yellow fog stung my eyes because they recalled the descriptions I had read of the London fog. England gave me a feeling of homecoming, not in terms of ancestors but of English literature. To hear a cuckoo for the first time or to go to a place known for its nightingales was not simply enjoyable but created a link between myself and the poetry that spoke of these birds.

I enjoyed also the sounds of English as pronounced by my new friends. In recent years, I understand, regional accents have come to be accepted, but at that time any undergraduate who did not speak the language appropriate to his privileged station would be urged to attend a school where he might improve his speech. I myself tried to speak as much like an Englishman as possible. This was not very difficult, and it enabled me to feel that I belonged in Cambridge. But sometimes it only earned me such sarcasm as, "How is it that you, an American, can speak English?"

Unpleasant comments about Americans formed part of the normal conversation of some of the people I met. It was annoying at first to be asked such questions as, "Is it true that American universities grant doctorates in dishwashing?" I gradually realized that there was generally nothing more than a pleasantry involved in these queries. The contrast between the austerity of life in Britain and the opulence of American life, as depicted in the films, must have been irritating to people brought up to the strains of "Rule Britannia"; and the "brain drain" of scholars to America was no doubt a reminder of the changes that had occurred in the comparative economic strength of the two countries. It would have been strange if there had been no resentment. But the courtesy of the British, far more than such momentary irritations, lingers in my memory.

During the winter vacation in 1948 my rooms in college were to be used by students taking examinations, and I decided to go to Rome, where I knew some people from the ship that had taken me to Europe. I had completed writing my doctoral dissertation, *The Battles of Coxinga,* while in Cambridge, and I decided to type it in Rome. I went first to Paris, then took an overnight train to Milan. The compartment was stuffy, and I thought I would take advantage of the wait in Milan to get some fresh air. I asked another passenger in the compartment if he would look after my suitcase and typewriter, and I then walked up and down the platform briskly for perhaps five minutes. When I returned to the compartment there was no man and no suitcase. At first I couldn't believe it. I thought that it must be a nightmare from which I would presently awake. I went to the police, and in my poor Italian explained what had happened. I urged them to look for the man, who must still be in the station, but they laughed at my guilelessness and insisted that I complete a form. Name of father. Name of mother. Names of grandparents. Profession of father. And so on. By this time I was almost hysterical, but there was absolutely nothing I could do.

I never saw the manuscript of my dissertation again. I returned to Cambridge with nothing but the few clothes I had bought in Italy. I was shaken by the disaster, but it led to the formation of my most important friendship in England.

It was still the Christmas vacation when I got back to Cambridge, and there were very few people in the college. I told everyone I met of the disaster that had overtaken me in Milan; this seemed to be the only way of dissipating even slightly my frustration. The response was heartwarming. One person arranged for me to stay in a warm and comfortable room that was empty during the vacation, another found me a typewriter on which to write a new version of the stolen dissertation. One of the few friends who was actually in Cambridge at the time, William Dickins, was the son of one of the dons at Corpus Christi College. His mother, by way of expressing her sympathy, invited me for lunch, and the invitation was extended day after day until the college kitchen started to function again.

It was no small favor to invite a guest to meals during those days of rationing, and I was profoundly grateful. More than that, Mrs. Mary Dickins became a close friend, a relationship that lasted until her death. She was the eldest of the five daughters of Sir Herbert Grierson, the great scholar of English literature. Her sisters, all of whom were exceptionally interesting women, lived in Oxford, The Hague, New York, and Paris. They had grown up in a household where scraps of poetry were used as a kind of shorthand communication, it being assumed that the relevance of the quotations to the situation at hand would immediately be understood. I confess that I did not always recognize the quotations, but that hardly mattered. It was exciting to talk with anyone from whom ideas tumbled so rapidly that ordinary prose could not keep up the pace.

Among Mrs. Dickins's achievements was that of being a great cook. She was able to find ways of preparing delicious meals from items (such as sheeps' heads) that were not rationed because almost no one knew how to cook them. Years later, when she decided to live independently, her skill as a cook was recognized by higher and higher levels of employers until she was finally cooking for the royal family at Balmoral.

Of the many subjects we talked about, painting seemed closest to her heart. Sometimes we went to galleries together. It was her practice to look at only one or two pictures during a visit, but to stay before each until she felt she really understood it. She had no interest in what was merely decorative; unless a painting spoke to her directly, she soon moved on. I recall that when I went with her to the Frick Collection in New York, she seemed to absorb into herself the great El Greco portrait of St. Jerome. Only then did she give me the benefit of her perceptions of what El Greco wished to reveal in the portrait. Or at the Metropolitan Museum she stopped before a Goya showing two women who sit on a balcony, smiling down on the scene before them, while a third person, somberly dressed, looks away. Mrs. Dickins instinctively felt that the women were watching an execution. I have no idea whether or not Goya in fact intended to suggest this, but it made perfect sense to me.

I suppose that one definition of a friend is someone with whom one always has something to talk about. That was certainly true of Mrs. Dickins. After my first year in college I lived in her house for two years, and although we met at mealtimes every day, there never seemed to be enough time for all we both had to say.

I managed, thanks to my friends in Cambridge, to rewrite the dissertation that spring. One friend who had read both the old and new versions told me that the new one was a great improvement. Perhaps he was only trying to comfort me. Even more important than his praise was the friendship with Mrs. Dickins that had stemmed from my loss. Perhaps I should really have thanked the thief in Milan.

*****

Among the other acquaintances I made during my first year in Cambridge was Bertrand Russell. This was his last year of teaching at Cambridge, and his lectures on modern philosophy were attended by a great many people, all resolved to tell their children at some future date that they had actually heard the great man lecture. After one of the first lectures of the term I went up to ask him to autograph a copy of his *A History of Western Philosophy*, which had been published a few years earlier. As it happened, I was the first in a fairly long line of people, each of whom had a book for him to autograph, and Lord Russell used my pen to sign them all. After the last person had gone away he realized that he had kept me waiting and, after apologizing, suggested that we have a beer together.

Needless to say, I was enchanted at the idea. We went to a nearby establishment and drank together for about an hour before he had to go off to dinner in Trinity College. I have unfortunately no recollection of what we talked about, but I was overjoyed when, after we had finished our beers, Lord Russell said something like, "Young man, I like your company. Let us have beer together after every lecture this term." And that is precisely what happened. Friends who saw me walking from the lecture hall to the hotel where we were to drink said that they had never seen anyone look so happy.

What was it that so captivated me? Of course, it was highly flattering to think that a great man had singled me out from among all the undergraduates attending his lectures as his drinking companion. But it was more than that. Bertrand Russell spoke with a pronunciation and a precise choice of words that made me think of eighteenth-century English literature. He would ask me searching questions, as if he were really interested in me, and when I asked him a question would consider it, as if it were worthy of thought. He was also quick to discover when I was only pretending to know something in the hope of keeping him from being disillusioned about me. For example, on one occasion he asked, "You remember how *Henry V* begins, don't you?" "Of course," I answered, though my mind was a blank. I had read the play several times and the film with Laurence Olivier was one of my great favorites, but I simply could not recall that it opens with the Archbishop of Canterbury planning to save church lands by backing Henry V's invasion of France. "I see that you do not know how *Henry V* begins," Lord Russell said with a smile.

How I wish that I had kept a diary or even a memorandum of

the substance of our conversations at that time! But I had always had such confidence in my memory that it never occurred to me that I might forget conversations that brought me so much pleasure. By accident, I still have a brief memo to myself on one conversation. Lord Russell told me about a Chinese student named Hsü whose teacher in China was distinguished both by his unusual knowledge of the classics and by the fact he had never taken a bath. When the teacher died, his family thought that he should be bathed before the funeral, but Hsü objected, "No, bury him whole!"

One conversation lingers with particular vividness. Lord Russell thought that the greatest danger to a lasting peace was Stalin, and that the Americans, while they still had a monopoly on the atomic bomb should use it on the Soviet Union to get rid of Stalin. People I have told of this conversation find it hard to believe. Lord Russell would be known as a passionate advocate of peace with the Soviet Union, and he was even credited with the slogan "Better red than dead!" I realize how unlikely it is that he should have expressed himself in such terms, but I have no doubt whatsoever that this is precisely what he said.

Another well-known writer I met in Cambridge during my first year was E. M. Forster. I had read most of his works before leaving America, and I asked Lionel Trilling, my old teacher and the author of a study of Forster's writings, for an introduction. I sent Mr. Forster a note enclosing the introduction, and one evening, while I was having tea with a colleague, there was a knock on the door and Mr. Forster entered. I introduced him to my friend, who was a member of King's College, and Mr. Forster said something to the effect, "We're at the same place." After arranging a meeting, he left. My friend asked, "Who was *that?*" It had not

occurred to him that the soft-spoken man who had rather timidly entered my room was a world-famous novelist.

I saw Mr. Forster from time to time during that and following
years. I imagine he was afraid of running out of things to talk
about with a teacher of Japanese, and that was why he always
invited an Asian of some nationality to keep me company. By
accident we eventually found a topic about which both of us
could speak with enthusiasm, our love of opera. As an undergraduate at Columbia I had hoarded my money to pay for a sub-
scription to the Metropolitan Opera. My seat was in the last row
of the top balcony, and even with the aid of opera glasses the
singers on the stage seemed very remote. But what singers they
were! It was the golden age of Wagner performances at the Met,
and I heard unforgettable performances with Kirsten Flagstad,
Lauritz Melchior, Lotte Lehmann, Kerstin Thorborg, Herbert
Janssen, Alexander Kipnis. Anyone who supposes that I am the
victim of nostalgia and that these singers were no better than
those one can hear today is urged to listen to the compact discs
that are now available of these legendary voices.

Mr. Forster, however, was more interested in Verdi than in
Wagner. He spoke with enthusiasm of *La Forza del Destino,*
which had recently been performed in London. The years immediately following the war were a marvelous time to hear opera in
London, even though the operas were generally sung in English
(except during the special international season in June). I heard
Elisabeth Schwarzkopf sing (in English) in *La Traviata,* and Victoria de los Angeles in *Manon.* I recall, too, a marvelous performance of *Boris Godunov* during which Boris Christoff sang in
Russian and everyone else in English, making for some rather
peculiar exchanges of dialogue. And no one who was present will
ever forget Ljuba Welitsch in the controversial production of *Sa-*

lome staged by Salvador Dalí, during which all the singers were costumed as birds and the whole set turned into an immense peacock at the end. The musical life was not by any means confined to opera. I remember especially the concert at the Royal Albert Hall at which Kirsten Flagstad sang the world premiere of Richard Strauss's *Four Last Songs*.

People sometimes ask me if I have a hobby. No doubt it would be interesting if I combined a love of Japanese literature with a passion for water skiing or for collecting rare butterflies, but the closest I come to having a hobby is a love of music, especially of operatic music. A day spent without once listening to music is a bleak day for me. On the other hand, I have no fondness for the rock music (and similar varieties of music) that give so much pleasure to young people. Sometimes I wonder whether I might not be a snob, and I have even tried to force myself to listen to music I dislike. But it does no good. It is much easier to violate all the rules that society imposes than those of one's own tastes.

The one person I wanted most to meet in England, even before I left America, was Arthur Waley. His translations of Japanese and Chinese literature had been my inspiration during the long years of learning to read these languages. I still have somewhere a copy of his *More Translations from the Chinese* with the Chinese texts laboriously (and clumsily) copied in my hand at a time when I was groping ahead in the dark toward the light that was Waley.

For some years I had thought (before I realized my own limitations) that I would imitate Waley in being a scholar of both China and Japan. However, though I admired his translations of Chinese poetry so much I had memorized some, I had never been able to read through his translation of the Chinese novel *Monkey,* though some people enjoy it most of all his works. This made me think again that perhaps I was cut out to be only half of Waley.

I preferred his translations from the Japanese, and sometimes I tried to persuade myself that he really liked Japanese literature better than Chinese. He once told me that his partial translation of *The Pillow-Book of Sei Shōnagon* was his own favorite among his works. I had been moved especially by the beauty of his translation of *The Tale of Genji,* a marvelous re-creation in English of a text a thousand years old. During the war I had tried to read the original in a class at the University of Hawaii, and this painful experience had aroused renewed admiration, even awe, for Waley's accomplishment.

I had been told before leaving America that Waley worked at the British Museum, but this had not been true for many years. As I was wondering how to meet him, I learned in January 1949 that he was to lecture in Cambridge and wrote inviting him to tea. I had no introduction, and only an ironclad desire to meet him can explain what gave me the courage to offer this invitation. Waley replied with a postcard, the message written in minuscule handwriting at the top, saying that I should introduce myself after his lecture.

That afternoon I was listening to a broadcast from Germany of a Wagnerian opera, when there was a knock on my door. "Come in!" I shouted unceremoniously, and an unknown man entered. "I am Dr. Waley," the man said. In great confusion, I switched off the radio, and stammered something about having been studying. I heard later from a friend with whom Waley subsequently spoke that he had been astonished that anyone could study to the beat of American jazz. I was miserable at the thought that Waley had formed a bad impression of me, and was sure he would never be able to take seriously anyone with such uncouth habits. Only later did I realize that my best qualification for being accepted as an acquaintance by this great collector of eccentrics was as the American who could study only to the raucous accompaniment of jazz.

His lecture that night was on the Ainu epic *Kutune Shirka*. All I knew about the Ainu was the stereotype of "the hairy Ainu," but Waley's rendering of the epic made me realize they had composed delicate and beautiful poetry. He read aloud in a rather high-pitched voice, interrupting himself occasionally to make some comment on the poetry, which he obviously loved. The possibility of discovering another variety of poetry had induced him to study the Ainu language, though he was of an age when learning a new language is by no means easy.

In the years that followed I visited Waley from time to time in London. I have met people who complained that they could never get a word out of Waley, but we always found topics of mutual interest, and sometimes we sat in his room talking until it became too dark even to see each other.

*****

Not long after I had firmly committed myself to teaching in Cambridge, the pound was devalued by about a third. My modest salary in terms of dollars became insufficient even to sustain life, to the consternation of family and friends in America; but as a matter of fact, I have no recollection of having suffered because of lack of money. Almost every item of food was rationed at a price that was calculated to the farthing, a quarter of a penny. Meals in restaurants never cost more than five shillings, though fancy establishments might add charges for such items as flowers on the table. Tickets to plays and concerts were still cheap enough for me to go regularly. In all the time I was in

Cambridge I never heard of the existence of a black market, though perhaps this academic community was not typical of the entire country. The only time I felt the strain of austerity was when, during vacations, I went abroad. The allowance for foreign currency was twenty-five pounds a year, hardly enough for travel to France, Spain, and Italy, the countries I wanted most to visit. All the same, I managed to go abroad almost every vacation without breaking any laws.

My teaching consisted mainly of reading classical texts with two or three students. I can remember only two—*Hōjōki* (which I would read with students at Columbia for about thirty years) and *Kojiki* (which I never read again). My one crisis as a teacher occurred during my second year of teaching. I was informed that if I wished to be promoted from assistant lecturer to lecturer I would have to teach a second Asian language. I had studied Chinese for almost as much time as Japanese, and suggested I might be able to teach that language, but I was told that the teaching of Chinese traditionally (on the model of Hebrew) could not be combined with the teaching of any other language. Was there not some other Oriental language I might teach? After some thought, I answered that during the war I had learned a little Korean, mainly from prisoners of war. "Excellent!" was the response. "Nobody will ever want to study Korean, and Korean goes well with Japanese, like Arabic with Persian." In this manner I became the lecturer in Japanese and Korean. The next summer the Korean War broke out, and in the autumn, when the university year began, I had seven students in my Korean class, most of them persons senior to myself.

I could not very well admit my virtual ignorance of the Korean language. Instead, I pored over the one book that was of help, a textbook of Korean grammar by a Finnish scholar. I also had a Korean-Japanese dictionary that I had picked up during the war. The text we read had been prepared at an American university, but was not accompanied by any teaching materials. The questions asked by my students were penetrating, each one seemingly designed to destroy the weak fabric of my self-confidence. Sometimes, when asked the meaning of a verb ending or particle that I did not know, I resorted to the desperate expedient of saying that it was only a meaningless sound. I really don't know how I got through that year, but one of the students went on to become a scholar of Korean, and I now think of myself (once in a while) as the father of Korean studies in Great Britain.

I was otherwise occupied with preparing for publication *The Battles of Coxinga,* and in the following year I published *The Japanese Discovery of Europe.* I decided then and there to publish a book every year, a resolution I found increasingly difficult to implement.

My first book, *The Battles of Coxinga,* was published in 1951. I was in Istanbul, attending the Congress of Orientalists, at the time of publication, and looked forward to my return to England, imagining I would see copies of my book in the windows of the bookshops in Cambridge. Alas, the book never made a window anywhere, and I can hardly recall ever having seen a copy on sale. It was reviewed in a few specialist periodicals and then left to disappear into the great void of unread books. Many young scholars have had the same experience, but nothing can prepare one or console one for the shock of having (with immense effort and expenditure of time) produced a book that no one wants to read. I marvel now that this experience did not make me decide never to publish another book, but perhaps (I have forgotten now) a spirit of never-say-die impelled me to write a book that would really be read and respected.

My second book, *The Japanese Discovery of Europe,* was a study of the interest that Japanese of the eighteenth century manifested in Europe. At the time their only access to the West was through the trading station of the Dutch on Deshima, a small, artificially built island in Nagasaki Bay. It was extremely difficult for the Japanese to learn Dutch (or any other European language) well enough to read books. There were no grammars and no dictionaries except for rough-and-ready word lists compiled by the official interpreters. The intellectual curiosity of the rangakusha, the scholars of Dutch learning, nevertheless compelled them to make great efforts to acquire a knowledge of a language that would make available to them the achievements of European civilization.

It may be that my interest in these scholars, first aroused, as I have noted, by the lectures given by my teacher at Columbia, Ryūsaku Tsunoda, was nurtured by a feeling that I was doing much the same as they—learning a difficult foreign language in the hopes of acquiring something not to be found in my own culture. Of course, it was much easier for me than for the rangakusha. I enjoyed the benefits of good teachers, dictionaries, and even a brief stay in Japan, but their knowledge of Holland and the rest of Europe had to be gleaned from whatever books happened to reach Japan and from casual contacts with the members of the Dutch trading station in Nagasaki when they made their annual visit to the shogun's palace in Edo.

While still in New York I had begun to study Dutch with an Indonesian friend who had learned the language while growing up in what was then a Dutch possession. Later, I was able to consult the Archives in The Hague where the records of the "factory" on Deshima were kept. I am afraid that I have very nearly forgotten Dutch now (along with various other languages I once could read), but I enjoyed doing research in materials which, I hoped, no other scholar had previously examined.

*

If anyone had read them it was surely Professor Charles Boxer, who had written a pioneering work on the rangakusha called *Jan Compagnie in Japan, 1600–1817*. Early in his career as an army officer he had become interested in seventeenth-century history, and he had learned Dutch and Portuguese, two languages essential for studying that period, both of them neglected by scholars in other countries. At the time I first knew him he was the Camoens Professor of Portuguese at the University of London. I wrote him about my research, and he kindly suggested books that might be useful. On one occasion he also invited me to spend a weekend at his house in Dorset, which proved to be a memorable experience.

The Boxers' house was an enormous relic of Edwardian times, much too big to be heated in those days of fuel rationing. Only a few of the hundred or more rooms were actually in use. One of them was devoted to Professor Boxer's collection of books, mainly huge folio volumes of the seventeenth century. His wife, whom I had known from writings published under her maiden name, Emily Hahn, had decided in "revenge" to collect the smallest books she could find. Certain rules of behavior prevailed in the house, and guests were expected to obey them. One was that there was to be no conversation at meals. Books and magazines were provided for those who chose not to concentrate on the food. The Boxers' house was not typical of England—Mrs. Boxer is in fact American—but, as I was to discover, a weekend at an English country house generally presented challenges. (One which baffled me to the end was being told at four o'clock in the afternoon, on arriving somewhere, "I expect you'll want to wash up. Dinner is at half-past seven." Is it really intended that one spend three and a half hours "washing up"?)

Once the silent meal was over, Professor Boxer let me prowl through his marvelous collection of books, many of them concerning the same period of relations between Japan and Europe that I was then investigating. His collection included Japanese books written by rangakusha, including some with illustrations that I would borrow when I published *The Japanese Discovery of Europe.*

It still fascinates me to think that during the period of seclusion, when the Japanese were isolated in every possible way from contact with the outside world, they nevertheless managed to learn of the scientific discoveries made in Europe, and some of them even attempted, for example, to reproduce the experiments in electricity about which they had read. They were impressed by the practicality of the alphabet which with only twenty-six letters could express every word of a European language, unlike the thousands of kanji and kana—the ideographic and phonetic characters—that were necessary for writing Japanese. Men like Shiba Kōkan were intrigued by the new possibilities in art opened by perspective and shading, and painted familiar scenes around Edo using these new techniques. Above all, the rangakusha were impressed by the European practice of publishing their findings and techniques, unlike the Japanese who had traditionally passed on the secrets of their art only to chosen disciples or to persons who paid sufficiently generous fees.

I have no recollection of the nature of the books in Mrs. Boxer's collection, but her conversation was quite the most fascinating I had ever heard. The conversation began with a surprise: I had heard that she smoked cigars, so I should have expected it when she lit one as the prelude to our after-dinner chat, but it startled me all the same. Even more startling were her subjects of conversation. A typical opening to a topic was along the lines of, "When I was on a Belgian troop ship going to the

Congo. . . ." She described how she and her husband had met in Hong Kong at a time when she was married to a Chinese. Not long afterward, when the Japanese captured Hong Kong, Charles Boxer was interned, but as the wife of a Chinese she not only escaped internment but could visit Charles. The Japanese jailors seem to have been lenient in the face of love.

I have forgotten much of the conversation, and I may have augmented it with what she has published, but I was intensely stimulated by Emily Hahn's absolutely matter-of-fact recitations of the most extraordinary experiences.

*****

My life in Cambridge was in most ways ideal for a scholar. My teaching load was light, and the vacations totaled more than six months each year. The collection of Japanese books in the University Library, at first restricted to the rare editions of the Tokugawa period given to the library by Aston and other pioneers in the domain of Japanese studies, had now been much augmented by purchases of modern books, and it was certainly adequate for my needs. I had friends like Mrs. Dickins in Cambridge and a few others elsewhere in England. In France and Spain I also had friends who made it possible for me to spend much longer periods in those countries than my annual allotment of foreign currency would otherwise have permitted. I knew how fortunate I was, and yet I sometimes felt discontented and depressed.

Probably the main cause of my discontent was my lack of satisfaction with my work as a teacher. After the initial excitement of the Korean War, which brought me the largest class I was ever to have at Cambridge, had died down, I went back to teaching classes of one or two students. If these students had been absolutely first-rate, they might have inspired me and persuaded me that I was fulfilling the traditional function of a teacher, passing on the torch of learning. The students were certainly pleasant and intelligent, but not extraordinary, and giving formal lectures to two people was frustrating. Like many others who have devoted themselves to the study of Japan, I had something of the propagandist in me. I wanted to communicate my enthusiasm for Japanese literature to others, the more the better, and two students failed to satisfy me.

The general lack of interest in my books was equally depressing. I had a statement from the publishers of my first book, *The Battles of Coxinga,* to the effect that at the present rate of sales it would take seventy-two years to exhaust the edition of a thousand copies. *The Japanese Discovery of Europe* had been somewhat more favorably received, but I never met anyone in the university who had actually read it. (I did not realize at the time that this was normal in academic communities.) And although I was still very much in love with Cambridge and its traditions, I was rather afraid of becoming like some of the scholars I knew, men who had published a brilliant book before they were thirty and nothing since. I learned not to ask (as one habitually did in America) what a scholar was working on, for fear of receiving an answer such as, "I've *written* my book."

Again, I enjoyed dining with the dons at the High Table in Corpus, where a valiant attempt was made, despite the rationing, to maintain some of the elegance of prewar days. After the meal, when we went to the Combination Room to drink port or madeira I would sometimes try the snuff that was passed around in a silver box, gingerly imitating the others. I never derived the least pleasure from snuff, not even a good sneeze, but I was eager to participate in all the traditional rites. The avoidance of "shop talk" on such occasions always depressed me. What, I wondered, could be more interesting than "shop talk"

with the scholars around the table? And what was less interesting than chit-chat on projected repairs to the college buildings
or the current state of the benefice made by some eighteenth-
century donor? I can hardly remember one topic of conversation
worthy of the learned men around me. Obviously, I was becoming restive but, having made up my mind to spend the rest of
my life in Cambridge, it did not occur to me that I might be
happier elsewhere.

In the spring of 1952 I offered a series of lectures on Japanese
literature at Cambridge University. The frustration I had begun
to feel over the fewness of my students and the general lack of
interest in my work had made me try to think of some way of
arousing interest in my subject and satisfying my vaguely sensed
desire to be a real teacher. It occurred to me that a series of lectures, open not only to everyone in the university but to the
town as well, might be the best solution to my problem.

I prepared five lectures, trying to make them as interesting
and intelligible as possible. Apart from the introductory lecture,
in which I presented my impressions of the characteristics of
Japanese literature as a whole, I gave one lecture each on poetry,
theater, fiction, and, finally, what I called "Japanese literature
under Western influence." When I think back on these lectures
now, I marvel at my daring in having ventured to present my
views on a literature that I had first begun to read less than ten
years earlier. But, reading the book that resulted now, I see that
what I lacked in knowledge, I made up for in enthusiasm.

I feel most dissatisfied now with the last lecture. I would not
call it "Japanese literature under Western influence" if I wrote it
today because I am aware of how much in modern literature cannot be explained in terms of influence from the West. At the
time, however, it was almost impossible to obtain books from
Japan, and the Japanese collection of the University Library,

though well provided with works of classical literature had extremely few modern novels. Arthur Waley gave me the copy of *Sasameyuki* (*The Makioka Sisters*) that the author, Tanizaki Junichirō, had sent him and this, together with *Ukigumo* by Hayashi Fumiko, were the only postwar works of fiction that I knew and discussed in my lecture.

On the day of the first lecture I waited nervously outside the hall for the time when the lecture was scheduled to begin. A young woman came up to me and asked if this was where the lecture on Japanese literature was to be given. I told her that it was. "Do you think it will be good?" she asked. I was too embarrassed to say anything, and to my disappointment she went away. When the hour finally arrived, I went inside. I saw that I had been given a very large lecture room, but that there were no more than ten people, all seated in a row. Of course, Mrs. Dickins was there, as was Professor Dickins. Most of the other people present were acquaintances, probably there out of a sense of duty or else (more knowledgeable in such matters than I) aware how few listeners were likely to assemble and anxious to spare me wounded feelings.

The audience for each of the five lectures ranged from six to ten people, huddled together in a room that could easily have accommodated two hundred. I was thoroughly discouraged. I had put into the lectures not only all of my imperfect knowledge of Japanese literature but my youthful love of my subject, and I felt rejected. I decided at this point to abandon Japanese, and I began in the autumn of 1952 to attend classes in Russian with the intention of shifting at some future date from Japanese to Russian literature. Fortunately or unfortunately, I made absolutely no progress with Russian; I had no trouble with the grammar, but the vocabulary refused to enter my brain. I concluded sadly that I was bound to Japanese for life.

Once again Bashō's words perfectly fitted my situation: incapable and untalented though I was, I was bound to this one course for life.

*****

It occurred to me at this time (the spring of 1952) that if somehow I could get to Japan, where I would be surrounded by Japanese culture, I would be able to break out of my loneliness as a scholar of Japanese literature. Travel to Japan, however, was expensive; the airplane fare was far beyond my resources. I made inquiries in England, but there seemed to be no funds available.

During the summer of 1952 I went back to New York to do translations for the volume *Sources of Japanese Tradition* which was then being compiled at Columbia. I took the opportunity to visit several foundations. The response was not encouraging. One foundation official told me in so many words that if he had to make a choice between two equally accomplished scholars, one in literature and the other in the social sciences, he would certainly award any fellowship at his disposal to the social scientist. But I made applications all the same.

That year I had an unexpected piece of good news from my friend Jack Cranmer-Byng, who was then studying Chinese at Cambridge and was the editor of the Wisdom of the East Series, founded by his father years before. The series included many works of Chinese, Indian, and Arabic philosophy, and a number of books of Chinese, Arabic, Persian, and even ancient Egyptian poetry, but only one Japanese title, a translation of *Tsurezuregusa* (under the title *The Harvest of Leisure*). Cranmer-Byng, after reading the manuscript of the lectures I had delivered in the spring, decided to publish them in the series.

I was absolutely delighted that the lectures, whose reception had been such a disappointment, would be reborn in this form. The little book that appeared in the spring of 1953, *Japanese Literature: An Introduction for Western Readers,* proved to be my first success as an author. Although the original British edition is no longer in print, the American edition still sells a few hundred copies each year to readers wishing to make their first acquaintance with Japanese literature; and the Japanese translation, made by Yoshida Kenichi, who a year or two later would become a close friend, has sold many more copies than the original. The book has been translated into various European languages as well. Greek and Romanian translations have recently appeared. It astonishes me to think that this book, by an inexperienced young scholar who had not read much Japanese literature, is still alive after forty years.

Best of all were the reviews. My favorite was in a periodical that I had never even seen. It concluded, "Now and again, you read a book which makes you feel grateful to the author. This is one of them." I have no recollection of whether or not I wrote the reviewer to express my appreciation. I tell myself now that surely I must have written. I hope I did, for the review filled me with joy. It—and other reviews I saw—restored my confidence as a scholar of Japanese.

During the years since then I have published many books, but I have never learned to take reviews in my stride. An unfavorable review wounds me as painfully as it would a beginner, and an ungenerous review, the kind that displays the knowledge of the reviewer at the expense of the author, arouses latent misanthropy. But a review of the kind I received—obviously meant, and not empty praise copied from the blurb on the dust jacket—can give a young scholar the courage to pursue the lonely path ahead.

CHAPTER FOUR

*****

(RE)DISCOVERING
JAPAN

In the spring of 1953 I received the unexpected and most welcome news that the Ford Foundation had granted me a fellowship to study in Japan. The subject of my research was to be the
survival of classical literary traditions in contemporary Japan. I
can admit now that I proposed this subject, rather than the
study of Bashō I really wanted to do, because I thought that
the foundation would be more likely to support a project with
contemporary significance than one of a purely literary nature.

My preparations for the journey involved getting visas not
only for Japan but for the various countries of Asia which I proposed to visit on the way. Being something of a pessimist, I
thought it unlikely I would ever again have enough money to
travel in Asia, and I was determined to take maximum advantage of my good fortune. I also wrote to my few friends in Japan,
announcing my forthcoming arrival and asking if they would
like anything from England.

One friend, a Japanese businessman I had met in Tsingtao,
replied that he would like a heavy winter overcoat. There were

none on sale in the shops in May, so I had no choice but to ask a tailor to make one to my measurements. This overcoat was to prove an immense nuisance at all stages of my journey. In those days one's baggage was carefully weighed before boarding the plane, and one had to pay considerable sums of money for each pound of excess baggage. My solution to this problem was to *wear* my friend's overcoat every time my baggage was weighed. But as I also carried with me my own overcoat, this meant that I had to wear two overcoats at the airports in Bombay, Bangkok, and various other torrid cities in July. The airlines personnel probably thought I was crazy, but nobody questioned my unusual appearance.

My journey by air to Japan was to take well over a month, what with stops in Italy, India, Ceylon, Singapore, Indonesia, Cambodia, Thailand, and Hong Kong. I had very little money and stayed at cheap hotels wherever I went, but being young, I was not fazed by the inconveniences, the heat, or even the tiresome officials I encountered every time I crossed a border. On the contrary, when I recall these travels now, after many more visits to the countries of Asia, it seems to me that I never again felt the excitement of discovery that I did when I traveled third-class everywhere. There are pleasures appropriate to each stage of one's life.

Obviously, I am romanticizing a bit. I certainly have no desire to repeat the attacks of diarrhea that plagued me in India. Nor do I yearn for the tension one experienced at that time in Indonesia when one never knew whether the men at the side of the road who stopped one's car were soldiers or bandits in disguise. But at this distance from the events they seem somehow endearing, and I am rather proud to have them in my past.

I finally reached Tokyo in August 1953. My first impression, after my travels in Asia, was that I had returned to Europe. Unlike the airports I had visited during the past month, filled with aimless wanderers, here everybody seemed busy, intent on his job. Haneda—the old Haneda—was certainly not picturesque. But I was in Japan at last, no longer a tourist but someone with a job to do in the country where it could best be done.

It was raining the night I arrived and from the bus window I could not get much of an impression of the city which I had last seen, very briefly, eight years earlier. The bus stopped at various hotels, where all the other passengers from the plane got out, but I continued on to Tokyo Station.

When I had traveled by train in India or Thailand I had felt the pleasant irresponsibility of someone who could not be expected to understand the language of the country or the regulations that passengers were expected to obey, but (as a teacher of Japanese) I was now embarrassed to ask stupid questions about where to buy tickets or the platform from which the train would leave or how much it cost for porter service. I also discovered to my annoyance that, after eight years of hardly ever speaking Japanese except in a classroom, some Japanese words I knew quite well did not come to my lips easily, and I seem never to have learned the kind of Japanese words used in a sentence such as "Do I have to get my ticket punched before I board the train?"

After making several mistakes and wandering here and there in the station, too proud to speak English, I managed eventually to buy a second-class ticket on what I was told was the last train that night for Kyoto. I sent a telegram to my friend in Kyoto informing him of the time of my arrival.

Eventually, I found the train and got a seat. The train, obviously of prewar vintage, was shabby and not air conditioned, and it was very hot. The man opposite me, seeing me attempt to fan myself with an old letter, took out a fan from his briefcase and gave it to me. The next morning, when we arrived in Kyoto, he insisted that I keep the fan. It was a small gesture, but I was touched, and even as I write these lines I wonder what ever happened to the fan. I remember now that the gesture made me feel happy that I had at last reached my destination after the long journey across the breadth of Asia.

Normally I am unable to sleep on a train, but that night I somehow managed to doze off. When I awoke early the next morning the train was standing in a station. I craned my neck to read the name on a sign. It was Sekigahara. I had known this name for years, ever since I read a book of Japanese history as an undergraduate. I had referred to the great battle fought there in 1600 in my books. I had even translated the name, for the benefit of readers who knew no Japanese, as "Moor of the Barrier." And now I was there. I felt as I imagine a Japanese student of English literature would feel on visiting the sites of the battles of Hastings, Agincourt, or Bosworth Field. I had no special interest in battles, but it was hard not to feel excited on reaching a place where many men had died and the course of history had been changed.

The name Sekigahara made me feel that I was not only really and truly in Japan, but that all of my studies of the past ten or more years had been pointed in this direction, and that this was where my studies would bear fruit. After the various discouragements that at times had even made me consider abandoning my study of Japanese, I had now had the reward for persisting. I felt such great exhilaration I wanted to tell someone about it, but my fellow passengers were all still dozing, and I decided to keep my joy to myself.

*****

My friend from Tsingtao days was on the platform in Kyoto when my train arrived. He expressed surprise that I had not spent even one night in Tokyo, but after a month of traveling ever since I left England, I was eager to reach my destination and to return to my books.

My friend took me to his house in the northern part of the city. He and his wife, his parents, and his children (one of the daughters born since I last saw the family in China) greeted me and I was led upstairs to a Japanese-style room. My friend had correctly guessed that I would prefer a room where I could study or sleep on the tatami, rather than a Western-style room with a bed. This was to be my room during my first month in Kyoto. My friend asked if I was tired and would spend the day resting, but I was so excited at being in Kyoto that I forgot about the fatigue of my journey.

Some years ago my friend in Cambridge, Mrs. Dickins, returned to me the letters I wrote her during my first stay in Kyoto. Reading them now brings back memories, though sometimes they contradict other memories built up over the years. I learned from reading my letter of August 28, 1953, that on my first day in Kyoto I went with my friend to the Ryōan-ji. I had forgotten that, probably because I went there many times afterward and could not keep the memories separate. According to the letter I said to my friend, "Now I understand the beauty of mathematics." He misunderstood me, thinking that I meant that the arrangement of the stones in the celebrated stone and sand garden was mathematically perfect. But (according to my letter) what I meant was that it is usually difficult to imagine beauty without emotional context, without spiritual attachment of some kind, but there is also a beauty in a mathematical solution. I went on, "An otherwise minor American poet said, 'Euclid alone has looked on beauty bare.' The garden has that effect."

Reading these words now makes me blush. Did I really say anything that pompous? Was I trying to create an impression, or perhaps to convince my friend that I understood the higher reaches of Japanese culture? I feel no organic connection between the person who wrote those fatuous remarks and myself. But another paragraph of the same letter accords with my memories of that first day:

"What impressions to record? Best of all was a walk last night with my friend and his two little girls through an old part of the city. The street was narrow, so narrow that one can touch the houses on both sides, but it was neither evil-smelling nor sinister, as narrow alleys are apt to be. The houses were illuminated with Japanese lanterns, and the street was filled with women in brilliant kimonos walking on high wooden pattens. This, evidently, must have been the geisha quarter, for in the rest of Kyoto most women wear Western clothes, probably not out of preference but because they cost so much less than a kimono. For the time that I walked through that narrow street I felt that it was possible to return to the past and not even be self-conscious."

I remember that walk through Ponto-chō, and the light from the lanterns at each door glinting in the gold thread of the robes the *maiko* (apprentice geisha) wore. When I go to Ponto-chō today and see the ugly coffee shops that have replaced wooden buildings in the traditional architecture, I feel lucky to have seen Kyoto when I did. But no doubt visitors who see Kyoto for the first time this year will have the occasion forty years from now to make the same comment.

The only way to describe my relationship to the city of Kyoto is to say it was love at first sight. Sometimes people told me that

Kyoto before the war was even more beautiful or that Kyoto in the days of gas rationing, when there were almost no cars in the streets, was even quieter and more charming. I refused to listen to such tales. As far as I was concerned, Kyoto could not have been more beautiful. Nowadays when I hear tourists gushing about the unspoiled charm of Kyoto I am tempted to say, "You should have seen it in the old days!" But probably Kyoto possesses the power to captivate visitors no matter how much it changes.

A letter I wrote to my friend in England at the beginning of September 1953 conveys my excitement: "Wonderful Kyoto! Yesterday an American friend took me shopping along little streets where each shop sells a special kind of doll or toy. The shops are enchanting, and the old lady who shows you the tiny badger or the doll with the parasol talks the delightful Kyoto dialect. Or perhaps you would rather go down the next street with its antique shops and its inns, where if one spends the night one has not only a room but a private garden. And as one walks in the narrow, beautiful streets, one sees ahead the great Yasaka pagoda and the green hills beyond. I didn't buy anything because I wanted everything. I want to buy all of Kyoto, or almost all (the alien registration office which I also visited yesterday can be omitted from the sale), and then give it away, bit by bit, century by century."

The street of the doll shops is still there. I went back a couple of years ago and bought a few things—tiny monkeys made of clay that link arm in arm to form a chain, a Bunraku chanter and his samisen accompanist. The young man in the shop complimented me on my Japanese, and I could reply truthfully that I not only was speaking Japanese long before he was born, but had visited his shop thirty and more years ago. The street (unlike much of Kyoto) has changed very little, but seeing it again naturally did not arouse the exhilaration that runs through my letter. One can only fall in love once in that way.

Now when I visit Kyoto I resent every change and recall nostalgically almost everything I can remember from the past. I think of the trams that often had two conductors as well as the motorman. Before each stop one of the conductors would call out its name in a polite, high-pitched voice, *"Hai, tsugi wa Maruta-machi de gozaimasu."* In the meantime, the other conductor would be making the rounds of the passengers, calling out, *"Gomendō shimasu"* ("Sorry to trouble you [for your ticket]").

Now, of course, one pays on boarding, and a stern-voice recording warns passengers that they must not carry dangerous articles. The streets are also announced by a recording, sometimes by strangers to the city who do not even know the correct pronunciations of the names. Perhaps, just as standard Japanese, constantly emitted from television sets, has gradually corrupted the Kyoto dialect, in time even the natives of Kyoto will say, as the recorded announcements now do, *Yonjō Karasumaru* instead of *Shijō Karasuma* for the name of an important crossing. I hope not. Some changes are of course both inevitable and desirable, but surely the old names can be permitted to survive even amid change.

*****

After I had lived about a month at the foot of Kinugasa-yama my old friend from wartime days Otis Cary, now a professor at Dōshisha University, arrived on his motorcycle and said he intended to take me to the place he had chosen as my residence in Kyoto. I got on the back of the motorcycle and soon we were cutting across the city from the northwest to the southeast. Again and again I thought I was going to fall off the motorcycle, especially toward the end of the ride, when we were going up a steep hill in the direction of Yamashina. At the time almost none of the streets of Kyoto were paved, and the dust kicked up by the motorcycle also made the journey something of a strain. But the destination, in the section of the city called Imakumano, made the adventure seem worthwhile.

We dismounted, and Cary slid open the door of a high wooden fence. We went down a flight of stone steps, circled around a large house, crossed over a little pond, and then stood before a beautiful small Japanese house. I later learned that the house (not in its present shape, however) had been brought to Kyoto about fifteen years earlier from the area of Takayama in the mountains. It had an enormous *genkan* (entrance), a floor of beaten earth, and four rooms. The largest room had an *irori* (open hearth) in the middle. This was where the owner used to gather friends for dinner parties (and where I also sometimes would invite my friends in the years to come). There was a *chashitsu* (the room where the tea ceremony was occasionally performed), a tiny room where I used to sleep, and a living room where I spent most of my time.

Standing on the *engawa* (a small veranda), one looked out over trees and hills. There was not another house in sight. In the foreground, just before the house, were cherry and maple trees and a low hedge of bamboo-grass. About ten feet farther on, the ground dropped sharply. I could hear the sound of a stream from the bottom of the valley. On the other side of the valley, I was informed, were the Imperial Tombs at the Sennyū-ji. I have never seen a landscape that pleased me more. I was to live in this little house and enjoy the view every single day for the next two years and then (after I began to teach at Columbia) during the summer vacations, which I always managed to spend in Kyoto.

Best of all was the owner of the house, Mrs. Okumura Ayako.

We became good friends over the course of the years, and some of my happiest memories of Japan are of our conversations. She was also a wonderful cook, and I looked forward each day to dinnertime. When I moved in she asked what kind of food I would like. I firmly replied, "Only Japanese food." I had decided that the experience of living in Japan would not be complete unless I ate Japanese food every day. But after a while Mrs. Okumura asked if I would mind having a Western-style breakfast; I had not realized how much time and trouble it was to prepare a Japanese breakfast. Naturally, I agreed. At a somewhat later stage I opted for *udon* (noodles) every lunch. The marvelous *tori namba* (udon with chicken and leeks) from the local shop (founded, I was told, in the Tokugawa period) has spoiled me for udon anywhere else.

I made one other, similar decision a little later on. It was not to use the gas stove but to depend on a hibachi for heating. I was determined to lead as Japanese a life as possible, and (thanks to Otis Cary) I had found the absolutely ideal place to realize this dream.

When I made application to the Ford Foundation for study in Japan I specified that I planned to attend Kyoto University. I had absolutely no information concerning admission requirements, but I assumed that, as the recipient of a Ford Foundation fellowship, I would probably be allowed to register even in the middle of the Japanese academic year. The only thing I knew about the teaching of Japanese literature at Kyoto University was the name of Professor Noma Kōshin, thanks to having read an article by him while writing my doctoral dissertation. I must confess that, with so much to see and do in the city of Kyoto, I was not really eager to attend lectures, but once I was settled in

With Mrs. Okumura on the engawa *of my home in Kyoto*

"my" house in Imakumano, I decided I would go to the university and take the necessary steps to get admitted.

I no longer remember exactly what I had to do in order to be enrolled, but the formalities were exceedingly brief. Foreign students were still a rarity at Kyoto University, and exceptions to normal admission procedures were readily made. I asked for a catalogue of the courses offered, but there was none. Someone told me that Professor Noma was offering a course on a certain day but that classes might not start for another couple of weeks.

Everything seemed extremely vague. This was disconcerting, but I was not displeased. I had done my duty by registering at the university, and now I was free to sightsee without interference from a guilty conscience.

The first class I attended was in October. That year Professor Noma was reading with his students Chikamatsu's play *The Love Suicides at Sonezaki.* While doing research for my doctoral dissertation on Chikamatsu's *The Battles of Coxinga* I had also read *The Love Suicides at Sonezaki,* and I was glad to have the opportunity to read the text in class. (I translated the play later on during my stay in Kyoto.)

I confess, however, that the classes did not much interest me. The professor would call on a student and ask if he was prepared, and if he said yes, the student was asked to translate a passage from Chikamatsu's text into modern Japanese. My ears were still not fully attuned to Japanese, and I had trouble in following the translations, which were usually delivered at breakneck speed. But this problem did not last long. After the second or third class Professor Noma ceased to appear. The students, including myself, would assemble at the assigned hour and wait for him each week. By November the classroom was cold, and there was no heating. We would sit on our hands to keep them warm until someone said after we had waited half an hour or so, "It doesn't look as if he is coming today." Then we would all get up and go home.

Under other circumstances I might have been disappointed and even much annoyed, but I was attending classes mainly to fulfill my promise to the Ford Foundation to study at Kyoto University, and I had derived very little from the two or three classes I had attended. Later on, I learned why Professor Noma appeared so infrequently. At the time the salaries paid to professors at national universities were so meager that they were forced to teach elsewhere in order to make ends meet. Professor Noma was scheduled to teach in Nagoya at more or less the same time as his Kyoto classes, and he apparently was under greater pressure to appear in Nagoya. I discovered also that he believed classroom teaching was less important than individual guidance, and he gave me guidance generously when I needed it the next year, after I began to compile my anthology of Japanese literature.

*****

Some months before leaving England the thought had occurred to me that there was nothing resembling an anthology of Japanese literature, and this might be a good time to compile one. I wrote to the company in London that had published *The Japanese Discovery of Europe* and asked if they would be interested in an anthology of the kind I had in mind. After some time I had a reply saying that they would publish such a book providing that it covered all periods of Japanese literature and was in fewer than two hundred pages. The limitation of two hundred pages seemed to me absurd, and I wrote back, pointing out that Japanese literature had a history as long as that of English literature, and that the volume was comparable. To this I received a frosty answer to the effect that the publishers knew their market better than I did.

I had more or less given up the idea of compiling an anthology when I heard from a wartime friend, a former translator of Japanese. He was now working for Grove Press, a small but adventurous company that was publishing books that the large commercial houses were unwilling to risk. I wrote him about my proposed anthology, and received a very positive response. They were willing to publish a book five hundred pages long. This was still not enough, but it was a distinct improvement on the British offer. At this point, for some reason that I have forgotten, Grove Press consulted Sir George Sansom, the great historian of Japan, who was then teaching at Columbia. He suggested that two volumes would be more appropriate, and Grove Press accepted the suggestion. I was to be allowed approximately five hundred pages each for classical and modern literature.

When I think of it now, I can only marvel at my audacity. My knowledge of Japanese literature was limited. Apart from the texts I had read in Tsunoda-sensei's classes and other texts that I had taught in Cambridge, my acquaintance with the classics was spotty, and I knew hardly anything about modern Japanese literature. I counted, of course, on using the marvelous translations by Waley of *The Tale of Genji, The Pillow-Book of Sei Shōnagon* and the Nō plays, but there were extremely few other translations that were good enough to reprint in an anthology. (The excellent prewar translation of the *Manyōshū* by a team of Japanese translators and a British poet was one exception.) I wrote to various people I knew who were engaged in scholarly research on Japanese literature and asked their help. Most valuable of all was the cooperation of Edward Seidensticker, another product of the Navy Japanese Language School, who was at the time teaching and translating in Tokyo. But still there were great gaps that I would have to fill by making my own translations. It was at this stage that I sought and received advice from Professor Noma and from various young Japanese scholars whom I had met at Kyoto University.

Preparation of the anthology was to be my chief occupation while I lived in Kyoto from 1953 to 1955—apart from sightseeing, attending the theater, etc. The work involved not only choosing and translating (or asking other people to translate) representative works of Japanese literature, but also typing the whole manuscript. I think I still am the holder of the world's record for the longest manuscript ever typed while sitting Japanese-style on the tatami.

The compilation of the anthology also had the happy result of bringing me into contact with the future Nobel Prize winner Kawabata Yasunari, who was then the president of the Japanese PEN Club. I wrote him sometime in the summer of 1954 to ask his help in obtaining permissions from living authors for the use of their works in my anthology. His reply, dated September 8, 1954, was extremely cordial. "I am happy and grateful that your work on the anthology of Japanese literature in English translation has been progressing. It is a great joy to us, too, that, thanks to your efforts, a splendid volume will be born, for the first time."

Kawabata's handwriting was superb, but it was not easy for me to read. During the war I had specialized in reading handwritten materials, such as the diaries of Japanese soldiers, but I had rarely encountered handwriting of this quality or such an abundance of *hentaigana,* the archaic variants on the kana. In the end, I generally was able to decipher everything, and it gave me particular pleasure to think that Kawabata-sensei, far from assuming that a foreigner would be unable to read his writing, favored me with the same beautiful calligraphy he would have sent to a Japanese friend. Sometimes, I am sure, I misread his writing, but the general sense was clear.

The letter continued, "I am willing to negotiate with the modern authors you have chosen, with the exceptions of Tanizaki, Shiga, Mishima, and Kinoshita [Junji], with whom you will deal with directly." It surprises me now that I considered myself to be on such familiar terms with Shiga Naoya (whom I only met once) that I could approach him directly. I am surprised also that I seem already to have been in contact with Mishima, though according to my recollections I would not meet him until November of that year. If only I had kept a diary!

The next point in the letter makes me wince with embarrassment. "I am willing for you to shorten my story 'The Izu Dancer,' but I would like to know which sections you have shortened and whether Mr. Seidensticker, the translator, has been consulted." I recall now that when I first read Seidensticker's excellent translation of the story, I suggested to him places in the text that should be abbreviated. In part, I suppose, I was trying to save space, having only a limited number of pages at my disposal. For that reason I had cut substantial sections from my translation of *Oku no Hosomichi* (*The Narrow Road of Oku*) in the volume devoted to classical literature. I had also, as the editor, eliminated a story by Mori Ōgai that I myself had translated.

In the case of "The Izu Dancer" it was not simply a matter of saving space. I believed that the story would be more effective in translation if certain passages were omitted, thereby tightening the story. Naturally, I consulted with Mr. Seidensticker before changing anything, and he did not always agree with me. But it astonishes me now that a young and inexperienced translator like myself should have dared to "improve" the work of a master. It puzzles me too that Kawabata-sensei should have accepted such cavalier treatment of his text. Perhaps it was because this was the first anthology of modern Japanese literature, and he wished to cooperate in making the volume a success. But I think it even more likely that this was a manifestation of the kindness and gentleness that he was to show me over the years, almost to his very death.

I had other letters from Kawabata-sensei in the spring of 1955. The fact that I was living in Kyoto at the time meant that, instead of telephoning (it took well over an hour for a call to be completed between Tokyo and Kyoto), he wrote me, sometimes in pen, sometimes with a brush. When I wrote him that I was planning to visit Tokyo in March, he invited me to visit him in Kamakura. He also suggested I attend a meeting of the PEN Club that month at which Edmund Blunden would be present.

I attended the PEN Club meeting. I never enjoyed such meetings, partly because I often had trouble in following what was said. Although my Japanese was adequate for most situations, I knew so little about activities of the literary world that the names of people mentioned meant nothing to me, and I could not keep my attention focused on matters of procedure. I was glad to meet Edmund Blunden, however. I knew some of his poems and liked them. I had also seen examples of his poetry in various parts of Japan, composed on the spot in response to a host who, placing a paper and a pen before Blunden, asked for "anything at all." None of these poems was of distinction, and the rhymes were sometimes ludicrous. But the very fact that he complied with such requests for poems, knowing in advance that probably they would not be good, was proof of his generosity.

Blunden told me that he had been reading some English translations of modern Japanese poetry. I had recently been making translations, and wondered if the selection Blunden had read was similar. To my surprise, I discovered that he had in fact been reading my translations. A Japanese acquaintance, a former student of Blunden's at Tokyo University, had previously written to ask if I had any translations of modern poetry, and I sent copies of what I had. The man had presented them as his own translations!

Kawabata-sensei's letter inviting me to the PEN Club meeting also suggested that I visit him at the place in Tokyo where he worked: "I will be staying at my lodgings in Tokyo until about the 28th or 29th of the month in order to write. I will be in the midst of writing, but I can find time to see you, so I will be very glad if you will get in touch with me by telephone and then come to see me at my lodgings. I sleep in the mornings." His "lodgings" were at the elegant Fukuda-ya in Yotsuya, and the detached room where he worked is still pointed out to visitors.

I never had the slightest difficulty in conversing with Kawabata-sensei. I had heard of people who found it impossible to elicit a response from him, even of a woman reporter who went to interview him and, after minutes of silence during which he merely gazed at her with his unusually large eyes, had burst into tears and left precipitously. But somehow I always found it easy and enjoyable to talk with him, and his kindness was exceptional. For example, when I visited him at Fukuda-ya and remarked in the course of the conversation my ignorance of modern Japanese poetry, he at once telephoned the publisher of a set of books of modern poems, and arranged to have them delivered to my place in Kyoto. Some cynics may suppose that his kindness was motivated by a desire to have me translate his works, but as a matter of fact, all I ever translated of Kawabata was one brief article on flower arrangement. The kindness was not affected or inspired by ulterior motives; it was an integral part of the man.

I met Kawabata-sensei in New York twice. The first time was in 1956 when he traveled around the world to persuade eminent writers in various countries to attend the Congress of the PEN Club that was to be held in Japan the following year. His efforts were extremely successful. I have attended several congresses since then, but none could compare with the Tokyo congress with respect to the quality of the participants. Kawabata-sensei usually looked so frail and otherworldly that it seemed unlikely he would ever become involved in practical, this-worldly matters; but he served untiringly for many years as the president of the Japanese PEN Club, though this involved many political problems during the 1950s and 1960s.

When Kawabata-sensei visited my apartment in New York, he told me that while in England he had met Arthur Waley and attempted to persuade him to visit Japan (whose literature he knew so well) for the first time. He had been unsuccessful. Moreover, Kawabata-sensei had brought with him a notebook of Lafcadio Hearn which he intended to give to Waley, but when Hearn's name came up in the conversation Waley had dismissed him as a hopeless romanticist who had never understood Japan. Kawabata-sensei had returned the little notebook to his pocket, but in New York he presented it to me. I was touched, but because I felt it belonged in a library rather than in private hands, I gave it to the Columbia University library.

Kawabata-sensei's second visit to America was in 1960, at the invitation of the State Department. When I met him, I was surprised to see how much younger and more cheerful he looked than ever before. He wore a sports jacket that gave him a rather dashing appearance, and he spoke of his excitement at walking the streets of New York. I remember in particular his account of how, wanting to find out what the ordinary workman in New York ate for lunch, he had bought himself a slice of pizza. Even now, I find it hard to visualize Kawabata-sensei eating pizza.

But Kawabata-sensei was far more complex a man than the side of himself he showed to me. When I dedicated my translation of Dazai Osamu's novel *The Setting Sun* to Kawabata-sensei (as a mark of appreciation for his help with my anthology), I did not realize that he and Dazai had been on bad terms. Kawabata had attacked Dazai's writings for their unhealthiness, and this had cost Dazai the coveted Akutagawa Prize. But there was an element of unhealthiness in Kawabata's writings too. This is obvious from his writings, not only the early, surrealistic works but such novels of his full maturity as *The Lake* or *The House of the Sleeping Beauties*. And behind his gentleness there was also surprising strength.

I also have many happy memories of Kawabata-sensei at his home in the beautiful resort town of Karuizawa. I remember one visit to Karuizawa especially. I had been forewarned that Kawabata did not get up until two in the afternoon, and I timed my visit accordingly. I arrived just as he was about to eat breakfast, and he cordially invited me to join him, though I had already eaten lunch. We talked for about an hour or so. All this time I had noticed a man pacing back and forth in the garden. I wondered if he might be a bodyguard, and, finally, unable to master my curiosity, asked who the man was. He replied with a smile, "He's come from the newspaper to pick up today's installment of the serial I'm writing." Kawabata-sensei showed not the least sign of wishing me to leave so that he could write the installment, and I kept wondering what would happen if he failed to write the manuscript. Perhaps somebody on the newspaper staff would be obliged to write the installment instead. I could not help but admire Kawabata's unhurried manner even with a man in the garden serving as a reminder of the needed manuscript.

Another memory is of meeting Kawabata at a fashionable bar in Tokyo. To tell the truth, going to bars has never given me any pleasure, but I used to go occasionally when some friend insisted. Kawabata-sensei was seated at the bar, and greeted me with a smile. We only said a few words because I had to devote myself to the friends who had brought me and to the various hostesses. The next day I had an appointment with Kawabata-sensei. He expressed his admiration for me: "I was afraid that you were interested only in old books, so I was glad to see you in a bar. It shows you know about modern Japan too." I did not disillusion him.

On another occasion I took to Kamakura the distinguished Indian novelist R. K. Narayan. Narayan is a delightful, unpretentious man whom anyone should be happy to meet, but when he asked my help in arranging a meeting with Japanese novelists, I was met with refusals from everyone, even two who had recently been in India. They explained that they did not know Narayan's work and would not have anything to talk about. The only writer who was willing to meet Narayan was the most distinguished of all, Kawabata. As a matter of fact, the two men did not have much in common. Despite the famous statement of Okakura Tenshin, all of Asia is definitely not one. But Kawabata went back and forth to his study fetching books of Indian art and anything else he could think of. Narayan subsequently published in *The New York Times* an article describing his visit. Kawabata had made a profound impression on him—as he did on almost everyone he met.

The last time I visited Kawabata's house in Kamakura I went with two young women. One was the British novelist Angela Carter, who was spending some time in Japan, and the other a former student of mine who had written her M.A. essay on Kawabata's style. We were ushered into the new Western-style house which he had built next to his Japanese house. I noticed in the dining room the set of eighteenth-century furniture he had bought in Sweden after winning the Nobel Prize. It no doubt was of excellent quality, but somehow did not accord with my conception of Kawabata's taste. We sat in the living room, furnished with massive black leather sofas imported from Italy. This accorded even less with my picture of the aesthete Kawabata, but he told us proudly how he managed to buy the furniture the last day of the year.

He was obviously pleased to have the company of the young women and to be able to show them his treasures. In keeping with the Western-style architecture, the objects of art were all in untraditional tastes, unlike the masterpieces of Japanese art in his Japanese house next door. I remember especially his Meiji-period glass objects, an unusual kind of art for anyone to be collecting at that time. But, even more than the art, I remember how, every time anyone moved on the new leather sofa, it let out heartrending squeaks. This rather constrained our movements.

Afterward, Kawabata took us by car to a temple where we were to eat vegetarian food. He waved me into one car, and got into another car with the two women. A misty rain was falling as we reached the temple, and by now it was almost dark. From the top of the stone flight of stairs a priest carrying a lantern descended to welcome us, the light flickering in the rain, and his figure only dimly illuminated. It was like a scene from a Kawabata novel. I seem to remember that the room where we ate was lit by candles, but perhaps this is only a subjective addition on my part. But I definitely remember the hanging scroll in the *tokonoma* (alcove) with the character *michi,* meaning "path" or "way," in Kawabata's unmistakable handwriting.

We were told that the temple had stopped serving the vegetarian food for which it was deservedly famous. I had the feeling that perhaps we were approaching the end of old traditions—of temples like this one, of food prepared in the manner of the past, of writers whose calligraphy was as beautiful as Kawabata-sensei's. I recalled his moving statement after the defeat: "I consider that my life after the war consists of 'remaining years' and that these remaining years are not mine but a manifestation of the tradition of beauty in Japan." Truly, he had lived to preserve the tradition of beauty in Japan, though it was fast disappearing.

I learned at some time in the 1960s of Kawabata-sensei's chronic insomnia and of the sleeping medicines on which he had come to be increasingly dependent. As anyone who has suffered from insomnia knows, it is a curse. Especially if one knows one must be alert the next day, it is tormenting when, unable to sleep, one sees from one's watch it is three in the morning and there seems to be no chance of falling asleep that night. Under such circumstances one is likely to turn to anything that will help bring sleep, but the danger is that, even if it works, one will have to keep increasing the dose. This is what seems to have happened to Kawabata. I recall Serizawa Kōjirō's interpretation of Kawabata's suicide in terms of his desperation over not being able to sleep. When sleeping pills and whiskey had failed, he may have inhaled gas in the attempt to sleep.

Kawabata's suicide in 1972 did not arouse much consternation in Japan, perhaps because so many writers of modern times have committed suicide, but I was profoundly upset. It was sad to lose a friend, sad, too, that the first Japanese to win the Nobel Prize should not have been enabled by this recognition to endure the afflictions he faced. It was puzzling that his splendid collection of paintings had not consoled him. Why else should one collect works of art?

As I recall, the last time I saw him was at the National Theater in November 1971 when Mishima's *Yumiharizuki* was being performed by the Bunraku company. We met accidentally in the lobby. Kawabata-sensei was one of the few Japanese friends who always shook hands with me, and on this occasion he kept my hand in his and led me to the circular bench in the middle of the lobby. We sat, and he described in tones of pleasurable anticipation the international gathering of Japanologists that was to take place under the sponsorship of the PEN Club the next year. I did not detect any sign of depression. Even now it seems impossible that Kawabata could have been contemplating suicide when he spoke to me. I can understand, or at least analyze, Mishima's suicide but the meaning of Kawabata's still eludes me. Perhaps, as Ōoka Shōhei, another great writer, once suggested, the award of the Nobel Prize to Kawabata, rather than to Mishima, was responsible for the suicides of both.

This may be so. It may be that Kawabata despaired of again writing anything of the quality he deemed appropriate for a Nobel laureate. Or, the real cause may have been insomnia. But if so, what caused the insomnia? Perhaps his never satisfied yearning for the beautiful and his unchanging sadness over the world. His last completed novel, though not one of his best, bore a title that seemed to suggest these two characteristics of his life, *Beauty and Sadness.*

*****

Compiling a two-volume anthology of Japanese literature should have been a full-time occupation. There seemed to be no end to the correspondence involved with each translator or copyright holder. Worst of all were the times when, having solicited a translation, I decided I could not use it either because it was inartistic or because the translated work proved to be insufficiently interesting to a non-Japanese audience. I do not think I made any enemies, but I might well have.

But despite all the problems involved in the anthology, I somehow had a surprising amount of time for other activities. When I first arrived in Kyoto and was living near the Ryōan-ji, I (along with half a dozen small children) took lessons in calligraphy from a neighborhood teacher. After my move to Imaku-mano, I looked for another teacher. The nearest big temple was Chishaku-in, and I reasoned that this Shingon temple probably preserved the traditions of Kōbō Daishi, the master of calligraphy. I arranged to take lessons there from a priest who was a renowned calligrapher, though of Sanskrit rather than Japanese writing. My handwriting certainly benefited by this practice, but even more important were the friends I made among the priests at the Chishaku-in.

I had not totally forgotten my original plan, for which I had received funds from the Ford Foundation, of studying the survival of the traditional culture in modern Japan, and to this end I decided to learn a traditional art. My first preference was the *kokyū,* a melancholy-sounding instrument that appealed to me, but I was informed that before studying the kokyū it was necessary to know how to play the samisen.

I gave up the kokyū, not being sufficiently ambitious to learn *two* musical instruments. My next choice was better. I had become fascinated by the delivery of Kyōgen actors whom I saw at the Nō theater. The ringing tones and the somehow endearing verb *gozaru* with which most utterances in these medieval comedies conclude attracted me especially. As a child I had been stagestruck and had loitered about a film studio in the neighborhood hoping that someone would spot me and decide that I was the young actor the world was searching for. This did not happen, but a residue of my old yearning seems to have lingered within me. At any rate, my desire to study Kyōgen was eventually transmitted to the head of the Ōkura school in Kyoto, and because this was the first time a foreigner had ever studied Kyōgen, the second son of the head was delegated to be my teacher.

I had lessons once a week. The first play I studied was called *Shibiri,* the name for the feeling of pins and needles that one gets when one's legs are "asleep." This was a suitable introduction to the art of Kyōgen because, after long sitting in formal Japanese style during a lesson, my legs generally fell asleep after the initial, painful first ten minutes. My teacher, Shigeyama Sennojō, would declaim one phrase or sentence in his powerful voice, and I would feebly repeat after him. This continued until I had mastered his inflections perfectly. After many years of studying from books, I was not accustomed to learning through my ears, and it was at first difficult to remember the words. The movements—every one prescribed—were also unlike anything I had learned before. But in the end I learned three or four roles and even performed them. Learning Kyōgen was perhaps my happiest single memory of Japan, and it gave me admirable training for classroom lectures.

But more important to me than the classes at Kyoto University, my calligraphy lessons, or even my delightful Kyōgen lessons were my evening meals at Mrs. Okumura's house. After I had been living in the *hanare* (detached cottage) in the garden for about a month I was told by Mrs. Okumura that an assistant professor at Kyoto University who had just returned from five years' study in the United States had moved into the main house. This news filled me with dismay. I was sure that he would want to practice his English on me. Or perhaps he would wish to regale me with stories of the big car he drove while in America. I later learned that when he was informed that there was an American professor of Japanese literature in the hanare he was equally dismayed, supposing that I would grill him on obscure points in Japanese literary history.

When I left my house to go to the street I had to pass in front of the rooms of the assistant professor. I tried to do this as inconspicuously as possible. Sometimes (since he got up later

than I) he would just be eating breakfast, and I would pretend
to be absorbed in deep thoughts that made me oblivious to him
and his soft-boiled egg. But one evening Mrs. Okumura apologetically informed me that because there were guests she would
like to have the two of us eat together. I could not object, and I
am glad I did not try, for after an hour or so of conversing with
my neighbor I had made a friend for life. The friend was Nagai
Michio, who was then teaching education at Kyoto University.
Later, he would become well known as a writer of stimulating
books about the present and future of Japan, and still later as
minister of education. He is now the director of International
House, among many other responsibilities.

Until I met Nagai-san I had really not been much interested
in contemporary Japan. I suppose that I had been influenced by
Arthur Waley, who had steadfastly refused to visit Japan, saying
that he was interested only in the Japan of the Heian period.
The general contempt that then existed in Cambridge for the
study of contemporary life had also affected me. When Mrs.
Okumura asked me what newspaper I would take, I grandly replied that I had no time for reading newspapers. I maintained
my purity in still another way: when I began about this time to
write little articles in Japanese for various magazines, I always
used the historical kana and the orthodox form of the kanji
rather than the abbreviated characters that almost everybody
else by this time was using. The greatest pleasure that life in
Kyoto gave me was discovering buildings or gravestones or com-
memorative monuments that told of the past.

Even after Nagai-san and I became friends, eating dinner together almost every night, I still retained my absorbing interest
in the past, but I became aware also of the importance and vital-
ity of contemporary Japan. Four or five years later, when I wrote

a book called *Living Japan,* I thanked Nagai-san in the dedication for having enabled me to realize how fortunate I was to be in Japan at that time, of all times of history.

Our conversations each night brought me many other rewards, and I enjoyed them so much that, even when I knew that he was eager to get back to his room to write a manuscript or prepare his teaching for the following day, I sometimes would detain him by asking one more question, or offering one more interpretation of some phenomenon that had intrigued me. We never ran out of things to talk about.

*****

In 1953 there were so few foreign students in Kyoto that the newspapers considered us to be worthy of special attention. I was interviewed by reporters from the Kyoto offices of various newspapers, usually on such boring subjects as whether or not I could eat Japanese food or whether or not I slept on a futon. One reporter referred to me in his article as the "blue-eyed Tarōkaja" (the name of the comic servant in the Kyōgen I was studying) and this nickname remained with me for some years. My eyes have never been blue, but at that time some Japanese believed that all foreigners had blue eyes and red hair. At first I protested that my eyes were not blue, but in the end I accepted the nickname and even used it for the title of the first book I published in Japanese.

Another reporter told me about a group he had formed of artists of different professions who met regularly to consider the role the traditional arts might fulfill in contemporary Japan. He invited me to become a member, and I accepted with enthusiasm, eager to make the acquaintance of the others. In this way I came to know a variety of artists, most of them about my own age. There were potters, a Kabuki actor, a woodblock artist, a painter, and so on, plus some scholars who were particularly interested in the arts.

I was treated with cordiality from the outset, and I still occasionally meet some of the members, but I gradually became aware of a contradiction between my reason for attending the meetings and the reason why the others were happy to have me present. I was eager to identify myself as completely as possible with Japanese culture and to feel that in some sense I was contributing to it, but I was constantly being asked what foreigners thought of this or that aspect of Japanese culture. Of course I was a foreigner, and their questions were natural, but I wanted to forget my foreignness, and to be reminded of it each time anyone spoke to me was frustrating.

Most upsetting of all was the tendency to ask me not my personal opinions but what foreigners thought, as if I were capable of speaking for all the non-Japanese in the world. I protested that my tastes were not typical of any country or any class of people, but that was not what the others wanted to hear. I wished I had a mask to conceal my foreign features, or that I could speak Japanese so effortlessly people might forget I was a foreigner, but finally I gave up and stopped attending the meetings. I regret this now. I am sure that if I had been more patient the others would in the end have treated me not as a guest but as a friend.

Fortunately, when I felt discouraged by these and similar setbacks in my efforts to find a place in the intellectual and artistic life of Kyoto, I could confide my griefs at dinner to Nagai-san, who with unfailing good sense always managed to put them into proper perspective. He recalled, for example, that when he was studying in America he would be asked such questions as, "Does it ever rain in Japan?" Or, when he went swimming, Americans who had heard of the "flying fish" Furuhashi Hironoshin, and assumed that all Japanese were champion swimmers, would express disillusionment when Nagai-san slowly made his way one length of a pool. Years later I read this memorable remark by the surrealist poet Jacques Vaché: *"Rien ne vous tue un homme comme d'être obligé de représenter un pays"*—nothing kills a man like being obliged to represent a country.

*****

When I think back now on my life in Kyoto between 1953 and 1955 my first recollections are of the house I lived in, the friends I made, my daily visits to temples and shrines, my Kyōgen lessons, and all the other pleasures of my life at that time. These recollections are not romanticized; I really was happy. It takes some effort to remember the incidents that from time to time depressed me, though when I talk with Nagai-san these days he seems to remember most vividly the days when I badly needed comfort.

The worst incident started auspiciously. I was asked by the editor of an important literary magazine to write a review of a recently published book on the classics of Japanese literature. It was flattering to an unknown like myself to be asked to write for this magazine, and I gratefully accepted the request. But as I read the book I found it extremely uncongenial. The three authors were moved by the same determination to prove that Japanese classical literature of whatever period was good only to the extent that it was "democratic." The author of the section on Heian literature was the most doctrinaire, presumably because he was dealing with literature that was for the most part aristocratic in authorship and manner. He totally ignored some works, like the great collection of poetry *Kokinshū,* harshly criticized other works, such as *The Pillow Book of Sei Shōnagon*, because the author was haughty toward the lower classes, and interpreted *The Tale of Genji* as a ruthless exposure of the contradictions in the ruling class.

I wrote the review as requested. It was critical but not, I think, excessively, and I did my best to praise what could be praised. The review was not published for several months, and when it finally appeared it was accompanied by another review of the same book by a critic who acclaimed it as a masterpiece. The editor of the magazine seems to have been afraid that if a "reactionary" review like mine appeared without a corrective it might alienate readers. In the next issue of the magazine the most extreme of the three authors published a reply to my review. He dismissed what I had written as an "unsolicited contribution." The editor of the magazine, who surely remembered he had asked me for the review, let this pass without correction. The article otherwise consisted mainly of a personal attack. I was denounced as an "aristocratic, petit-bourgeois, decadent Westerner."

It is hard to imagine anyone writing in such terms today. It even amuses me now that I should have been denounced as being both aristocratic and petit bourgeois, but I was not amused then. I wrote a rejoinder, but the editor never acknowledged it. I asked various people who knew me and my work to respond on my behalf, but they all refused, either pleading an ignorance of classical literature or expressing the opinion that ignoring the attack was the best strategy. As a matter of fact, I realize now that ignoring it *would* have been the best strategy, but I was too incensed to realize this. I felt terribly let down by my friends. Yet when I think of these events now I am embarrassed to think how presumptuous I was. Why should anyone have stuck out his neck merely to assuage my feelings?

The incident passed, and eventually not only I but everyone else forgot about it. The editor and I became friends again. But while it was still on my mind, Nagai-san no doubt heard more than he desired of what seemed to me to be a great calamity.

When I think back on the pleasures of my life in Kyoto in 1953 and 1954 I see how many of them were the small pleasures of daily life that have largely disappeared and now arouse my nostalgia.

I used to enjoy, for example, the sound of *geta* (wooden clogs), particularly in the evening when people would be going to and from the public bath down the hill. This was for me the typical sound of Japan, even more than the *uguisu* (song thrush) or the *semi* (cicada), and certainly more than the present roar of traffic. In those days, when there were no "mansions" (as the ubiquitous modern apartment buildings are called) and everyone lived much closer to the ground than today, the clop-clop of geta just the other side of the garden fence could transport me back to the Meiji era. I myself enjoyed wearing geta, and practiced until I could make the slurring sound of the habitual geta wearer. Some people still wear geta, but I hardly hear their sound anymore. It makes me sad, like thinking of the fate of the *toki,* the bird that is soon to become extinct, though once it was considered to be so typically Japanese that its Latin name is *Nipponia nippon.*

The *furoshiki* (cloth wrappers) were another small pleasure of life. Of course, some people still carry them, but it is rare to see them except when people are returning from a wedding with souvenirs. These beautiful objects have been replaced by plastic shopping bags. I bought one in a Tokyo subway station when I found that the various small parcels I had acquired were becoming unmanageable. This shopping bag had for its design not a calligraphic or a floral pattern of the kind that was normal when a furoshiki was silk, or the arabesques used for cotton furoshiki, but instead a bold inscription diagonally inscribed: MIND KID. Underneath, in smaller letters, were the words: IT'S TIME NOW, AMAZING AND AMUSEMENT. Other examples of plastic shopping bags I have seen were no doubt inscribed by the proverbial monkeys chained to typewriters. I confess that these do not possess for me the charm that the quaintly mistaken English of the Meiji era possessed, and the contrast with the elegance of the furoshiki is painful.

I miss too, in the extravagance of contemporary Japan, the frugality of the Kyoto of forty years ago. Frugality is not the same as stinginess; in fact, only the frugal can be really generous. I remember the custom, which has probably not entirely disappeared, of putting something inside, even a sheet of paper, when one returned the furoshiki in which a gift had been wrapped, a symbolic gesture embodying the adage, "It's the thought that counts."

At the time the minimum fare for a small Renault taxi was 60 yen (about 16 cents). Most people in Kyoto knew exactly how far one could travel before the meter went up another 10 yen, and were careful to ask the driver to go only that distance. The streets of Kyoto were largely unpaved, and the owners of shops along the streets spent hours every day watering them to keep the dust down. These unpaved streets were bumpy, but if one elected to travel only on paved streets it made for a circuitous route. When I got into a taxi at Kyoto Station and gave directions to my house, the driver generally asked, "Shall I take the good road?" The meaning of his question was that if he took the shortest road it would cost the minimum of 60 yen, but if he went by the "good road" it would cost 70 yen. What a delightful sensation of extravagance one could enjoy by opting for the good road!

*****

The pleasures available to me in 1953 with my modest grant from the Ford Foundation included the purchase of books. How incredibly cheap they were! New books usually cost no more that 250 yen, and secondhand books could be obtained for as little as 20 yen if one searched the dusty bookshops along Tera-machi or Maruta-machi. I penciled in the prices for some of the secondhand books I acquired; the same kind of book would cost close to one hundred times as much today.

I decided to collect first editions of the works of Tanizaki Jun-ichirō. At the time first editions were generally cheaper than second or fifteenth editions because, being older, they had become dirtier. I paid less than 100 yen each for most of my Tanizaki first editions. The highest price I paid for a Tanizaki first edition was 700 yen for the first volume of *Sasameyuki* (*The Makioka Sisters*), privately printed in an edition of two hundred copies during the war. My copy bears not only Tanizaki's autograph but a poem in his handwriting. It would be hard to find such a book today, regardless of the price. Naturally, I now regret I didn't buy the first editions of books by other authors as well!

Travel was also cheap. As a student at Kyoto University I had a *gakuwari* (student discount) which entitled me to travel a certain number of times for half price on the national railways, which were cheap even without a discount. Before traveling to another part of the country I would buy coupons from the Japan Travel Bureau. For 1,500 yen one could stay at the best inn anywhere, and that included two meals. I remember especially the inn in Matsue where I stayed in an enormous room that was said to have been the novelist Shimazaki Tōson's favorite, commanding a splendid view of the lake. At one hot spring in Wakayama prefecture, the proprietress of the inn came to me apologetically to say that the most expensive accommodation was only 1,200 yen. What was she to do with the extra 300 yen? Less attractive but perfectly decent accommodations (with two meals included) were available for 600 yen a day at a time when the exchange rate was 360 to the dollar.

I could go on indefinitely with these nostalgic remembrances of a vanishing Japan. Even at the time I seem to have been dimly aware that sooner or later paradise would be lost. In an essay I published in Japanese a few years later after visiting the castle at Matsuyama, I wrote, "When I reached the foot of the castle I found a line of the usual souvenir shops and loudspeakers were blasting forth a baseball game. These were the same kind of shops one finds wherever one goes in Japan. But an amusing thought flashed through my head. I had never met an old man who, reminiscing, said, 'Tokyo in the old days was boring,' or 'Restaurant food in New York in the old days tasted terrible.' If, when I become an old man, I say, 'The souvenir shops at Matsuyama Castle were dreary,' I won't be living up to my role as an old man. It would be better to say, 'In those days, not like now, the salesgirls were all polite, and they would show you with a smile the wonderful things on sale. There were delicious cakes made with real sugar, handmade dolls of a kind you don't see anymore, and towels made of a fabric called cotton. I can't tell you what a marvelous feeling it gave you when you wiped yourself with a cotton towel.'"

I was not being serious when I predicted a future in which

everything was synthetic, but I was not far off the mark, and it was an unusual prediction to have made in 1957.

*****

I learned in September 1953 that the renewal of the Great Shrine at Ise, normally performed every twenty years but delayed this time because of the war, was to take place the next month. At the end of *The Narrow Road of Oku* Bashō mentions going to Ise to witness this ceremony, and I was eager to follow in his footsteps.

I had no idea how to get invited to the ceremony, so I visited the nearest major Shinto shrine, the Kitano Temmangū, to ask for advice. I met the chief priest and this led to establishing friendly relations with him and his family that lasted throughout my stay in Kyoto. In October we went together to Ise.

The beauty of Ise, from my first glimpse of the Isuzu River and the magnificent trees, quite overwhelmed me. There had been a heavy rain the night before, but the water in the river was pellucidly clear. I followed the other worshippers in washing my hands and rinsing my mouth before approaching the shrine buildings along the gravel path. I had visited other Shinto shrines, but the experience here seemed totally different because of the special, holy atmosphere.

When I reached the Great Shrine, I followed the others in dropping a coin in a wooden box. No—it was probably a bill rather than a coin; in those days the only coins were of 5 or 10 yen and 10-yen bills were more common than coins. I bowed my head and clapped my hands. I don't remember what I prayed for. It could hardly have been for more than what I was actually enjoying, the peace and beauty of Ise.

The ceremony of the renewal of the shrine would not take place until it grew dark, but for hours before people sat on matting, patiently waiting. The invitations to the ceremony specified that men must wear either formal Japanese costume or morning suits, while women had their choice of *monzuki* (crested kimono) or a *robe montante*. I am not sure I would recognize a robe montante if I saw one, but it was evident that the people around me, dressed for the most part in nondescript clothes, could not afford such costumes. The postwar recovery of Japan was under way, but it was not yet reflected in the clothing.

After some hours of waiting I was startled to hear a loudspeaker bray, "*Donarudo sama! Donarudo sama!*" I decided that the name being called must be my own, and went where the loudspeaker directed. A seat had been found for me among the dignitaries, and I was to leave my place on the matting. I asked why I had been summoned by my first name rather than by my surname, and someone replied, "If we asked for Keene, people might think a Korean had come." (As pronounced in Japan, "Keene" sounds rather like "Kim," a common Korean surname.) This response was so surprising and so unworthy of the occasion that I could think of nothing to say.

The ceremony began with the faint sounds of *gagaku,* the ancient ritual music, and torch flares in the total darkness. Slowly one torch was joined by others, and a procession wound its way down the stone steps of the old shrine to the gravel path leading to the new shrine. The climax of the procession was when the divinity was moved to the new shrine inside a long silk canopy borne by the priests. As the canopy passed before the worshippers, they clapped their hands in reverence, and a wave of sound moved laterally in parallel with the procession, dying out in one section of worshippers to be taken up by the next. Of all the religious ceremonies I have seen in Japan, this moved me most.

*****

My first trip to Tokyo from Kyoto was with Professor Noma and a group of students from Kyoto University. Our purpose was to examine documents in the Toshoryō, the library of the imperial palace. The overnight train journey took close to eight hours, and I stood much of the way, but I was young and able to endure the strain. Perhaps my years of experience in standing room at the Metropolitan Opera (especially for performances of Wagner) had given my legs the strength to endure this minor ordeal.

I have no recollection of what books I saw at the Toshoryō. Probably they were manuscripts in a script so elegant I couldn't decipher a word, but no doubt I managed to make appropriate comments to the effect that I was deeply grateful for the privilege of having been allowed to see such precious documents.

Far more important than this attempt to establish myself as a serious scholar of Japanese literature was the visit I paid to Shimanaka Hōji. Nagai-san had been friends with Shimanaka-san from kindergarten days, and when he heard I was going to Tokyo he had written a letter of introduction. Shimanaka-san was about my age, but he had been the president of the publishing firm of Chūō Kōron Sha ever since the death of his father in 1949. He himself had intended to become a scholar, but when his elder brother died as the result of maltreatment by the Japanese military during the war (the company was considered to be dangerously liberal and all publications were halted in 1944), he had no choice but to give up his academic career and assume charge of a large company.

Sometimes I wonder what I would have done if I could not have become a scholar. I cannot think I have ever been capable of running an organization. Perhaps the best I could have managed was to serve as a tourist guide in Kyoto. But Shimanaka-san had managed to make a successful transition from one world to another.

He asked how he could help me and I responded (remembering my obligation to the Ford Foundation to make a study of the survival of Japanese traditions in contemporary literature) that I would like to meet some authors whose writings made use of traditional materials. It was thanks to Shimanaka-san's introduction that I met Kinoshita Junji whose play *Yūzuru* (*Twilight Crane*), based on materials in Japanese folklore, had enjoyed extraordinary acclaim. I recalled that members of the traditional arts group in Kyoto had often cited *Yūzuru* as the model for the use of traditional materials in creating, say, new dance plays or puppet dramas. It was in fact successfully adapted both as an opera and as a Nō play.

Kinoshita-san's plays were embodiments of the use of Japanese traditions in modern works, and the dialogue was written not in standard Japanese, or in any one existing dialect, but in a special dialect he himself had created, borrowing elements from many dialects, and in this way imparting universality to the plays. I enjoyed talking to him, and we even considered doing a joint translation into Japanese of an Elizabethan play. We disagreed, however, on one point. His interest in Japanese tradition was focused on folk tales and the like, whereas I was even more interested in the purely literary traditions. I remember asking him if he would not consider writing about Ono no Komachi, the Heian poet who was known for her beauty but also for her cruelty toward her lover, but Kinoshita-san was not interested. It was not long afterward that I learned of a Japanese dramatist

who had already turned the story of Ono no Komachi into a
modern play—Mishima Yukio.

*****

My first meeting with Mishima Yukio occurred on the steps of
the Kabuki-za in Tokyo in November 1954. The meeting (and
probably the place, the most famous theater in Japan) had also
been arranged by Mr. Shimanaka of Chūō Kōron Sha, knowing
of my desire to meet contemporary writers who had derived materials from traditional Japanese literature. That day at the Kabuki-za a play by Mishima, based on a humorous sixteenth-
century tale of a court lady who fell in love with a sardine ven-
dor, was being presented. This was exactly the kind of use of
tradition that most intrigued me, at a time when many Japanese
denied that anything in their own past was still of interest.

The place of meeting also foreshadowed an aspect of the
friendship that soon developed between Mishima and myself: we
would go to the theater many times together, not only to Kabuki but Nō, Bunraku, modern theater, and even opera. We
watched this performance (and many others, later on) from a
glassed-in box at the rear of the auditorium. The glass wall in-
terfered with the audibility of the actors' voices, but it permitted
Mishima to make comments on the performance without fear of
bothering other spectators. Mishima's knowledge of Kabuki was
professional. He was acquainted with the many different traditions of the roles, and was unerring in his choice of actors who
would one day gain great distinction. Only last year I read the
notes Mishima had kept of Kabuki performances he saw during
the war years, when he was still in his teens. There cannot be
many people today who possess his expertise.

I remember, even more than the performance, my pleasure in

166

Mishima's company. I had read only a few of his stories when I met him, and I was afraid that my ignorance of his major works might annoy him, but that evening, having dinner together, I felt the special excitement of having made a new friend.

It is difficult for me to remember what Mishima looked like at that time because of my vivid memories of his appearance in later years, when he wore his hair cropped very close and he cultivated a resolute expression (at least when his picture was being taken); but the photograph of Mishima on the cover of the English translation of *Kamen no Kokuhaku* (*Confessions of a Mask*) probably shows how he looked when I first met him—with an engaging smile. Mishima was a man of extraordinary willpower, who would deliberately control the facial expression he presented to the world, but I remember most of all his laughter, his delight in parody or humorous exaggeration.

But perhaps the laughter also reflected his willpower rather than genuine mirth. One of his Japanese acquaintances told me that Mishima laughed only with his mouth, never with his eyes. I am not sure one can really read anything in a person's eyes, but perhaps to say this merely indicates that I was insufficiently sensitive to his moods. Early in our acquaintance he made it clear that he did not welcome "sticky" relations, and he never confided any secrets to me. Only once, almost the last time I saw him, did I have the impression that I could see something in his eyes that contradicted the loud laugh and the self-assurance that he deemed to be appropriate to a writer, proud of his craft, but I hesitated to ask him "sticky" questions.

After that first meeting in November 1954, Mishima and I saw each other every time I visited Tokyo from Kyoto. It is hard to believe it now, but sometimes he would be waiting on the platform when my train arrived. He maintained an old-fashioned sense of correct behavior, and at that time seeing off

Mishima Yukio

and welcoming friends at the railway station was still very much a part of Japanese etiquette.

We usually had a meal together, either before or after attending a performance at some theater. He invariably would invite me to first-class restaurants, and I worried about the cost. I tried to persuade him that his conversation gave me more pleasure than even the most elaborate meal, but in this respect, too, he was old-fashioned: he never forgot that there was a proper way to treat guests.

Perhaps the worst mistake I made during the course of our friendship was not to follow his suggestion that we drop polite language and talk in the informal manner of old friends. Mishima said that he could not really feel close to anyone if he had to employ honorifics. But to tell the truth, it was (and still is) much easier for me to speak polite Japanese than the language appropriate to old friends. I had learned my Japanese as an adult, and never had the occasion to use it in conversing with younger siblings or with classmates. I did not feel the slightest closer to someone if I called him *kun* instead of *san.* I imagine I felt rather the way that Japanese feel when foreign friends ask their permission to call them by their first names. But, whatever my feelings may have been, I should have responded to Mishima's request and used the language that *he* preferred. If I had, he might not have treated me always as an honored guest but as someone with whom he could relax.

During the seventeen years that I knew Mishima as a friend we never had any serious misunderstanding (as he did with many other friends), but there were moments of tension. For example, years later, when Mishima had begun to desire the recognition signified by the Nobel Prize, he believed that the more works of his that were translated the better his chances would be of obtaining the prizes. He knew that I admired his novel *Ai no Kawaki* (*Thirst for Love*) and asked me to translate it. I was reluctant to agree because I was fully occupied with my history of Japanese literature, but I promised to make the translation, provided there was no deadline. Just at this time I happened to see Abe Kōbō's play *Tomodachi* (*Friends*), which I enjoyed so much I felt impelled to make a translation. When Mishima learned this, he expressed his annoyance. He wrote that, although he admired Abe's play, he thought I was morally bound to translate his novel first. At this distance from the events, I have to admit that he was right; but at the time translating the play seemed far more enjoyable and less work than translating

Mishima's novel, and I did what I pleased without taking his feelings into consideration. I regret it, as I regret so many other mistakes in my life, and not only those connected with Mishima.

About a month after we first met I read in the 1955 New Year issue of *Shinchō* Mishima's modern Nō play, *Hanjo*. I was so excited by its literary and dramatic quality that I decided to translate it. Perhaps I thought that translating a modern drama that was based on a Nō play of the fifteenth century would satisfy the Ford Foundation that I was really doing the work for which I had been granted a fellowship.

I don't remember when I actually made the translation. All I know is that I received in May 1956 a letter from Stephen Spender, the editor of the British literary magazine *Encounter,* saying that he was anxious to publish the translation of *Hanjo* as soon as possible, but he was "absolutely overwhelmed" by accepted material, and it might take six months before *Hanjo* appeared. In the meantime, I translated *Sotoba Komachi,* another of Mishima's modern Nō plays.

I received a letter from Mishima in November 1956 expressing his pleasure that *Hanjo* would at last appear in *Encounter.* He mentioned also that Harold Strauss, the editor in chief at Knopf, at the time the leading American publisher of translated literature, had written him to the effect that Grove Press would probably be the best place to publish the translation of the entire *Modern Nō Plays.* I interpreted Strauss's remark as meaning that Knopf was unwilling to take a chance on anything so unconventional as a collection of modern Nō plays, but that Grove Press (the publishers of my anthology of Japanese literature), which had already acquired a reputation as a publisher of unusual books, would make a more appropriate publisher. This suggestion appears to have disappointed Mishima. The Japanese series that Strauss had initiated at Knopf no doubt seemed a more distinguished place for his book than the rather eccentric Grove Press. Mishima wrote that he hoped Strauss, when he actually read the translation not only of *Hanjo* but of *Sotoba Komachi*, would change his mind.

One of the problems in publishing translations of Mishima's modern Nō plays was that Western readers might think of them simply as one-act plays and remain unaware of their special relationship to the original Nō plays. For that reason, Mishima wrote me, "When the book is ready to appear I would be extremely grateful if you would write an introduction. It is probably necessary to explain such things as my having Komachi sit on a park bench as the equivalent of her sitting on a *sotoba,* or the coincidence that Komachi's being ninety-nine years old puts the work back precisely in the age of the Rokumeikan."

The Rokumeikan, a ballroom where Japanese of the 1880s danced with Europeans and ate Western food, was much on Mishima's mind at that time. He wrote in the same letter, "I am extremely busy now with rehearsals of my new play *Rokumeikan,* which opens on November 27, and with the story I am writing for the New Year issue of a magazine. At the end of *Rokumeikan* I have Japanese gentlemen and ladies of the 1880s dancing a waltz. No doubt if Western audiences were to see this Japanese version of *The King and I* they would burst out laughing at this aping of Western ways."

My next letter from Mishima, written early in December, expressed his joy that Knopf had decided to publish all five of the modern Nō plays. I evidently had informed him of Strauss's decision. In my letter I also had mentioned the difficulty I had experienced when translating *Aya no Tsuzumi* (*The Damask Drum*) because the character Hanako had no surname. In Japanese it is quite sufficient to say *okusama* alone, but in English one simply cannot say Mrs. without a surname. It is possible to say Madam, but unfortunately there was another character in the play who was referred to as *madamu*. Mishima therefore created for the English translation the name Tsukioka Hanako.

The letter also contained suggestions for the performance of the plays in America. The park in *Sotoba Komachi* should be Central Park in New York, and the teacher of *Nihon buyō* (Japanese dance) in *Aya no Tsuzumi* should be a ballet teacher. "I think it best when the plays are performed that it not be attempted to give them any peculiar Japanese flavor." In the performances of these plays staged in New York in later years Mishima's directions were in general obeyed. Most often the plays were set in an indeterminate place that might be contemporary New York, but the opera based on *Sotoba Komachi* was set in London at the beginning of this century. I remember how much Mishima disliked it when Japanese actors performing in European plays put on false noses, dyed their hair red, and spoke an unnatural, foreign-sounding Japanese. Mishima's modern Nō plays have been performed in translations into many languages in every part of the world, but as far as I know it has never been attempted to make the performers resemble Japanese. These were probably the first Japanese plays to be widely performed abroad.

*****

During my second year in Kyoto I began to write manuscripts in Japanese. The only compositions I had previously written in Japanese were letters to friends. These were apparently intelligible to the recipients, but I certainly did not feel confident that I could write a learned article in Japanese. I was told by the editor of the magazine *Bungaku* (who had requested the article) that if

I delivered the manuscript by a certain date, he would have it translated, but if I failed to meet the deadline, I would have to submit it in Japanese. For some reason, I was unable to meet the deadline, and so I had no choice but to write the article in Japanese.

At first I considered writing the manuscript in English and then translating it into Japanese, but I discovered that this led to extremely unnatural Japanese if translated faithfully, and if translated freely, I felt impatient with the English version. So I decided to write in Japanese from the start. I suppose that, whether or not I was conscious of it, I was translating anyway, as I became aware when I wanted to express something for which I knew the English but not the Japanese word. But there was a difference too: unless one is a really gifted translator from English to Japanese, he will not come up with the double negatives, rhetorical questions, and so on that are so much a part of normal Japanese expression. Machine translation may be quite sufficient for many purposes—scientific papers, news reports, official proclamations, and so on—but I doubt that it ever will be able to make the discriminations in usage that are crucial to literary expression.

When I finished the manuscript, I asked my friend Nagai-san to read it over. He made various suggestions, all of which I accepted, but I am sure that he must have been anxious not to hurt my feelings by making too many corrections and for this reason let pass some dubious usages. He also may have found it somewhat irritating that I insisted on using the old kanji and the historical kana spellings. I wrote in that style because it was the Japanese I had learned during the war, and I had not previously had any need to modify it. I suppose, too, that, like most other people whose first language is English, I was reluctant to change historical spellings. (Voltaire, despairing of pronouncing

English correctly with only the archaic spellings to guide him, declared that he hoped ague would take half the English language, and the plague the other half.)

Although writing Japanese was far more difficult than reading it or even speaking it, I felt that my efforts had been rewarded when a manuscript I had written in Japanese appeared in print. Print gave authority to the words over which I had struggled, and I felt pleased that (like Joseph Conrad) I had become a writer in an adopted language. But for a time editors to whom I submitted manuscripts in Japanese insisted on adding in brackets at the end *gembun no mama* (printed as originally written). I am sure that never happened to Conrad! I discovered that there were actually some foreign writers of Japanese who asked to have *gembun no mama* printed at the end of their articles. One such man was known to translators as *gembun no mama-san* for this reason! My aim was to write Japanese well enough so that it would not occur to anyone to ask if it had been translated.

After I had been writing articles in Japanese for about six months, I was asked by the editor of *Chūō Kōron* if I would write a monthly article reviewing recent Japanese works of literature and criticism. I was flattered by the request, which I eagerly accepted, and the first article appeared in the January 1955 issue. I asked the editor, my friend Shimanaka Hōji, to read my manuscripts before publishing them to make sure that there were no awkward or unnatural expressions (or downright errors, for that matter). He kindly did so, but was reluctant to change too much. He said that he hoped the very unnaturalness of expression would stimulate a fresh use of language on the part of Japanese writers. I have no reason to suppose that my articles stimulated anyone, but it was agreeable at the time to think that my little book reviews were likely to precipitate beneficial changes in Japanese prose style.

I have continued to write articles from time to time in Japanese along with many more that I have written in English with the expectation that they would be translated. At first people were reluctant to believe that I myself had actually written the articles in Japanese, but more recently I have been asked again and again why I don't write in Japanese *all* the articles I intend to be read by the Japanese public. I suppose that laziness and the press of other obligations makes me want to write in the way that is easiest for me, using the twenty-six letters of my native alphabet rather than the far more complicated Japanese script. But that is not the only reason. I have been lucky enough to find Japanese translators who render my words accurately and with an understanding better than my own of what Japanese readers would want to know. It has not infrequently happened that the Japanese translation has seemed to me superior to my original article.

Finally, and perhaps most important, there is a psychological factor. As long as I felt uncertain about my capacity for writing Japanese, I wanted to prove it by writing as much as possible. Now that I know that I can do it reasonably well, the allure is gone. I have also come to feel the pressure of time in a manner quite unlike my former busyness. I ask myself how many more years I can hope to keep writing before old age overtakes me. I am easily led astray by temptation of any kind, but I always regret anything, however pleasant, that keeps me from doing my work.

The same is true of lectures. The first lecture I ever delivered in Japanese was at Dōshisha University in Kyoto. I can't remember the subject, but I remember exceedingly well the nervousness aroused by my fear that the audience might not be understanding me. That fear returns once in a while even now, but normally I feel more or less confident that the general drift of my remarks is intelligible. I have lectured over the years in all but two Japanese prefectures. But now that I know it is possible for me to hold the attention of a Japanese audience for an hour and a half at a time, it seems less and less exciting a prospect when I am asked to deliver a lecture at some remote place. I see with my mind's eye the waiting room at Haneda—nowhere at all to sit or only next to someone smoking fiercely— the rush to get on the plane, the tedium of watching for the thousandth time the demonstration of how to use a life preserver (and some-times the hunger of flights at lunchtime), and, at the destina-tion, the exchange of calling cards and the question, "How was the flight?" I crave madder music.

*****

I remember very well my first visit to the house of Tanizaki Juni-chirō in the summer of 1954. I brought with me the translation of *Some Prefer Nettles* that Edward Seidensticker (who lived in Tokyo) had asked me to deliver to Tanizaki in Kyoto. I had gladly complied with his request, for Tanizaki was the one living Japanese writer whose works I knew. I had read several of his short stories while in Hawaii, and in England (as I have men-tioned) Arthur Waley had given me the copy of *The Makioka Sisters* that Tanizaki had sent him. Probably Tanizaki hoped that the translator of *The Tale of Genjii* would also wish to translate the "modern version" of the great classic, but Waley had said in giving me the three volumes, "I found it rather flat." I can imag-ine why someone who had translated the original *Tale of Genji* might have felt that way about a modern novel, but I was grate-ful for the gift.

I read the first volume of *The Makioka Sisters* during a journey by jeep from England to Turkey in the summer of 1950. I should have realized that a copy of the first edition, not only signed by the author but inscribed to Arthur Waley, was too valuable an object to take on a long and dusty journey, but I was eager to read it. I soon encountered unexpected problems. Most of the conversations in the book are in Kansai dialect, which I had never learned, and I was sometimes baffled by the expressions. Naturally, there was nobody on the road between London and Istanbul to whom I could turn for assistance. But I persisted anyway, and eventually I read the entire book.

I had known Seidensticker at the Navy Japanese Language School and afterward at Harvard University, where we both spent a year studying Japanese literature. His translation of *Some Prefer Nettles* had been made at the request of Harold Strauss, the editor in chief at Knopf. Strauss himself had learned some Japanese during the war, and his enthusiasm for Japanese literature led him to publish a series of translations. With the exception of Hino Ashihei's *Earth and Soldiers,* these were the first translations of modern Japanese novels to be published in America in almost thirty years.

The opening work of the new series was *Homecoming* by Osaragi Jirō, a novel that describes the rediscovery of Japanese culture by a Japanese who had forgotten what it was like. This was a good choice for beginning a series of translations of modern Japanese literature. Most American readers would be unfamiliar with Japanese culture, and they would therefore be in the same position as the hero. *Homecoming* was well received by the critics, and this encouraged Strauss to publish the translation of *Some Prefer Nettles,* also a work that describes a rediscovery of traditional Japan, though it is literarily much superior. Eventually, the Knopf series would include works by most of the leading contemporary Japanese novelists.

When I arrived at the gate of Tanizaki's house in the Shimogamo district with the manuscript of Seidensticker's translation under my arm, I felt rather nervous. Someone had told me of Tanizaki's aversion to guests, and I was afraid I would be no exception. When I finally mustered the courage to ring the bell and go into the house, I was met by Mrs. Tanizaki, whose charm soon put me at ease. In the years that followed, until her death, I would see her from time to time, and I never failed to be struck by her charm, which did not desert her, even after she had become quite old. It was easy for me to understand how Tanizaki himself had been captivated by so enchanting a woman.

Mrs. Tanizaki showed me into the living room, and I waited there for Tanizaki-sensei to appear. I looked around the room and at the garden outside. Every so often I heard a hollow sound like blocks of wood struck together. Later I was informed that it was caused by water falling into a *shishi-odoshi,* a simple device originally intended to frighten away deer. Everything about the house seemed in elegant Japanese taste. Nothing suggested the fascination with the West (and with China) that had characterized Tanizaki in earlier years.

Soon afterward Tanizaki entered. We spoke for a while about the new translation, which he was eager to read. Tanizaki could not have had many opportunities in recent years to practice his English, but he expected not only to understand the translation but to appreciate its stylistic qualities. The conversation shifted to *The Makioka Sisters.* I had supposed that most of the incidents in the novel had been invented by an author whose inventive powers were celebrated, but at times while reading the work certain events seemed to be at the same time so special and yet so real that I thought they must have been derived directly from his experiences. I asked Tanizaki if they had actually taken place, and to my surprise he cheerfully confirmed that they were all closely based on real life. Years later, at his funeral, I had an even more startling experience when I saw the four sisters of the novel before my eyes as one after the other they offered incense at the altar.

As I listened to Tanizaki I had a strange feeling of already knowing much about his family, thanks to having read *The Makioka Sisters*. Of course, for artistic reasons elements of fiction were added to the portrayal of the characters in the novel, but I couldn't help identifying each person I met in his household with someone in the novel. When, for example, I met Mrs. Tanizaki's younger sister, I felt sure she was the Yukiko of the novel. This habit of thinking of each person in terms of the novel had an embarrassing consequence. When I learned of Tanizaki's death in 1965, I rushed to a nearby post office to send a telegram of condolence to Mrs. Tanizaki. I knew that her name was Matsuko, but in my state of shock over the news, I unintentionally addressed the telegram to Sachiko, using the name of the character in the novel who closely resembled her.

I was occasionally invited to dinner by Mr. and Mrs. Tanizaki. Tanizaki's gourmet tastes seem to have been known throughout Japan, and I got the impression that whenever someone caught an unusually fine fish or harvested unusually delicious fruit, the first thought was to send it to Tanizaki-sensei. Mrs. Tanizaki was determined that he eat nothing but "the best in Japan," no matter what it was. Once when she and I ate in a Kyoto restaurant, she commented on how delicious the tofu was. Afterward, she asked the waitress where she might purchase it. She must have decided that the tofu that Tanizaki-sensei had previously been eating was not "the best in Japan" after all.

Another memory of Tanizaki's house concerns the toilet. Having read the description in *In Praise of Shadows* of the traditional Japanese toilet, dark and fragrant with the scent of cedar boughs, I decided to visit the toilet in his Kyoto house, though it was not absolutely necessary. To my disappointment, it was of gleaming white tiles.

Of all the mistakes I made in the past, I think the worst was not having kept a diary. If only I had recorded even the general gist of the conversations I had with Tanizaki-sensei, it would give me pleasure to reread the diary now and might even be of use to scholars who plan to write about him. I am sure that nothing momentous was said—I would have remembered anything that greatly impressed or surprised me. All I can remember are isolated fragments of our conversations.

I remember, for example, his comment that during the years he had lived in Kyoto he had not made one male friend. Probably he was already at an age when it is difficult or even impossible to make new friends, but the fact that he specified male friends suggested that he had succeeded in making female friends in Kyoto. Needless to say, although he was friendly when I visited his house, I did not presume to be considered a friend. Not only were our ages too far apart for us to meet on terms of equality, a necessary condition for friendship, but I had the impression that Tanizaki-sensei was really not much interested in men. I remember one occasion when I arrived at Fukuda-ya, the inn at Toranomon where Tanizaki-sensei stayed while in Tokyo, just as he was about to leave. He was entirely surrounded by women, not only maidservants but members of his family, and he looked entirely in his element.

But I should not wish to leave the impression that he was anything less than extremely kind to me. When I was about to leave Kyoto in 1955 he asked what kind of present I would like. I regret now that I did not ask for a sample of his writing or at any rate something tangible that I might look at now and treasure as a memento of him, but I asked instead that Mrs. Tanizaki perform for me a dance. That seemed to me to be more elegant than anything material. I was invited for dinner shortly before my departure and Mrs. Tanizaki danced for me. It was a memorable occasion.

Mr. and Mrs. Tanizaki were among those who saw me off at Kyoto Station. When I think back on it now, it seems incredible that this great author should have left his work to say good-bye to an unknown young man, but in later years he showed further proofs of his kindness. He wrote a preface for the first book I published in Japan, *Aoi Me no Tarōkaja* (*The Blue-Eyed Tarōkaja*), in 1957 and then again for my book on Bunraku, published in 1965. Even though it is an indisputable fact that he wrote these prefaces, it never fails to surprise me when I open one of the books and see his name. How incredibly lucky I was that this great writer did this to please me!

Sometimes, though, I couldn't help feeling that Tanizaki-sensei was confusing me with somebody else. He was sure that I couldn't eat eels, though I like them very much, and that my favorite among his novels was *The Mother of Captain Shigemoto,* though there are others I prefer. I did not correct him. I was happy to think that he thought of me at all, whether rightly or wrongly.

*****

My experiences in Japan as a writer and lecturer made me realize there was an aspect to myself I had not adequately recognized. When I was in high school I wrote short stories and dreamed of becoming a novelist, but since then I had written only on academic subjects, at first term papers, later articles submitted to learned journals. I supposed that I was not capable of writing anything in a more popular vein, but in Japan my articles had appeared in many different publications. Again, my public lectures at Cambridge, which I hoped would appeal to everyone interested in Japanese literature, had attracted very few listeners; but in Japan I had discovered that my lectures kept the attention even of fairly large audiences. I was still persuaded that the life of a scholar—the life of a secular monk, as I supposed—was what I wanted, but I now knew there was something inside myself that craved greater attention.

I sometimes thought of returning to America, but this was the time of the notorious Senator McCarthy's investigation of un-American activities, and although I had done nothing that seemed likely to attract his attention, I thought the atmosphere in America created by him would be unconducive to study. (One of his henchmen had visited the American Cultural Center in Kyoto and demanded that works by Keats, Shelley, and various other sinister aliens be removed from the shelves of the library.) I still expected to return to Cambridge and to spend the rest of my life there, but the excitement of Japan and the discovery of possibilities within myself I had not suspected made me reluctant to leave as the end of my first year approached. I wrote Cambridge asking permission to remain in Japan another year, but it was not granted.

Just at this point I had a letter from Columbia offering a position as an assistant professor of Japanese. I was apprehensive about the academic life in America at a time when some scholars lived in fear of being denounced as Communists. I also remembered my dissatisfaction with New York when I lived there. But when I was assured by the people at Columbia I could remain in Japan another year, that decided matters. I wrote to Cambridge informing the university of my intention of resigning my position.

Once the decision was made, I had many second thoughts, and more than once considered asking Cambridge to take me back. Cambridge was too beautiful to leave. I had been happy in Cambridge and had no idea how I would respond to New York. But each time I wavered, the prospect of another year in Kyoto gave me new resolution. Recalled at this distance in time, the decision was a good one. My second year in Kyoto was far more fruitful than the first. As an incurable pessimist, I doubted I would ever again have the opportunity to spend so long in Japan. This was a miscalculation, but never again would I be young enough and malleable enough to absorb all this wonderful city has to offer.

It was painful to leave Japan in May 1955. From the airport I sent Mrs. Okumura a telegram in Kyoto dialect expressing my thanks. To put off as long as possible my separation from Japan, I persuaded Nagai-san to accompany me as far as Hong Kong, but from Hong Kong on I had only books to remind me of Japan. On the plane I read Nagai Kafū's *Sumidagawa* (*The River Sumida*). I found that I was weeping, not because of the story but because of the beauty of the Japanese language and the evocations of the country I was leaving.

*****

Several months before I left Japan in May 1955 I met a couple who would play a very large part in my life during the years that followed. The husband, Faubion Bowers, was a writer whose chief interest was Kabuki. He had lived in Japan before the war and learned to speak Japanese well. During the days of the American occupation he had served for a time as an interpreter for General MacArthur, but his chief accomplishment was to have saved Kabuki from the American authorities who had decided to purge it of its feudalistic and militaristic elements. He succeeded in getting permission for *Chūshingura,* the play describing the vendetta of the forty-seven retainers of the Lord of Akō, to be performed, and the Kabuki actors were deeply grateful. He had returned to Japan in 1955 to examine the changes that had occurred in Kabuki since his departure five or six years earlier.

Bowers's wife was the Indian writer Santha Rama Rau. Her father had been the first Indian ambassador to Japan after India gained independence, and she had lived in Japan during the postwar period. Santha had published a successful book called *East of Home* that described her adventures during the overland journey when she returned to India from Japan.

I was captivated by their conversations, and it was exciting to meet their friends, especially the Kabuki actors. When they were about to leave Japan to see theaters in other parts of Asia they suggested that we meet in India and I gladly agreed. On my way to Japan in 1953 I had spent several weeks as a tourist in India. I did not know one person in the whole country, and my prior knowledge was more or less confined to what I had learned about Indian art from a survey course on Asian art taken at Columbia. I had nevertheless enjoyed what I saw in India and thought it would be wonderful to see it in such company.

We met, as arranged, on the station platform in Madurai, near the southern tip of India. From there we drove up the east coast of India to Madras and ultimately to Calcutta. In addition to the three of us there was an American photographer who did much of the driving. He probably did not realize it, but he served an important role in the close friendship that was established at this time among the three others: we found him so objectionable that we drew together in a way that would normally have taken years. For example, he could never start the car without saying, "We're off like a flock of turtles!" After hearing the tenth or twentieth repetition of this memorable declaration, each time he put the key into the ignition we could only grit our teeth and flash signals to one another with our eyes. On one occasion the car ran out of gasoline. Santha and I leaped out, took a jerry can from the back and happily started to walk to the next gasoline station, hoping it would be miles away. Anything was better than being with that photographer. To our disappointment, there was a pump just over the next hill.

The low point of the journey occurred at a place called Guntur. We arrived too late for the last ferry over the river and had to spend the night at a guesthouse whose facilities were primitive. There was no restaurant, but a man offered to buy some food for us. He came back with a can of meat, a can of cream, and a can of milk. Somehow, instead of annoying us, everything contributed to our gaiety. We composed the libretto of a Wagnerian opera about Guntur. We laughed as though we were quite drunk, though we hadn't had touched a drop. Days later, we discovered that the photographer had a suitcase full of provisions from which he had secretly supplied himself while we were in Guntur.

I said good-bye to Santha and Faubion, who somewhere along the way departed by train for Delhi, and continued my journey to Calcutta in the car driven by the photographer. We headed directly for the airport where he created a scene by insisting that he simply *had* to be on the next plane to London. I knew this was untrue from our conversations, and hid behind a column, fearful that people might associate me with him. I am sorry to say that, as the result of his antics, he got a place on the plane, but this relieved me of the necessity of spending any more time with him.

The next day I myself took the London plane. I have no recollections of the journey, though it is not hard to imagine the thoughts that passed through my head as the plane approached

Europe. I was returning to England after two years in Japan, but only as a visitor this time, on my way back to New York, a city I had hated for many years. No doubt I pondered many times the decision I had made. Probably I was so immersed in such thoughts that I paid little attention to the stops the plane made.

I returned to Cambridge and to the house where I had lived for two years, the first house I had ever owned. (A colleague and I had each bought half of a house that had originally been built as lodgings for undergraduates.) I considered for a time sending to New York some of the furniture, notably the desk Sir Herbert Grierson (the father of my friend Mrs. Dickins) had used when making his monumental edition of the poems of John Donne, but in the end I decided to send to New York only my books, persuading myself I would return every summer to Cambridge. Alas, the colleague sold the house while I was in America—we had agreed that if one wanted to sell the other could not oppose—and the desk and various other things I had prized were sold at auction for derisory sums.

I left England by ship from Southampton. I have no recollection of this voyage either, no doubt because I was once again so preoccupied with my future that the present made little impression. I do remember the first sight of New York, as the tops of the skyscrapers gradually became visible on the horizon. It was (literally) thrilling to arrive in New York by sea; people who arrive by air can have no idea of this unique experience.

I had arranged with Tsunoda-sensei, who was then in India, to stay in his apartment for the first few months in New York. I could have stayed with my mother, but she lived over an hour's distance by subway from Columbia, and I begrudged the time. Even more than that, I had come to realize that my mother and I could not be happy living together. I kept this as a guilty secret from my Japanese friends, who assumed as a matter of course that I would be eager to return to my old home and look after my mother. But I had many memories of the clashes that had occurred because we were too much alike, in some ways at least. I dreaded going back to conditions that, more than the city itself, had made me hate New York. But how could I possibly have explained this to a Japanese?

My decision was probably right, but even believing this did not alleviate the feelings of guilt I continued to experience. My new life in New York commenced, then, with doubts about myself from which I had been insulated for seven years while I lived in England and Japan.

CHAPTER FIVE

*****

BOOM AND BUST

My return to New York could not have occurred at a more propitious time. The series of translations of modern Japanese literature published by Alfred A. Knopf had already attracted favorable attention from the critics, and my own anthology of Japanese literature, compiled in Kyoto, was about to appear. The first major exhibition of Japanese art, held in Washington, New York, and other cities in 1953, had been an enormous success. Zen was the rage among intellectuals—and not only intellectuals: I saw an alphabet book that began with the usual *A* is for *Apple* and ended with *Z* is for *Zen.* The Japan "boom" had begun.

My teaching load at Columbia was heavy. In addition to a one-year general survey of Japanese literature, I taught Japanese History before 1600, and Second-Year Japanese. I also taught the East Asian segment of Oriental Humanities, modeled on the course in reading the great books of the Western tradition that had become a basic part of undergraduate education at Columbia. Finally, when I discovered that the one advanced graduate student in Japanese literature had taken all the courses offered in the language, I instituted a special reading course for her.

I undoubtedly was very busy preparing for classes, but that was not my only activity. I had met in Japan the publisher of New Directions books, James Laughlin, when he was preparing a special Japan issue of a magazine. On the basis of the translation I had made for him of Dazai Osamu's story "Villon's Wife," he asked me to translate one of Dazai's novels. I chose *Shayō* (*The Setting Sun*) and translated it with what for me was great rapidity. Although Dazai and I share no points of resemblance, as far as I can tell, as I translated his work I felt almost as if I were writing a book of my own. I have had this experience only twice as a translator, with the novels of Dazai and with *Tsurezuregusa* (*Essays in Idleness*) by the priest Kenkō. Translation for me is generally a painful process, consisting of equal parts of despair and resignation, but in the case of these two extraordinarily different authors, it was close to pleasure.

My busyness during my first year as a teacher at Columbia was compounded by another feature. Faubion and Santha Bowers were back in New York and leading an extremely active social life. They invited me to their apartment at least three or four times a week, especially to "celebrity parties" attended by people whose names and photographs I had long known but never expected to meet. It was startling to be introduced, say, to W. H. Auden, George Balanchine, J. Robert Oppenheimer, Adlai Stevenson, or Leopold Stokowski, and I yearned to utter some brilliant witticism that would make an indelible impression. Needless to say, the brilliant witticism would occur to me, if at all, long after I left the party.

My most unforgettable memory of these people whose acquaintance I briefly made is of the time I took Greta Garbo to the theater. I felt when I first met her as if I had known her name ever since I had known anyone's name. I could even remember, as a junior high school student, jocularly referring to her as Greasy Garbage. I must have seen all or nearly all of her films and I could recall how she looked in each, especially *Camille,* in which her mysterious beauty was set off by the vulgarity of the other actors. I had met Gigi, as she was called by her friends, at parties, but had been unable to pronounce a word before her. It can easily be imagined how I felt when I was asked on the telephone by Jane Gunther, a close friend of Garbo, if I would like to take her to the theater. My answer was instantaneous. I was then informed where to meet her, and told that if I absolutely had to refer to her by name, I should call her Miss Brown.

We met as scheduled and went to the theater where a matinee of *The Diary of Anne Frank* was playing. We entered just as the lights were being dimmed. During the intermission "Miss Brown" held her program around her face so that no one could see her. (She must, however, have drawn the attention of some people by this unusual way of spending the quarter of an hour of the intermission.) We left just as the play was ending, while the theater was still dark. We stepped outside and I signaled for a taxi. During the five or so minutes until one came along, pedestrians gathered silently around us, and many cars in the street stopped. Although Garbo had not appeared in a film for twenty years, her face could still halt traffic.

I saw her only once again. It was at a party held at the house of John Gunther. She sat silently on a corner of the sofa as the usual gossip was being exchanged, but as soon as another guest, the distinguished Indian novelist R. K. Narayan, started to describe a mystical experience, her face showed intense interest. When she was silent and brooding over some private matter she no longer looked beautiful, but when her attention was engaged she suddenly and magically became the Garbo everyone remembered. How wonderful to think I actually met her!

Very few of the people I met at the celebrity parties became even nodding acquaintances, but meeting them was an extraordinary experience for which I was most grateful to Santha and Faubion. It made me realize for the first time that New York was, as so many authors have stated, a city of wonders, where one might meet almost anyone.

It was also a city of theaters. When Faubion bought theater tickets he always bought one for me too, and I saw more plays in those first eight months than all I had previously seen combined. We went to the opera too. The way I repaid the Bowers for their kindness was by standing from six o'clock in the morning at the Metropolitan Opera to buy tickets to operas in which Maria Callas was to appear.

When I think back on my first year of teaching at Columbia, I wonder how was it possible for me to do so much at the same time—teaching, translating, partygoing. I recall, too, that for the first time in my life I drank rather heavily. This was not because I needed the liquor or derived much pleasure from it; the atmosphere of the parties demanded that I drink. Hardly had I entered the apartment where a party was being held than I was asked what I wanted to drink. It was almost impossible to refuse without arousing consternation. Sometimes, when I went to the theater after a cocktail party, I had difficulty in focusing my eyes on the actors, and saw two of each of them. But, miraculously, the next morning I was always ready to teach and never suffered from a hangover.

Teaching gave me more pleasure than it had in Cambridge, if only because there were so many more students. I am afraid, though, that I was interested only in the good students, and did not make much effort to guide the poorer ones in their efforts to master the Japanese language. I now feel very warmly toward the twenty or thirty students who have taken advanced degrees under my supervision, but I doubt that, like Mr. Chips, I shall have the names and faces of students of the forty years of teaching at Columbia file past me on my deathbed. Occasionally I have letters from students of former years, especially those who were in a relatively large undergraduate class and whose names I have forgotten, telling me that in retrospect the course they took with me gave them the most pleasure. Nothing could be more gratifying to a teacher, but I sometimes wonder why this should have been true. Perhaps it was because the students sensed that I really enjoyed my subject, that if I had to (and could afford it) I would pay to teach Japanese literature. I think *that,* rather than the content of my lectures, has lingered with them.

The daily routine of my university teaching was of course less exciting than the nightlife, but it gave me pleasure to think how little my students could have suspected that the professor with whom they laboriously read Japanese texts on Tuesdays and Thursdays had conversed the previous evening with Garbo. But this was still a very different pleasure from the kind I had when meeting writers or actors in Japan. In the case of celebrities like Garbo or Margot Fonteyn, it was quite sufficient simply to gaze on them, but I wanted to learn from the Japanese.

My anthology of Japanese literature was well received. The first edition was two thousand copies. The publishers, fearing that so many copies would never sell, entered into an agreement with the Japan Society, which agreed to purchase unsold copies. If, on the other hand, more than two thousand copies sold, the publishers promised to pay the Japan Society a small amount of money for each additional copy. The first edition was exhausted by Christmas, and the book has gone through many printings since. Not infrequently graduate students have told me that their interest in Japanese literature was first aroused by the anthology. Its success brought home to me again the discovery I had made in Japan, that I was really not cut out to be a scholar who produces one perfect research article every decade and that my greatest strength lay in communicating to other people the excitement I felt on reading works of Japanese literature.

My least pleasurable teaching was Second-Year Japanese. I hated the textbook. It presented so many new items of vocabulary in each lesson that I was sure nobody could retain them. Once, to test this conviction, I asked the students to read in class not the lesson they had prepared the night before but one that we had gone over a week earlier. The results were disastrous. I switched from the textbook to a local Japanese newspaper. It was better, but the characters were small and smudged. I switched then to *Sanshirō* by Natsume Sōseki, and from then on the course was fun.

Contrary to my experiences in England, I was not embarrassed to tell people that I taught Japanese literature, because I was sure they would not ask me why I was wasting my life on anything so remote from normal human experience. Instead, I was often asked permission to attend my lectures. Very few people who asked permission in fact appeared, but the display of interest, however superficial, was reassuring.

The Japan boom was just beginning. Zen especially had become fashionable. At one party I attended Suzuki Daisetsu-sensei sat on a sofa delivering words of wisdom to the assembled, elegantly attired Americans sitting on the floor at his feet. One gentleman of about sixty asked the master, "Dr. Suzuki, I wonder if you can help me? I am a successful architect, esteemed in my profession. I have a devoted wife and children, and live in a house with everything I desire—books, records, objects of art. I still feel confident that in the future I will achieve even better things than what I have done in the past. But why am I unhappy?" After this long question Suzuki Daisetsu thought a moment and then said, "Eh?" The architect repeated the question almost word for word. This time Suzuki-sensei answered, "Happiness is doing unto others as you would have done unto yourself. Golden rule, I think you call it?" From the opposite end of the room a voice called out, just loud enough for us (but not Suzuki-sensei, who was rather deaf) to hear, "Oh, no, we call that the silver platitude." I could not decide if Suzuki-sensei's answer had been deliberately intended to ridicule the question or if he really meant what he said. At that time even the "platitudes" of Christianity were welcomed by the New York intellectuals, provided they came from a Zen master.

The beatniks were especially intrigued by Zen. At one party the guest of honor was Munakata Shikō, and most of the people present were beatniks, including the leaders of the movement, Allen Ginsberg and Jack Kerouac. As I entered the room Ginsberg was saying to a young Japanese that he had just composed a haiku and he would like the young man to translate it for Munakata-san's sake. The haiku was: Three poets urinate in the snow. The interpreter did not understand the English word *urinate,* so Ginsberg gestured, made sounds, and in the end all but urinated on the carpet. I hastily intervened and supplied the Japanese word. Ginsberg asked who I was, and when I gave my name, he praised my translation of *Hōjōki* (*An Account of My Hut*). As we talked Ginsberg suddenly went over to Munakata-san, took his hand, and bit it. I nervously explained that this was a traditional American gesture of friendship. In the meantime

Kerouac kept shouting my name from across the room, demanding that I translate into Japanese the names of various technical terms of Buddhism which he gave in their Sanskrit pronunciations.

The Japan boom had many other ramifications. For example, Japanese films were discovered for the first time and, although I knew almost nothing about filmmaking, I was the closest thing to an expert, and distributors frequently asked my opinion of films, especially those I had not seen. I also had telephone calls from dealers in prints, asking me the value of items in their collections. When I truthfully informed one such dealer that I had no idea, he answered, "But I was told you knew *everything* about Japan." I was asked by the president of a major broadcasting system to recommend a reliable Japanese couple to serve as butler and maid in his domicile.

Such requests were obviously absurd. Would one ask a professor of French literature to recommend a cook? But, I confess, I rather enjoyed the attention, which contrasted so sharply with the indifference to my work I had sensed in Cambridge. The interest was largely superficial, hardly more than a passing vogue, but I benefited by it. I was asked to write articles by magazines and gave lectures to women's clubs. I also enjoyed attending social gatherings at which I was the only academic, invited because I knew something about a country that had suddenly become fashionable.

But, all the same, I missed Japan. Japanese visitors to America were still infrequent because of currency and other restrictions, and weeks sometimes went by without my speaking Japanese except to my students. I worried lest I lose my facility with the language. More than that, I missed the unexpected kindness or even affection that I often experienced in Japan, even from strangers. I remembered, to cite one instance, how an old lady had come up to me as I waited for a train somewhere in Nara prefecture, and asked when I was going back to my country. I told her, and she replied, "Take me with you!" The moment was funny rather than touching, but I recalled it again and again, always with pleasure.

I lived in Tsunoda-sensei's apartment until he returned. I then had to find a place of my own, no simple matter at the time. Someone introduced me to a politician who kept an apartment near Columbia where he did not actually live, in order to maintain the fiction that he was a resident of that particular electoral district. He agreed to let the place to me under two conditions: the first was that if anyone telephoned I was to say that Frank (his name) had just stepped out, and the second was to stay away from the apartment on Wednesday afternoons when he met his girlfriend there. I complied with these conditions, though I found it unconvincing when I told someone who telephoned at seven in the morning that Frank had just stepped out.

The apartment was large and reasonably well furnished, but faced an inner courtyard, and Frank, in order not to have the walls painted more than absolutely necessary, had had them painted a dark blue, which did not show the dirt. At noon on the brightest day the apartment was dark and depressing. How often I contrasted it with "my" house in Kyoto! The stillness of the apartment should have been beneficial to my work, but as soon as I opened the door and stepped in, I felt a wave of gloom pass over me, and there was nowhere in the impersonal, unloved apartment where I could even read a book, let alone write. I simply had to return to Japan.

Finding money to go to Japan became a major preoccupation during the following years. The Columbia summer vacations were over three months long, which made it possible to spend a useful period of time in Japan, but my salary was inadequate to pay for the airline ticket. In 1956, for example, I was given money by *Newsweek* to write a series of articles about contemporary cultural life in Japan. I wrote them; but only one, on Ishihara Shintarō's novel *Taiyō no Kisetsu* (*Season of the Sun*), ever appeared in print. I was paid anyway, and this enabled me to spend the summer in Kyoto. In other years I managed to obtain funds from foundations or (for several years) from Columbia, in order to work in Japan on my translations of the plays of Chikamatsu. Somehow, I managed to find the money every year.

*****

Perhaps the most memorable of these summers in Japan was 1957, when I was chosen as a member of the American delegation to the PEN Club Congress held in Tokyo and Kyoto. I was pleased to have this first recognition from the American literary world, though I was aware, of course, that I had been chosen not on the basis of my published works but because I could speak Japanese. The congress that year was particularly brilliant. Kawabata Yasunari, then the president of the Japanese PEN, made a trip around the world to induce famous writers to attend the congress and he was largely successful. Even the European and American writers who normally would have avoided anything like a PEN Club Congress, were eager to have a look at Japan and gladly accepted the invitation. For the Japanese, it was a great occasion, the first international cultural event to be staged in Japan since the end of the war. Even schoolchildren contributed money to make the congress a success.

The American delegation was headed by John Steinbeck, who would win the Nobel Prize a few years later, and included John

Dos Passos, John Hersey, Ralph Ellison, and other writers whose works I knew well. I was excited to be a member of this delegation, and I met equally famous members of other delegations.

To my great surprise, I was an object of special attention from the Japanese reporters, simply because I could respond to their questions in Japanese. At first I was highly pleased by this attention, but it did not take long to grow tired of responding again and again to identical questions. I remember crying out in exasperation at one point that I had already answered many times the question, "What do the foreign delegates think of Japan?" The reporter replied, "That was for other newspapers. I need your opinion from you directly." My irritation was not assuaged, and as I was preparing to make some sarcastic answer, I noticed a distinguished member of the British delegation slowly and patiently describing, probably for the twentieth time, what he thought of Japan. I realized that I was not cut out to be a celebrity.

A few memories stand out. I remember, for example, a party at an expensive restaurant in Akasaka to which a group of delegates was invited by a publisher and his wife. One European delegate somehow got the idea that we were in a brothel, and he asked me in a low voice when the publisher's wife would leave and the "geishas" appear. It was typical of the misconceptions about Japan that were current even among foreign intellectuals.

The congress began with an address of welcome by Kawabata Yasunari. As I recall, he spoke in quietly humorous tones, reassuring the foreign delegates that although September was a month of typhoons that often caused great damage, the oldest wooden buildings in the world still stood in Nara, an indication of the resilience of Japan in the face of storm winds. Perhaps he also meant us to catch behind his words the implied meaning that Japan had successfully emerged from the terrible storm of the war years. However, Kawabata's words were not greeted with smiles of appreciation, probably because the interpreter, who stood rigidly erect by the side of the stage, interpreted Kawabata's words in tones that suggested a monstrous typhoon was imminent, sending a thrill of fear through the audience.

There were other moments of misunderstanding, some of them invented by the press. For example, after a performance of the Nō play *Funa Benkei* which (as far as I could tell) had greatly moved the international audience, reporters approached the delegates with such questions as, "You were bored, weren't you? You wanted to leave, didn't you?" Similarly, the newspaper accounts insisted that the foreign delegates, after a delicious and filling vegetarian meal at a temple in Kyoto, were not satisfied with such fare and went off afterward to eat steaks. At the time it was normal for newspapers to print photographs of foreign dignitaries using chopsticks for the first time, by way of comic relief perhaps, and it was therefore not surprising that writers, though they are more likely than politicians to be cosmopolitan in their tastes, were also portrayed as being baffled by the refinements of Japanese civilization.

Many pleasant memories linger from that PEN congress, though I have almost not a single memory of the one held in New York a few years ago. When I meet someone who was present at the Tokyo congress, it is hard to resist spending some minutes in recollections. I remember, for example, going with Alberto Moravia, Stephen Spender, and Angus Wilson to various temples in Kyoto. At the time there were still extremely few privately owned cars in Kyoto, but one belonged to a friend of mine, a priest at the Shōren-in, and he took us to places he thought we would enjoy. At the Koke-dera we were each asked to write a poem on a cardboard square (*shikishi*). I hope that the temple still has them. During the following thirty years I would meet these three men occasionally in different places, and I was grateful to the congress for having made such acquaintances possible.

The congress called the attention of the international literary world to the existence of an important modern Japanese literature. Two years earlier, when William Faulkner visited Japan, he was asked if he had ever read any work of Japanese literature, but he could not remember. It is doubtful whether many of the delegates to the congress were aware of more than a haiku or two. Even those who might have read Waley's translation of *The Tale of Genji* probably had not read a single modern Japanese novel; but their visit to Japan brought them in contact with Japanese writers and their works, making them receptive to the translations that would appear during the following years. Their reviews, prefaces to translations, and praise helped to establish the place in the world of modern Japanese literature.

*****

Although there were occasional moments of stress in my friendship with Mishima Yukio, almost every memory I have of the times we spent together is a happy memory. His many-faceted talents, his sense of humor, and his extraordinary perceptivity made for captivating conversations, and I think he is the only genius I have ever known. I do not use the word *genius* lightly. Some Japanese are ready to call anyone who speaks two foreign languages a genius, but I have known a fair number of unintelligent persons who (for various reasons) could speak three or four languages with ease, and there are many professional linguists who have mastered a dozen languages without being geniuses. A genius is someone who can perform with little or no effort actions that are impossible for ordinary persons.

A manuscript written by Mishima was like pages of music in Mozart's hand. There were almost no words crossed out or other corrections. When about to write a novel or other major work, Mishima would draw on a large sheet of paper an extensive outline of the plot. This achieved, he would (in his own words) merely add flesh to the skeleton. For Mishima this was extremely simple; indeed, he could not understand why other writers had to struggle with their words. I remember that when I wrote him that I had completed the first draft of my translation of his play *Madame de Sade,* he answered with a telegram wishing me a myriad, myriad years of life (*banbanzai*). He evidently did not realize that in my case the first draft was only the beginning of the hard work of turning a translation into readable English.

Mishima arrived in New York shortly after the publication of my translation of his *Five Modern Nō Plays* in the summer of 1957. The publishers arranged for an interview with a reporter from *The New York Times* as publicity for the book. The reporter, though fairly well known as a chronicler of the literary scene, proved to be a dolt. His first question, made while looking at the information about Mishima provided by the publisher, was something like, "It says here you have already published a novel in this country, and now you're publishing some plays. Which are you, anyway, a novelist or a playwright?" At first Mishima answered the man's questions in English, but as the questions became more and more stupid, he switched to Japanese, leaving me the unenviable task of interpreting.

Mishima in the letters he wrote me at this time often mentioned the inadequacy of his English, but it was surprisingly good. Unlike most of his contemporaries, he had learned English conversationally, rather than from books of grammar, and he eagerly picked up whatever English words were currently in vogue, giving people the impression that he spoke the language fluently.

An article based on the interview appeared in the newspaper and had the desired effect of attracting attention to the plays. Before long, many producers expressed interest in staging them. Mishima chose from among them two young men who were in television. Both were exceptionally intelligent and likable, and they had good ideas on how the plays should be performed. The men were sure they would have no trouble in raising the money needed for the production. Their only concern was that there not be any strings attached to the money, and their ideal, as they reported to Mishima and myself, was a wealthy button manufacturer who did not have a wife with theatrical ambitions.

Unfortunately, they never found the ideal button manufacturer, and Mishima waited impatiently for something to happen. At this point the producers had a bright idea: in Japan, they read somewhere, comedies called Kyōgen are presented in between the tragic Nō plays, and they would be grateful if Mishima would write a modern Kyōgen. Mishima did exactly that. I have the manuscript, just as he wrote it, and there is hardly a word changed anywhere.

This still did not attract any button manufacturers. The producers decided that the problem was that the three Mishima Nō plays they intended to produce were one-act plays, and Americans disliked one-act plays. They asked Mishima to rewrite the three independent plays into a single three-act play. Mishima once again obliged, though most playwrights would have insisted that it was impossible, and again the manuscript is without corrections.

Knowing such a man not solely as a writer but as a friend was one of the reasons why in the years that followed I felt I had to return to Japan each year, no matter how difficult this might be financially.

*****

Although Mishima would one day write that the only thing he missed while in New York was Kabuki, his stay in 1957 must have been lonely and frustrating. In part this was my fault. I tried to see him as often as possible, but I was teaching and had other obligations. I also felt hesitant to invite him to the kind of restaurants where I normally ate, remembering the splendid restaurants in Tokyo to which he always invited me. I should have realized that it was better to eat with a friend in a poor restaurant than to eat in a good restaurant alone.

Mishima was not completely dependent on me. His publisher occasionally invited him to dinner or to a weekend in the country, and he made other acquaintances. But Truman Capote, whom Mishima had entertained in Tokyo at the beginning of the year, chose not to see him. This did not surprise me. Capote was surely one of the most disagreeable and untrustworthy persons I had ever met. But one would have thought he would have had at least the courtesy to return hospitality.

Another source of irritation for Mishima must have been his growing shortage of funds. At the time it was difficult for Japanese to obtain foreign currency, and Mishima was obliged to leave the comfortable hotel where he had been living for a much cheaper one. But the worst aspect of his stay in New York was that he could not write. He told me that he could not write naturally unless he was surrounded by people speaking Japanese. He had in fact written a modern Kyōgen, and occasionally composed newspaper articles, but for someone whose daily routine normally included long hours at his desk, not to be able to write was surely frustrating.

The stay in New York was not, however, a total loss. Mishima attended every single play that was being performed, from the great hits of the year, *My Fair Lady* and *West Side Story*, down to amateur productions in tiny theaters. Perhaps some of them provided pointers he would use in his own plays. He also did research for the sections of his novel *Kyōko's House* set in New York. His stay probably also helped to make him the first international Japanese writer. Long before his sensational suicide attracted the attention of the world he was the best-known Japanese writer. He was chosen as one of the "hundred men of the world" by *Esquire* magazine, and was asked to write articles by American magazines of wide circulation. Intellectuals who could not name another Japanese writer knew Mishima's. His reputation was established initially by the publication of the translation of *Confessions of a Mask* in 1958 and of *The Temple of the Golden Pavilion* in 1959, but his personal contacts with American and other writers undoubtedly contributed much to his celebrity.

*****

Mishima returned to Japan from New York and Europe on January 10, 1958, and was at once caught up in a furious round of activity. He wrote, "Night after night there are parties welcoming me back; I have been obliged to write an account of my travels in over one hundred pages; the phone rings without stop all day long; and in between I have appeared on television three times, have had a film shot at my house, and have in addition seen plays of every kind. I simply didn't have the time to write. What a country—what a busy country!"

His letter does not say so, but after the months of waiting and loneliness in New York, he obviously reveled in this attention. In works of literature that depict Japanese living abroad, they are almost always pictured as being so aware of the differences separating them from the people of the country where they are temporarily residing that they yearn to return to Japan as soon as possible. These Japanese inevitably tend to idealize Japan, much as Americans in Europe or Europeans in America idealize their own countries. But this was not true of Mishima, who took pleasure in the variety of experiences that can happen only in an unfamiliar world and who enjoyed the company of foreign people. All the same, he was happy to be back in Japan.

"Friends dragged me off from Haneda Airport to Tōyoko Hall where a benefit performance of *Rokumeikan* was being staged. They took me backstage, and when I appeared for curtain calls I gave a talk relating my feelings on returning to Japan. Ah, I thought to myself, in Japan all these people have been waiting for me to return, and looking out at the audience I felt really happy. It made me realize quite keenly that I have been a spoiled child of journalism, and that I am incapable of living a lonely life all by myself."

Walking with Mishima through the streets of Shinjuku or some other busy part of Tokyo was always a very special experience. Again and again he would be stopped by people who wanted his autograph, and he always complied with a smile. He told me once that a young woman, who had nothing else for him to write on, asked him to inscribe his name on her panties in *majikku* (Magic Marker). He obviously enjoyed the attention, and I think he was amused rather than annoyed when he was refused admission to a restaurant in the Imperial Hotel because he was not wearing a jacket, imagining how chagrined the employee would be if he realized he had refused a celebrated author. It can easily be imagined, then, how much he missed this attention in New York. After the interview with the *New York Times* man, who clearly had never heard of him, Mishima (who had already published two books in New York) asked me as we were leaving what one had to do to become famous in New York. I answered truthfully that even if Hemingway and Faulkner walked arm in arm through Times Square, nobody would recognize them.

Among the newspaper articles Mishima published after his return from abroad, one in the *Asahi Shimbun* had annoyed me by referring to the *taihai* of New York. It was unpleasant for me to see the city where I was born and grew up characterized as *taihai*, and I had difficulty reconciling this word (which, according to my Japanese-English dictionary, meant "corruption" or "degeneration") with Mishima's professed pleasure in living in New York. I was disappointed that Mishima had resorted to what I considered to be a stereotyped characterization of New York, and mentioned my disappointment in a letter I sent to an American living in Tokyo, an acquaintance of Mishima. This man decided (without asking my permission) to show the letter to Mishima in order for the "quarrel" to be discussed openly and in this way to be amicably settled.

Mishima wrote me on April 12, 1958, explaining his purpose in writing the article: "When I wrote in my article that New York was 'sick' or that it was *taihai,* the words were used in a good sense. The word *taihai* is entirely different in nuance from *fuhai,* which means corrupt. For many years, up to the present even, Japanese intellectuals have gone around saying that there is no decadence in America. This is exactly the same sort of thing as when they say, 'America is the new world and lacks the special smell of its own that an old country has, a smell that appeals to our own tastes, a smell like that of old wine.' Because we revere European decadence, Thomas Mann is more esteemed for his extremely typical and profound decadence than for his art."

On reading these words I realized the danger of accepting the definitions given in a dictionary of a particular word without taking into consideration the connotations that had accrued around the word as it was used by different segments of society. For Mishima *taihai* was desirable, though this had not been apparent to me. He went on to explain another word in the article that had upset me:

"When I used in my article the word *sick* I was contrasting it with the novels and lives of contemporary Japanese writers. Needless to say, this was not in the sense of merely being unwell, but it was sick in the sense of 'something living in the muddy depths of a culture that represents all the negative aspects of that culture and its tragic fate.' It is only at that point that a culture can achieve its finest expression.

"I believe that at present there is decadence in America too, in the true sense of the word. There is the ferment for creating the taste of old wine. I intended also to say that this is different from European decadence, and is a uniquely American development."

During the seventeen years of my friendship with Mishima this was about as close as we ever came to having a quarrel. Reading his letters, I see that in every instance of disagreement (as in the above case) he was right and I was wrong.

*****

During the late 1950s there was a marked upsurge in the study of Japanese and other "unusual" languages. The Soviet launching of the first satellite in 1957 had shaken American complacence, and led to the enactment of programs intended to improve the quality of American education. However, if these programs had been plainly identified as educational, they might not have been approved by Congress, so the enabling act was called the National Defense Educational Act, making it clear that education was valuable because it promoted national defense.

Because of this concession to legislators who might otherwise have refused to waste public funds on education, the program was well funded, and provided fellowships in many languages. Teaching staffs were also augmented, and this was how it happened that Ivan Morris joined my department at Columbia. I had met Ivan in Japan, and had been so favorably impressed that I thought of him when we learned we could increase our staff.

Ivan was born in England of an American father and a Swedish mother. He had spent some of his formative years in France, and his B.A. degree was from Harvard. He had learned his Japanese at the U.S. Navy Japanese Language School, and I have a picture showing him in American naval uniform. Yet I have rarely met anyone who struck me as being more English—in his diffidence, his sense of humor, his determination to see justice done. Even in externals—his clothes, his walking stick (one of them concealing a sword), and his pipe—little of New York seems to have brushed off on him during the sixteen years he spent there until his untimely death in 1976. He once told me that he had not intended to spend more than a few years at Columbia, but his stay imperceptibly lengthened.

Ivan's translations from the Japanese are in a class by themselves. When translating Saikaku's *The Life of an Amorous Woman,* for example, he painstakingly verified that every word used in his translation had been employed in the same sense in eighteenth-century English literature. The result was a translation that reads like Defoe. There are other good translations of Saikaku, but Ivan's is unique. His translations of *The Pillow Book of Sei Shōnagon* and *As I Crossed a Bridge of Dreams* (this is the title he gave to *Sarashina Nikki*) are superb examples of English prose that give new life to the originals without falsifying them. His *The Nobility of Failure* is a compelling account of the failed hero in Japanese history. His own favorite among his books was probably *Madly Singing in the Mountains,* essays he edited about Arthur Waley, his teacher and model. By a coincidence, his translation of *The Pillow Book* (dedicated to me) and my translation of *Essays in Idleness* (dedicated to him) were published on the same day in 1967.

On social occasions Ivan showed rare warmth and charm. He soon had a far greater circle of acquaintances in New York than I, and visiting British writers were often guests in his apartment, but he was shy and reluctant to talk about himself. I, too, am shy and hesitate to intrude into other people's affairs, and even when I could see that he was suffering, I could only wait for him to tell me the cause. This seldom happened. He once mentioned to me Akutagawa's phrase *bonyari shita fuan* (a vague uneasiness). His sudden death at the age of fifty left a great gap in my life and regret that I had done little to comfort him when he was unhappy.

*****

In retrospect, the late 1950s and early 1960s seem like a time when there was money for every scholarly project. At Columbia my colleague Ted de Bary initiated a program for the translation of the great books of East Asia, to be used in an Oriental Humanities course corresponding to the Humanities course in reading the great books of the West. I was asked to translate plays by Chikamatsu, and there were funds for my journeys to Japan each summer.

The only time I have ever asked the help of a Japanese scholar when translating a work of Japanese classical literature was while working on the plays of Chikamatsu. Professor Mori Shū of Osaka Municipal University would come to my house in Kyoto once a week, and we would go over together the questions that had accumulated. He would spread out on the table all the existing commentated texts of Chikamatsu's works (there were not very many), and before answering my questions would read through the troublesome passage in each text. More often than not, the commentaries provided little if any guidance. Sometimes we would manage to get through only one or two sentences during his visit.

The failing of the commentators was that they never told me anything that would help in making a translation. They generally confined themselves to repeating what earlier commentators had written or else added a definition or two from the Japanese-Portuguese dictionary of 1603, to demonstrate an awareness of modern scholarship. Confucius was regularly identified as "a great man of China," Edo as "the modern Tokyo," and *The Tale of Genji* as "a representative work of Heian literature," though it is hard to imagine anyone who needed such information reading Chikamatsu. The tradition of providing only useless facts has not died out. Real difficulties in the text are generally passed over in silence, as much as to say, "What's your problem? It seems perfectly obvious to me."

So I tortured poor Mori-san with such questions as "Is this word singular or plural?" "Why does she complain of having so

BOOM AND BUST

many children when she only has three?" "When Sōshichi says he and Kojorō are bound for Owari, are we to understand a pun on *owari,* meaning the (bitter) end?" And so on. This was the kind of information I needed in order to make an accurate translation, but naturally no commentator had ever troubled himself over such matters. Poor Mori-san, after carefully consulting the texts before him, would usually ask, "Might it not be . . . ?"

The problems in translating Chikamatsu did not end with finding English meanings for his words. I had somehow to make the dialogue sound like the utterances of real people. I also made at least a stab at conveying the intricacies of wordplay in the original. For example, this passage occurs in my translation of *The Love Suicides at Amijima,* Chikamatsu's masterpiece: "Ask your guest to keep you for the whole night, and show him how sweet you can be. Give him a barrelful of nectar! Good-bye, madam. I'll see you later, honey."

This may not sound very elegant, but I was trying desperately to convey the effect of the *engo* (related words). In the original, however, the related images are not sweet (as in my translation) but salty, including a cask of soy sauce and some pickled vegetables. I simply couldn't think of salty endearments in English.

*****

During the autumn I began to study the singing of the texts of Nō plays. I decided that I would study with a teacher of one of the less popular of the five schools of Nō, on the assumption that I would receive more individual attention (and that possibly the fee would be lower). This was a wise decision. I was introduced to Sakurama Michio, a leading actor (later a Human National Treasure) of the Komparu School, and began my weekly lessons. In some ways Nō was easier than Kyōgen. When learning Kyō-

211

gen I had nothing before my eyes to remind me of the words, but Nō was sung from a text that also had markings indicating whether the voice was to go up or down, or whether a given sound was to be prolonged or slid into the next one. I am completely incapable of carrying a tune in any other form of singing, but I think *anyone* can carry a Nō "tune," though some people obviously do it much better than others. In any case, it was pleasant to feel confident of my voice, for the first time since I was ten or eleven.

People who are really familiar with the performance of Nō plays can easily distinguish the styles of singing of the different schools, but to the end of my short career as a singer of the texts I seldom succeeded in differentiating one from another. Sakurama-san informed me that it was characteristic of the Komparu School for the actors to open the mouth wide when singing but not to expose their teeth. I tried doing precisely this, and I soon understood why the enunciation of the texts tends to lack clarity.

We began with *Hashi Benkei* (*Benkei at the Bridge*), a simple and essentially uninteresting play. I was impatient to move on to one of the more artistic plays of the repertory, and I told this to Sakurama-san. "What would you like to learn?" he asked. I had not really considered this before, but I answered, almost without thinking, "*Yuya.*" This is indeed a most beautiful Nō play, though not one of those I like best, and I surprised myself with the positiveness of my reply. Sakurama-san laughed and said that what I proposed doing was rather like going from kindergarten to the university with nothing in between. But, in the end, he agreed to teach me *Yuya* because my stay in Japan was limited and I might never have the chance to learn *Yuya* otherwise.

I enjoyed singing the text, which was far more lyric than the weighty measures of *Benkei at the Bridge*. *Yuya* is the story of the courtesan Yuya, the favorite of the despotic Taira no Munemori. She receives a letter from her mother in the country telling of her illness, which seems likely to be fatal, and she begs Munemori to let her go to her mother's side. He refuses: he has been looking forward to going with Yuya to see the cherry blossoms at the Kiyomizu Temple, and is unwilling to change his plans merely because her mother is ill. But after they arrive at Kiyomizu, she composes a poem that induces him to relent, and he allows her to go to her mother.

It was just at this time that I began to get letters from my own mother telling me of her illness. The nature of her illness was not clear, and I suspected that it might be mainly loneliness. I wrote her reassuringly, but the tone of her letters did not become any more cheerful, and I had no choice but to return to America halfway through my intended year in Japan. It was as if the ghost of Yuya, annoyed by my presumption in attempting to learn the play, was taking revenge by haunting me.

Rather like Yuya, I left Tokyo to go to the sickbed of my mother, but I did not go directly. I had long been planning to visit Southeast Asia in a relatively cool season of the year and, like Munemori in the same play, I was unwilling to allow other considerations to interfere with my plans. It baffles me now that I was capable of acting with such coldhearted indifference to my mother's illness, but I must have reassured myself that, as in a number of instances in the past, my mother's mental anxiety had given her the symptoms of some physical complaint.

In any case, instead of crossing the Pacific, I headed first for Manila in December 1961. My only previous visit to the Philippines had been just prior to the invasion of Okinawa, and at that time I had seen only Samar and Leyte. I did not know anyone in Manila, but through the PEN Club I met several writers, and my week in Manila was made enjoyable by their hospitality. I read novels and short stories by the people I met, and I was impressed by their exceptional skill. These writers wrote in English of great effectiveness, though for some it was a third language, after their native Filipino language and Spanish. I became so enthusiastic about Filipino literature that for a couple of years I wrote reviews of newly published books.

The attitude toward Japan, however, was almost uniformly hostile, mainly because of the great destruction and loss of life suffered during the final battle for Manila in 1945. Intramuros, the old section of the city, had suffered particularly. When I mentioned consolingly that the sixteenth-century St. Augustine Church still stood, I was told of horrors that had occurred even within that church. But I have mercifully forgotten much of what I was told, and I remember instead the Christmas stars in the windows of the houses, the Chinese restaurants where the menus were exclusively in Spanish, and, above all, the unaffected warmth of everyone I met.

I flew from Manila to Saigon. The war had not yet begun in Vietnam, but there were constant incidents of terroristic violence in the city, and the first U.S. advisers had started to arrive. I met a Vietnamese journalist who, in response to my request, took me to the classical theater. I naturally could not understand the sung and spoken dialogue, but my new friend would murmur from time to time what was going on. The plot seemed vaguely familiar, though I had never before seen a Vietnamese play and the story concerned (as I recall) a King of Ngui and a King of Han, costumed and performed in a manner resembling that of a Chinese opera. But I somehow seemed to know what was coming next. Finally, I asked the name of the play, and learned to my astonishment it was Shakespeare's *The Winter's Tale,* performed in traditional Vietnamese style.

While in Saigon I met a French priest who was a translator of Chinese literature. I told him of my plan to visit Hue, the old capital. He answered sardonically, "Yes, go to Hue! You will be disappointed, as everyone is disappointed, but go there anyway!" But I was not disappointed. I remember the forlorn old palace, the last remnant of Chinese-style monarchy, where one old custodian looked after the dusty buildings, amusing himself with a top which I think is called a diabolo. I remember, too, the magnificent bronze caldrons in the palace courtyard. Most of all, I remember the boats plying silently in the River of Perfumes. Did this beauty all disappear in the fighting a few years later?

From Saigon I flew to Siem Reap in Cambodia. The Royal Cambodian Airlines plane left before dawn, and I grew hungrier and hungrier during the flight. Finally, there came a promising odor of food being prepared in the galley, but to my disappointment, the stewardesses ate the food, ignoring the hungry passengers.

I stayed at first at the Grand Hotel of Angkor, as I had eight years before. The hotel was all but deserted, and every morning the staff of the hotel drilled with wooden guns, in preparation, it seemed, for a conflict to come. I arrived at the magnificent ruins of the twelfth-century temples at sunset, when the great expanse of buildings was tinted orange against a dark sky. I was stunned by the sight, but at that moment, from somewhere in my subconscious, the word *uncomplimentary* mysteriously floated up. For a moment I was baffled: what word could be less appropriate for the sight before me? Then I realized its significance.

Shortly before leaving Japan, I had been translating Mishima's novel *After the Banquet.* One scene relates how Kazu, the heroine, knows exactly the right tone to adopt when talking to customers at her restaurant. With men whose career is waning, she is careful to say nothing that might wound their feelings; but with men who are confident of their importance, she does not hesitate even to make *burei* jokes. Of course, I knew the meaning of the word *burei*—rude, impolite, discourteous, disrespectful and so on, but none of the dictionary meanings seemed to fit the context exactly. But at that moment, when I stood before the full splendor of Angkor Wat, the right adjective for my translation (though certainly not for the incredible sight before me) at last surfaced.

Over the years, I have again and again had the experience of being presented by my subconscious with a needed word or phrase. When I was translating poetry for my anthology of Japanese literature, I would sometimes, after making a rough version, go out for a walk, trusting that the words would rearrange themselves metrically in my subconscious. It didn't always work, but a number of the versions that were printed were the product of these walks.

I can hardly imagine anyone who would be uncomplimentary about Angkor, but I have recently seen photographs that show that the jungle is again taking possession of the massive ruins. While at Angkor (in those days, anyway) one was certain to learn two words of French: *fromager* is the name of the huge trees that over the centuries burst their way through the stone walls and towers of Angkor; the other word is *anastylos,* a term that does not appear in my Larousse dictionary, but refers to the process of reassembling fallen elements of masonry. It seems as if, with neglect, the fromagers are winning their struggle against the archaeologists who painstakingly cut down the wild growth of trees, unearthed the ruins, and restored them to their former grandeur (by anastylos).

There is, or was, a Japanese graffito on one of the walls of
Angkor Wat. It relates how a samurai from Kumamoto made
his way to Angkor in the middle of the seventeenth century, to
pray for the repose of his mother. But how did he learn of the
existence of Angkor if it lay buried in the earth until discovered
by archaeologists in the nineteenth century? There is probably a
prosaic answer to this mystery, but I don't want to know it. I
prefer to keep the graffito along with my other memories of the
beautiful, lost Angkor.

There was still one more site in Southeast Asia I wanted to see
before going on to Europe—Pagan in Burma. I had spent a week
there in 1955, but I wanted to return, convinced (in my usual
pessimistic way) that I would never have another chance to visit
this most marvelous of Buddhist ruins. When I stopped there in
1955, I was the only guest in the hotel, a rambling wooden
structure where one slept on an outside porch. Three times a day
I had exactly the same meal, a Burmese approximation of a British Sunday dinner, consisting of roast chicken and roast potatoes.
But the two thousand broken temples, some only a pile of
stones, others still splendid, made an unforgettable sight that
evoked in my mind Rome after the barbarians had sacked the
city.

I will never forget my first visit. I took a plane from Rangoon
to a place called Chauk, or rather to a field on the other side of
the Irrawaddy River from Chauk. When I got out of the plane I
was startled to see that there was nothing in the way of airport
facilities, nothing but a strip of flat ground used by occasional
planes, and absolutely nobody to tell me how to get across the
river. Fortunately, an Englishwoman and her small child were

on the same plane, and I timidly asked if she was going to Chauk. She was, and presently, when a boat came to fetch her, I too got aboard.

Her husband, on the Chauk side of the river, invited me to lunch "if I had no other plans." I was delighted by this example of British reluctance to interfere in other people's affairs, but I assured him that I had very few acquaintances indeed in Chauk and would be glad to accept his hospitality. After lunch he arranged for a car to take me to Pagan, about twenty-five miles away.

I was surprised by the size of the vehicle that arrived soon afterward. It was of the kind called by the military a "carryall," much too big for myself and my minimal baggage. But after we had gone about a mile or so, the car stopped, and some seven or eight armed soldiers got aboard. I was annoyed that *my* car should have picked up hitchhikers, especially these ferocious-looking men. Nobody spoke English, and I no Burmese. Every couple of miles the car would break down, and the driver would indicate with unfriendly gestures that I was to get out while he searched for tools that were kept under my seat. It took about five hours to travel twenty-five miles, and all the way I was terrified lest one of the desperadoes in the back of the truck would decide the moment had come to kill me and take my suitcase.

After I arrived in Pagan, the innkeeper, who spoke some English, informed me that I must pay not only the driver but also the soldiers, who had served as my bodyguards during the passage through territory controlled by various bands of Communist insurgents. The thought had not occurred to me that they might be my protectors.

But the wonders of Pagan made up for the uncertainty and even fear of the journey, and I shall not forget the kindness of the innkeeper either. He was a young man with a wife and two

children, but when it seemed as though the plane I was ex-
pecting to take back to Rangoon would not arrive, he dashed off
a note to his wife saying that he would be escorting me to Rangoon on the riverboat and might not be back for a week. Long
after I had abandoned hope that the plane for Rangoon would
ever arrive, it suddenly showed itself on the horizon, and I said
good-bye with emotion to the innkeeper who had been willing
to make a long and tedious journey just to make sure that I
reached my destination safely.

From Rangoon I went to Calcutta. I had briefly visited the
city in 1955, and had been repelled by the poverty, the crowds
of unhappy-looking people, and the gaunt cows wandering in
and out of public buildings. The experience this time was quite
different. I was met by a friend, P. Lal, and made a spectacular
entry into the city on the back of his motorcycle.

That night at his house there was a party of his friends, intellectuals of the city. They all spoke English not only fluently but
with such authenticity of expression that one wondered if they
spoke any other language, and their skill at argumentation was
virtuosic. That night the main subject of discussion was the mo-
rality of the Indian army's having taken Goa from the Portuguese a month or so earlier. To some, the use of force contravened
the Indian tradition of nonviolent opposition; others insisted
that there was no choice. But I got the impression that the heart
of the discussion was not Goa itself but the participants' love of
language and logic. I was even surprised they did not change
sides in the middle of the argument, to demonstrate even more
fully their virtuosity.

P. Lal is both a Sanskritist and a scholar of English literature,
combining the oldest and youngest traditions of India. He in-
sists that English is no longer a foreign language in India, but
the normal daily language of millions of people who use it to do

business, to carry on discussions, and even to make love. I confess that I was sympathetic to his views, in part because the idea of a confluence of cultures appeals to me, in part because nationalism, particularly as revealed in attempts to prove that one language is superior (or more eloquent or more heartfelt) to another, seem to me misguided and even pernicious.

From Calcutta I went on to Benares, the holy city of India. I arrived on the much-heralded day of the conjunction of five planets. Astrologers predicted the end of the world, but priests claimed that their prayers would avert disaster. During the day I walked by the Ganges, and saw pilgrims bathe in and drink its water. I saw at a distance a cremation and felt uneasily that perhaps this was a sign that the world was indeed coming to an end. That night I could hear from the old-fashioned English hotel where I was staying the sounds of chanting, and I saw elephants paraded through the streets. Nothing happened. Many people were undoubtedly relieved when they woke up safely, with no apparent changes in their lives, but others uttered imprecations against the diviners who had falsely predicted disaster. The latter naturally took credit for having saved the world from unspeakable calamity.

I have since visited India a number of times, always with pleasure and interest. I have close Indian friends whose cosmopolitanism makes me forget my ignorance of Indian history and traditions; but while in India I am always conscious of a kind of wall which, in my ignorance, I am powerless to penetrate. I feel I am a stranger as I no longer do in Japan.

The last country in Asia I saw on this journey was Lebanon. Beirut was as yet intact; the warfare that would destroy so much of the city was still years away. I made an excursion to the Roman ruins at Baalbek. The columns of the two temples stirred reveries, as ruins generally do, but I had expected more, and I was disappointed.

My next stop, Cyprus, on the other hand, was far more beautiful than I anticipated. I am sure I shall not forget the ruins of Famagusta, especially the walls and tracery windows of Gothic churches standing in green fields where sheep grazed. There are Roman ruins too, and an imposing fortress, said to be Othello's, marked with the winged lion of Venice. I felt extraordinarily happy as I wandered among the ruins.

But I should not have been happy. I should have been aware that my travels in Asia and in Cyprus were an escape from whatever was awaiting me in New York, where my mother lay ill. It did not occur to me that her illness might be really serious, even fatal. I in fact felt sure that my appearance by her bedside—if she was actually in bed—would miraculously cure her, and I was reluctant to give up what was perhaps my last chance to see the marvels of the world.

There was another reason to return to New York by way of Europe. Shortly before I left Japan I had a letter from Arthur Waley in London, typed with his left hand because his injured right hand was still "useless for writing." Beryl de Zoete, his long-time companion, was very ill with chorea, and "in a state painful to suffer and of course painful to witness." In addition, he had been informed by the University of London that he would have to leave the flat where he had lived for many years. "A last appeal for grace was not even answered." He spent much of his time reading aloud to Beryl and, he wrote, he had given up Orientalism.

I felt I simply had to see Waley, though I realized that there was not much comfort I could offer. It was particularly painful for me to think of Waley having given up his study of China and

Japan. He had long been my inspiration, though I had resigned myself to never being more than a fraction of Waley. My decision to go to London, rather than New York, recalls the choice made between father and friend in Natsume Sōseki's *Kokoro;* perhaps that is why this novel moves me more than any other by Sōseki.

I arrived in England on a cold, dark day in February 1962 and went directly to Waley's house in Gordon Square. He met me without any special display of emotion, but suggested I go upstairs to see Beryl. He warned me not to ask her any questions because, being able to understand perfectly what was said to her, she would stuggle to make a reply. "Just kiss her and say you're glad to see her," he said. But when I saw her, she was so terribly afflicted that I was incapable of kissing her. I felt miserable. I went with Waley to the kitchen, where he warmed up a tin of steak and kidneys. I asked him if he had really given up Orientalism, and he said he had. I offered to become his secretary and set down on paper his researches, but he shook off the suggestion. He said he intended to devote his remaining years to European literature. I wanted to say something of comfort, but could think of nothing.

Beryl died about a week later, and this was the last time I was ever to see Waley.

I went from London to Cambridge, where I found a letter from my aunt. She said that I should not be alarmed, but that my mother's illness had taken a turn for the worse. I decided to go to New York at once, and telephoned an airline in London for a ticket. It is baffling to me, considering how many important events and conversations I have forgotten, that I should remember exactly from which telephone booth I made the call. I didn't have the exact amount in change, and put in more money than was necessary, only to have the operator inform me that she could not accept an incorrect amount. In my agitated state, I was almost incapable of asking passersby if they would supply me with change.

The plane could not land in New York because of a snowstorm there, and for five hours I waited in the Montreal Airport, tormented by piped-in "music," for the plane to leave. The next day, when I finally reached New York, my mother was dying. She did not recognize me. I was told that if I had arrived even one day earlier she would have been able to speak to me. I left the hospital in a daze. The one thing that was clear to me was that I had been a bad son. Needless to say, I felt especially ashamed that I had traveled two-thirds around the world instead of going directly to her bedside. The pain I felt was not so much of bereavement as of guilt.

That night, back in my apartment after six months in Japan, the telephone rang. It was from my friend Shimanaka Hōji in Tokyo. He told me that I had been awarded the Kikuchi Kan Prize. I did not weep when my mother died, and I did not weep now, but I was torn apart.

I flew to Japan after the funeral. The plane was considerably delayed. This would have been upsetting to me in my overwrought state even if there had been no complications, but I had been informed that Ambassador Reischauer was giving a lunch in my honor and I was anxious not to be late. I headed directly from the airport to the embassy. The ambassador, who not long before had been wounded by a deranged man, was still recovering, and walked with the aid of a cane. He and Mrs. Reischauer received me warmly. There is a photograph taken that day showing the Reischauers, together with the principal officers of Bungei Shunjū Sha, the company that had made the award, Mishima Yukio, Shimanaka Hōji, and, standing next to me in a

At the ambassador's residence, from front left: Haru Reischauer, myself, Yoshida Keni-chi; middle: Sasaki Mosaku, Ikejima Shimpei, Mishima Yukio; rear: Edwin Rei-schauer, Tokuda Masahiko, Shimanaka Hōji.

characteristically contorted pose, Yoshida Kenichi. The only close friend missing was Nagai Michio, who was in Hong Kong.

At the presentation ceremony I of course expressed my gratitude. I said also, with complete sincerity, that Arthur Waley deserved the honor far more than myself. Throughout his career as a scholar of Japan he had denied himself the pleasure of visiting the country, insisting that he was interested only in its past glories. But, as I had already discovered, Japan had brought me comfort in the depth of my unhappiness, and it might have comforted him, too.

I went to Kyoto and spent a night in "my" old house there. I visited again the Chishaku-in, where I had studied calligraphy, and the Kitano Jinja, where the plum blossoms were in bloom. By the time I left Japan I had emerged from my gloom, and I knew now that if ever again I should be in the morbid state in which I had arrived a week or so earlier I could count on Japan to restore me.

CHAPTER SIX

*****

FRIENDS

In 1961 I received a grant from an American foundation to spend the year in Japan doing research on the Japanese theater. I reluctantly decided to live in Tokyo rather than in Kyoto. "My" house in Kyoto was unchanged, and Mrs. Okumura would have been glad to have me stay, but the view before the house had been radically altered. A tunnel had been dug nearby for the Shinkansen (the "bullet train"), and the excavated earth and stones had been dumped into the valley, turning the loveliest of prospects into a bleak landscape devoid of a blade of grass. It was painful to contemplate this victim of progress, and I swore I would never travel on the Shinkansen when it had been completed. (It did not take very long for me to violate this most sacred of oaths.)

When I had arrived in Japan for my year of research on the Japanese theater, I made the decision to live in Tokyo, and justified it not only in terms of the destroyed landscape in Kyoto but of the greater availability of different forms of theater in the capital. But I had difficulty finding an apartment I liked in

Tokyo, and although a stay in Japan had always elevated my spirits, this time I felt oddly depressed. My Tokyo friends, who usually were eager to see me as soon as I arrived, this time felt no need to hurry, knowing that I was to be in Japan for a whole year. I most often ate alone. I am sure that if I had had the courage to telephone my friends and say that I was lonely, they would have responded, but I was embarrassed to confess my loneliness.

My greatest pleasure each week came on Thursday nights when I would drink and eat with my friend, the scholar of English literature Yoshida Kenichi, and his friends, including the critic Kawakami Tetsutarō and the novelist Ishikawa Jun. The three men, though very different in personalities, all qualified as *bunjin* (dilettante man of culture) of the prewar variety, and the first requisite of a bunjin was that he be fond of liquor.

I had first met Yoshida shortly before the PEN Club Congress in Tokyo. I remember his telling me that he had resigned from the club in order to avoid being dragooned into service as an interpreter. Yoshida's English was extraordinarily good, not in the sense that he spoke a foreign language well but meaning that his English had a grace unmatched by most native speakers of the language. I usually prefer to speak Japanese with Japanese friends, even those whose English is very proficient, not because I want to show off my Japanese but because I enjoy hearing the friends express themselves in the language they know best. With Yoshida, however, I preferred to speak English, and we always did, except when other people were present who did not understand English. Sometimes he would captivate me with an old-fashioned locution such as "Has he the French?" where I would say much less elegantly, "Does he speak French?" When he was drunk, however, I found him equally unintelligible in English and in Japanese.

When Yoshida heard of my difficulties in finding a place to

live in Tokyo he kindly suggested that I live in his house. I regret now that I did not accept, but I supposed that he drank heavily every night (and day) and that I wouldn't get much work done if I were to become his drinking partner. Not until much later did I learn that he drank only one or two nights a week, though when he drank he did not easily stop.

Even before I first met Yoshida he had read the little book I published in England in 1953 called *Japanese Literature: An Introduction for Western Readers.* Probably some friend in England had sent it to him. He made a translation, which was not published until 1963. When the book appeared I wrote to express my admiration of his translation. In his reply he wrote, "I really enjoyed translating it and perhaps it's one of the best things in that line I have ever done. In fact, I started thinking in the middle of it that I was writing the book myself." This is surely why the translation was so successful.

I thought I would demonstrate my gratitude by translating something by Yoshida. I chose an essay on Oscar Wilde as a critic of literature, remembering how much he admired Wilde. But I found it almost impossible to render into English his convoluted style. Of course, if Yoshida had felt like it, he could have translated his works into English, but I imagine that he thought of the language he used—whether Japanese or English—as being an integral part of the work and essentially untranslatable.

My friendship with Yoshida was especially important to me during the autumn of 1961, when I saw few other friends, but it was not by any means confined to that period of my life in Japan. I remember the first time I was invited to his house. He and his family were living then in a house that had been built of concrete blocks during the immediate postwar days. On that occasion dinner consisted of a barrel of oysters and a barrel of saké. It can easily be imagined how quickly the guests got drunk.

On another memorable occasion at this house, I was invited to a gathering of the group of writers who constituted the Hachinoki no Kai. In keeping with the spirit of the Nō play *Hachinoki,* in which an old samurai sacrifices his most precious possession, three dwarf trees, to provide firewood on a snowy night for his guest, these writers originally began to meet at a time of shortages of food and drink, when the host had to sacrifice almost equally precious possessions to entertain the others. The group included Mishima Yukio, Ōoka Shōhei, Nakamura Mitsuo, and Fukuda Tsuneari, all of whom I would get to know much better in future years (unlike the people I met at parties in New York).

I had one, rather strange connection with the Hachinoki no Kai. My little book *Japanese Literature* contains a discussion of *renga,* or linked verse, and Yoshida, who had not previously heard of renga, suggested to the group that they keep a "record" of each gathering in the form of a renga sequence. Some years later, when I was helping to edit a "renga issue" of an American literary magazine, I wrote Yoshida to ask permission to publish some of the renga composed by the Hachinoki no Kai. He refused, saying that the participants were much too drunk by the time they got around to composing renga for their compositions to be intelligible, let alone literary. But if the manuscripts still exist, there surely would be *something* of interest in even the most frivolous quips of such distinguished men.

A few years after I attended the Hachinoki no Kai, Yoshida had a new house built. It was in an English style of architecture and much more elegantly furnished than the previous house, but the atmosphere, created by his personality (and that of his wife),

A meeting of the Hachinoki no Kai in February 1955, from left: Ōoka Shōhei, Mishima Yukio, Yoshida Kenichi, myself, Yoshikawa Itsuji, Jinzai Kiyoshi, and Fukuda Tsuneari.

remained exactly the same. Sometimes he would tell me he had paid a visit to Oiso, meaning that he had gone to the house of his father, Yoshida Shigeru. He would always return with some treasure from the former prime minister's wine cellar. On one occasion, when the cartoonist Shimizu Kon was a fellow guest, he opened a bottle of cognac whose faded label bore the date 1868, a century earlier. Of course it was delicious.

The Hachinoki no Kai broke up after quarrels had erupted among the different members of the group. Probably it was only to be expected that sooner or later there would be clashes among the various strikingly different personalities, but I was sorry to learn of the quarrels. I was sorry, too, that the quarterly magazine published by the group, *Koe,* ceased publication after ten issues. Yoshida had urged me to think of *Koe* as "my" magazine, and I had in fact published there two articles about Hanako, the Meiji period actress and model for Rodin. But above all I regretted the loss of the rare and special occasions for members of this group of highly distinguished writers to enjoy the company of equals.

Yoshida's years in England as a young man had left a permanent imprint on him, but this did not make him the less Japanese. He was like Nagai Kafū, the great chronicler of life in old Tokyo, in his preference for what he considered to be genuinely Japanese, as opposed to superficial manifestations of up-to-date tastes. However, he belonged to a younger generation than Kafū and for him the 1930s (a time Kafū detested) seem to have been the last "genuinely Japanese" period. Most of his friends, older than he, had flourished in the 1930s and shared his nostalgia for Tokyo when the city was still laced with rivers and canals. They also lived up to an ideal that he shared with Kafū, that of the bunjin of the past. The bunjin were gentleman scholars who enjoyed drinking and composing poetry together—not cries from the heart but witty poems that referred to a shared acquaintance with literature and the world.

The bunjin by definition were uninterested in money, and as soon as they obtained some, spent it with prodigality. I was once invited to the restaurant of the old Akasaka Prince Hotel with Yoshida, Kawakami Tetsutarō and Ishikawa Jun. Kawakami and Ishikawa were bunjin after Yoshida's heart, and probably that is why he ordered champagne and caviar. He was in a cheerful mood and, like a true bunjin, he did not spare money when he entertained friends. While we ate, an orchestra was playing. Yoshida called the leader to our table and asked him to play something, pressing a thousand-yen note into his hand. I forget what he requested, but (as I recall) it was nothing unusual. When that piece had been played, Yoshida again summoned the leader and, requesting another piece, pressed another thousand yen into the man's hand. After this was played, he again summoned the leader. This time he said, "Anything at all," and again pressed a thousand yen into the man's hand.

I was rather shocked by the extravagance. A thousand yen was worth a lot more thirty years ago than it is today, and I couldn't help recalling essays Yoshida had written about being a "beggar prince." (As the son of Yoshida Shigeru he was a kind of "prince.") But I redeemed myself on another occasion, when he took me to a teahouse on the Sumida River. Drinking in such a place was in keeping with bunjin traditions, but the smell of the river was oppressive. I did not mention the smell during the course of the evening and this (as he informed me) earned me Yoshida's respect.

I always enjoyed Yoshida Kenichi's company, and I admired him as a literary critic, but I was by no means equal to the task of associating with him as a bunjin. I had a greater capacity for liquor thirty or even fifteen years ago than I have now, but even so, the day after drinking with him and his friends was generally a blank.

The Thursday night meetings with Yoshida, Kawakami, and Ishikawa began with drinks at a bar called Sophia, followed by a meal at Hachimaki Okada. Yoshida normally ate almost nothing. He ate with his eyes—he enjoyed looking at food, particularly Japanese food that was artistically prepared and served on beautiful plates and bowls. He wrote books on food, and no doubt he sometimes ate, but a restaurant was for him a place to drink. When drunk he always looked extremely happy.

On one occasion, when I had received money for an article, I invited him to dinner. At his suggestion we went to a Hungarian restaurant where he ordered the most expensive dinner, including lobster and steak. He also ordered two bottles of Tokay. He did not touch either the lobster or the steak, but the Tokay soon disappeared.

On another occasion Shinoda Hajime, a massively built man, joined us at Hachimaki Okada. He, Yoshida, and I returned by taxi. Somewhere on the way Yoshida suddenly called out for the driver to stop: *"Tomare!"* and the taxi stopped. Yoshida got out, but Shinoda followed him, picked Yoshida up in his arms, and deposited him back inside the taxi. This happened several times in exactly the same manner.

Among the various friends of Yoshida Kenichi I met, I was initially most attracted to Kawakami Tetsutarō. I was much impressed by the range and depth of his interests, extending to many aspects of both Japanese and European civilization. I felt frustrated, however, that his remarks each time we met would tend to get blurred as liquor took effect on both of us. I have the impression that at our regular Thursday gatherings he drank even more than Yoshida or Ishikawa Jun. On one occasion, when the four of us were eating at a Western-style restaurant, I was busily talking to Yoshida and did not notice that Kawakami had left the table. I thought that he had probably gone to the toilet, but after some minutes I felt something bump against my feet. When I looked under the table, there was Kawakami, to my astonishment. In his drunken state he had evidently slipped off his chair. I had often heard the expression "to drink someone under the table," but had not realized that such things actually happened.

I must confess, on the other hand, that when I visited him at his ancestral home in Iwakuni, I was the one who did the lion's share of the drinking, and Kawakami had to send out for more saké. The next day I had a splitting headache, but Kawakami had promised to take me in his sailboat to Miyajima, and that is what he did. I was afraid that my hangover might cause seasickness, but the sea was calm. In fact, as we approached the great torii of the shrine, the wind died down completely and we were becalmed. Under other conditions I would have been delighted to have an uninterrupted conversation with someone as brilliant as Kawakami, but sitting there in a motionless boat under the glaring sun I could think of absolutely nothing to say.

The worst was yet to come. Kawakami urged me to see Hiroshima. I should have refused, considering my condition, but perhaps I was led by a feeling of "a desire to see the worst" into accepting. The most unfortunate thing arose from Kawakami's kindness. He couldn't go with me, so he arranged to have a geisha as my guide. I went with her to the museum that displays the effects of the atomic bomb—the watches stopped at the same fatal hour, the shadow of a man burned into stone, and all the other terrible evidence of a moment of unspeakable horror. And I had to walk from exhibit to exhibit in the company of a young woman in a brightly colored kimono who kept up a flow of cheerful chatter intended to entertain me or perhaps to absolve me, as an American, from my share of the guilt involved in the bomb.

A most pleasant visit had been soured by a meaningless experience which, more than thirty years later, still haunts me.

I was determined to have a serious conversation at least once with Kawakami, and if possible without any liquor. He graciously agreed to a meeting one afternoon at his house, and though we consumed some liquor (as a modern bunjin he probably would not have felt in the mood to talk about literature without some alcohol), our conversation was orderly and did not trail off into drunken joking. He made a tape recording of the conversation, and it later appeared in a newspaper. My part of the dialogue, as it was styled, was merely to ask questions, mainly about the course of development of modern Japanese literature. Kawakami's answers were to the point and well expressed. I left with the greatest admiration for his critical judgment.

I suppose that this was the high point of my acquaintance with Kawakami. For some months more we met as usual, in the company of Yoshida Kenichi and Ishikawa Jun, but one night a trivial incident changed our relationship. The four of us had gone to an elegant geisha establishment in Shimbashi and, as usual, had quite a lot to drink. That night for some reason I thought as I listened to Kawakami speak I could detect in him his samurai ancestors—not of the distant past but of the early Meiji period, when the leaders of the new government from Chōshū would meet and drink at just such places as the one where I found myself. I found this foreign to myself, there being nothing of the samurai in me. As the evening wore on, Kawakami suddenly cried in a loud voice, "*Kaerō*!" ("I'm leaving!") He then put his feet on the shoulders of the geisha sitting beside him and shouted, "*Kaerō*!" in an even louder voice.

I cannot explain this, but I felt a profound sense of alienness. Probably the geisha was accustomed to such behavior, and the others present showed no signs of dismay. My own reactions were no doubt intensified by the liquor I had consumed. But I felt it was impermissible to treat another human being that way. When I met Kawakami again, as a sensitive man he must have detected my changed feelings, even if he was unaware what had brought about the change.

In the years that followed I saw him infrequently. Nothing unpleasant ever happened between us, and I had occasion to regret that, because of an instinctive reaction over which I had no control, I had deprived myself of a learned and highly gifted friend. Fortunately, the last time I saw him my feelings were assuaged. It was at the wake of Yoshida Kenichi. Of course, this was a sorrowful occasion for both of us. At first I did not see Kawakami, but suddenly we stood face-to-face. He said, "It was good of you to come," and shook my hand. That was all, but I felt a warmth behind his words that melted the coldness of a whole decade. I am sorry I never saw him again.

Ishikawa Jun, the remaining member of the Thursday night drinking parties, was perhaps even more learned than Yoshida Kenichi or Kawakami Tetsutarō. He had at first devoted himself to French literature, but he later had read to such an extent in Edo literature that he once said he had his "study abroad" conducted in Edo. This probably referred to the years when (as described in his story "The Song of Mars") dismay over the war hysteria had caused him to take refuge in the saner world of the Japanese past. He longed for the days when bunjin met at a teahouse overlooking the Sumida River to compose poetry in classical Chinese. Old-fashioned terms from the Edo period appeared not only in his writings but in his speech. For example, knowing of my mother's illness, he asked politely about *go-kendō*. I confess that the word—a rather pedantic word for "mother"—meant nothing when I first heard it.

Ishikawa had a reputation for eccentricity, and sometimes (I was told) his normal, courtly behavior would give way to contempt when he decided he was talking to a fool. I was told that his front teeth had been knocked out by a reporter who resented something Ishikawa had said. My most memorable experience of his eccentricity took place at a Czech restaurant in Tokyo. Ishikawa suddenly gave forth several loud sneezes and, apparently not having a handkerchief, wiped his nose with the bill and crumpled it up.

I found his writings difficult to understand at times, but nevertheless absorbing, and translated his novella *Asters*, probably the first translation of one of his works into a European language. As a mark of his appreciation he gave me a volume from the famous Kōetsu editions of the Nō plays. That was why, when I published a book on the Nō theater some years later, I asked him to write an introduction, and he kindly wrote one.

I had one painful experience with Ishikawa. After the volumes of my history of Japanese literature devoted to the Edo period had appeared, Ishikawa was asked, as a great admirer of the literature of that period, to do a dialogue with me. He consented, and for about two hours, with a shorthand writer taking everything down, he informed me of every single error in my book. The one thing any author wants most when his book is published is praise, and although I appreciated the trouble Ishikawa had devoted to correcting my mistakes, I was miserable, knowing the dialogue would appear in print. Later, an editor, consoling me, said if Ishikawa had not respected me as a scholar he would never have agreed to take part in a dialogue. I hope this was true.

Yoshida Kenichi sometimes also invited younger friends to our Thursday evening sessions. I remember especially my first meeting with Shinoda Hajime. After having drinks at Sophia, we went as usual to Hachimaki Okada. When it came to ordering, I chose two or three items, but Shinoda ordered *everything* on the menu. He told me years later, when I asked about this, that he had assumed that the portions of each dish would be small, and he was correct. Even so, it took courage when dining with men who drank rather than ate, to display such a healthy appetite.

I confess now that when I first met Shinoda I supposed that, because he was a very heavy man, approximately twice as big as myself, he could not be a sensitive critic. I soon realized, however, that I had been foolishly prejudiced. I have never met anyone more devoted to books, who read as many works of literature in as many languages. At this point in his career he was still relatively unknown, but Yoshida must have detected his extraordinary ability.

I recall my first visit to his house. I had stupidly forgotten to bring his address or telephone number with me, and although I remembered the name of the nearest station, once I left the station I was at a loss where to go. I tried various shops—the grocer's, the rice merchant's, and so on—giving his name and indicating his great bulk, and before long I found someone to guide me. I doubt that it would have been so easy if he had been a more normal size!

At the time he, his wife, and two sons were living in a small apartment. We had dinner in a room in which we were surrounded on four sides by books that reached up to the ceiling. I wondered what would happen if there were an earthquake. Perhaps Shinoda considered that being buried under thousands of books would be an appropriate way for a scholar to meet his end. Later, when he and his family moved to a much bigger apartment, his wife tried for a time to keep one room free of books, but it did not take long for the books to start encroaching, relentless as water hyacinths on the Congo River.

Shinoda's books were not those of a bibliophile. I doubt that a first edition signed by the author was of greater value for him than a paperback. Books were to be read, a source of knowledge and pleasure, not an investment or a mania. He collected records with almost the same fervor. He told me once that he had intended at one time to become a scholar of music rather than literature. He certainly knew a great deal more than I about contemporary classical music, always a weak point with me, and his judgments on performers, though sometimes severe, were proofs of his sensitivity. How wrongly I had first judged him!

*****

I remember the 1960s now mainly in terms of the books I published during the decade. At the end of 1961, just before I left Tokyo for New York, I had the pleasure of receiving the first copies of my translation of plays by Chikamatsu and of my translation of three modern Japanese novellas. In 1963 the translation of Mishima's *After the Banquet* appeared, and in 1967 of his *Madame de Sade.* Two books of a quite different nature, studies of Nō and Bunraku, illustrated with magnificent photographs by Kaneko Keizō, appeared in 1965 and 1966. *Essays in Idleness,* probably the best of my translations, appeared in 1967, and at the end of the decade I published a translation of Abe Kōbō's *Friends.* There were naturally articles in magazines and learned journals, and lectures that eventually also got published. I had more or less lived up to the dream I first conceived in Cambridge of publishing a book every year. This happened in my forties, a period that the Japanese call *hataraki-zakari,* a term inadequately rendered in English as "the prime of life."

I traveled a great deal too. In those days a round-the-world plane ticket did not cost much more than a New York–Tokyo– New York round trip, and on several occasions I took advantage of this. The most memorable of my journeys was to Africa in the summer of 1963. I had mentioned casually to a friend of mine, an American anthropologist who had recently traveled in Africa, that I would like to go there someday. I probably said that with no greater hopes of realization than I might say today I would like to visit the moon, but, to my great surprise, the friend made all the necessary arrangements with a foundation for me to go to Africa, the only condition being that I give lectures wherever requested. I had no "business" in Africa, obviously nothing immediately related to my work, but the lure of the unknown was too strong to resist.

I flew from New York to Paris and from Paris to Abidjan in the Ivory Coast. I really had no idea what to expect, but the beauty of the city of Abidjan astonished me. The gleaming white, strikingly modern buildings, set against a dark blue sky, created a first impression of Africa that was totally unlike the gloomy Africa of childhood geography books. I traveled also in the hinterland, to the monastery at Bouaké, with two American women who had a car. On the way we stopped at a restaurant, where we ordered steaks, among other things. The two ladies asked for well-done steaks, and I (as usual) asked for rare. After I had eaten about half of my steak, one of the ladies informed me that it was not safe to eat undercooked meat in Africa because of the parasites. What was I to do at that point? With a show of bravado, I ate my steak to the end without any disastrous consequence.

Of the countries I visited, I was most impressed by Nigeria. I traveled in the interior with Ulli Beier, a German ethnologist who knew the region well. I had supposed that the African jungle consisted of impenetrable growths of trees and vines (as in the Tarzan movies), but the spaciousness of the vistas, like rooms in some gigantic palace, enchanted me. I gave a lecture at the university in Ibadan, followed by a bit of Kyōgen. I wouldn't be surprised if this was the first "performance" of Kyōgen in African history!

After my lecture at the University of Ibadan there was a reception in my honor at which I met several important Nigerian writers. One, the poet Christopher Okigbo, "rescued" me when he saw that I was at the mercy of an elderly woman who wished to tell me everything about Japan, another was the playwright Wole Soyinka. A few years later, when the country was torn by the terrible Biafran war, Okigbo was shot attempting to smuggle arms into Biafra. Soyinka was imprisoned for a year without any charges ever being brought against him. As a member of Amnesty International, which I had joined at Ivan Morris's invitation, I wrote a letter to him in prison. It was delivered eight months later, when he was released. He wrote me that he would probably have been executed if he had not received many such letters as mine. A few years ago he was awarded the Nobel Prize in Literature.

I remember many other people and places of my African journey, the beauty of the scenery, the magnificent physiques of the people walking along the roads, the display of indigo-dyed cloth in the markets. Tannarive in Madagascar (strictly speaking, not part of Africa) lingers in my mind because of its red buildings and the sad mementoes of the Malgache royal family, one of them addressed as "Dear Cousin" in a letter from Queen Victoria I saw. My lecture in Tannarive attracted the biggest crowd of my African tour. I later discovered the reason. In 1915 a Malgache journalist published an article comparing Madagascar and Japan, ending with the rhetorical question, "Whose fault is it that, although Japan and ourselves were at the same level of civilization fifty years ago, the Japanese have forged ahead while we have stayed as we were?" This naturally did not please the French colonial officials, who confiscated not only the magazine but everything else related to Japan, including pictures of Mount Fuji and of geishas standing on the Sanjō Bridge in Kyoto. Japan became established in the minds of the people of the island as the land of liberty, and I benefited from it!

My visit to Mauritius was equally memorable, if only for the newspaper that appeared on my birthday in June. The top headline on the front page proclaimed (in French) the visit of an American professor of Japanese. To the left, in articles whose headlines were in smaller type, were reported the funeral of the pope and the launching of two Russian cosmonauts. Relegated to the bottom of the page was the Profumo case, which at the time was agitating England. Never again will I enjoy such celebrity!

One other journey of the 1960s lingers in my mind, the month I spent in Mexico City, where I taught Japanese literature at the Colégio de México. I had not used for at least twenty years the Spanish I had learned in high school, and it was painful trying to express myself, but I fortunately could still understand other people. I met again my old friend the poet Octavio Paz, perhaps the most cosmopolitan person I know (though, at the same time, intensely Mexican). I would meet him again in India, when he served as the Mexican ambassador, and in Tokyo, when he gave a lecture at Sophia University. Wherever he goes he seems capable of extracting something precious and unique from the culture, and he writes with marvelous insight and command of language. He, too, was awarded a Nobel Prize in Literature. I have been singularly fortunate in my friends.

*****

It was in the 1960s, too, that I made my last friends in the Japanese literary world. I first met Ōe Kenzaburō about thirty years ago, but he has changed extremely little. For many years he remained the youngest writer of importance, and even now, when writers younger than Ōe have gained recognition and Ōe himself occupies a central position in the world of Japanese letters, he seems to belong with the younger writers rather than with his own generation. This is not merely a matter of appearance (though that, too, remains youthful) but of temperament. I can hardly imagine a time when Ōe will reminisce nostalgically about the years of his youth, or contrast them with an inferior present.

I first met Ōe when we went on a lecture tour arranged by Chūō Kōron Sha. Itō Sei and Hirabayashi Taiko were also members of the group. At the time (January 1964) I was suffering from diarrhea contracted in India, and I remember that Itō solicitously recommended a medicine that looked and tasted like charcoal, but helped to suppress the characteristic effects of this malady. I ate very little during the tour, a fact I remember especially because in later years I often ate and drank with Ōe. On this occasion I was in no state to eat or drink with anyone.

But this tour was memorable especially because it enabled me to become friends with Ōe-san. I had felt some tension before meeting him, supposing from the tone of his articles that he would be an outspoken and perhaps intemperate critic of my political opinions, which at this stage might properly have been described as "confused liberal." On the train from Osaka to Nagoya we sat opposite each other, Ōe-san holding a copy of *Esquire* in his hand, and I a Japanese literary magazine. This stern confrontation did not last long. Surely few people in the world have as winning a personality as Ōe-san. Far from denouncing my opinions, he spoke politely and with a sense of humor that exactly matched mine.

I remember one part of Ōe's lecture on that tour in particular.

He was probably inspired by the presence of Hirabayashi Taiko to recall her participation during her anarchist days in a magazine with the curious name of *GE.GIMGIGAM.PRRR.GIM-GEM.* Ōe pronounced the unpronounceable syllables of this name with evident pleasure, even with a touch of impishness, a quality not normally associated with lecture tours in Japan. He has never completely lost this quality, although he has, of course, been deeply involved in causes that are of the utmost seriousness. He told me, after he had spent one summer studying at Harvard, that Kissinger had referred to his "wicked smile."

We got along well from the first. This rather surprised me for a peculiar reason. I had seen at the old Bungei Shunjū building, after he won the Akutagawa Prize, the manuscript of the winning story, and I had taken an instant dislike to his handwriting. It was not that I was comparing his writing to that of a great calligrapher like Kawabata, but the handwriting seemed characteristic of someone antagonistic to the traditions of Japanese calligraphy. I was right: Ōe belonged to a different generation from the writers I had hitherto met, but that, as much as anything, gave him his particular appeal.

My recollections of Ōe Kenzaburō include many different scenes—drinking *hirezake* at a *fugu* restaurant in Tokyo (hirezake is saké in which toasted fins of the intoxicating fugu, or blowfish, have been placed, giving it a special flavor), crossing the Hudson on one of the last ferryboats, eating oxtail that he himself had prepared, or (more recently) attending a meeting where, after someone in the German literary world had referred to him as *unser* (our) *Kenzaburō Ōe,* he gave imitations of how a Frenchman or a German was likely to pronounce the name Ōe. All of these recollections confirm the general impression of a man whose basic seriousness does keep him from having a sense of humor.

Perhaps the greatest charm of Ōe-san is his youth. This is not merely a matter of age, for he is no less youthful now than when I first met him, and I imagine he will remain equally young for many years to come. Usually it makes me feel very old when I am with young people, but Ōe-san's enthusiasm is infectious, and after a while with him I no longer feel any difference in age. I do not agree with everything he advocates, but I almost always share the spirit behind his opinions. While I am with him I miraculously shed the indifference or even cynicism that has replaced my idealism of the past, and I feel receptive again to new possibilities.

I confess it took some effort before I became an admirer of Ōe-san's writings. I sensed the strength behind the early stories, but their style repelled me, no doubt because my tastes had been formed by such writers as Nagai Kafū or Tanizaki Junichirō. But in the end Ōe-san's style not only imposed its authority but convinced me of its necessity. After reading *A Personal Matter* I was so impressed I cabled a New York publisher urging him to undertake the translation. *The Silent Cry* struck me especially by the superb, almost musical construction.

Music, as it happens, forms one of the closest bonds between Ōe-san and me. One night in a *sushi-ya* Ōe-san, Abe-san, and I argued the question of whether or not Japanese can appreciate opera. Abe-san, always so international in his outlook, surprised me by insisting that it was impossible, but Oe-san, who seems much more conscious of what is peculiarly Japanese, insisted that it was certainly possible for Japanese to understand opera. I sided with Ōe-san, and the next day, as I uncomfortably made my way through a downpour without an umbrella, I decided on sudden impulse to send Ōe-san the recording of Verdi's *Don Carlo,* one of my favorite operas. Nothing gives me greater pleasure than spontaneously giving a present to a friend, and this pleasure is crowned if my choice is genuinely appreciated. When Ōe-san told me he had been memorizing the Italian text of the first act of *Don Carlo* I felt as if something important had occurred between us.

I enjoyed best being invited to his house and, after having imbibed a suitable amount of liquor, listening to records with him. I remember especially listening together to Maria Callas's *Lucia,* sometimes singing with her, both of us utterly drunk, not only with wine but with the incredible beauty and intelligence of her voice. (He later wrote an article on Callas which he dedicated to me.)

I can hardly imagine having a similar experience with Mishima Yukio, though I felt no less intimate with him. Perhaps it was because Mishima-san, even when a young man, lacked Ōe's special quality of youth.

The relations between Ōe and Mishima were complex. Of course they were political enemies, but Mishima unstintingly praised Ōe's writings. I think Ōe was the only younger writer he ever praised in this manner. Ōe for his part obviously considered Mishima the best Japanese writer. He particularly admired *Runaway Horses,* and for the jacket of *Spring Snow* wrote a beautiful tribute which, for reasons unknown to me, was not used. Ōe seemed always aware of Mishima, whether seriously or ironically. When, for example, he sent the first episode of *The Silent Cry* to his New York publisher, he carefully pasted a picture of Mishima on the text. And for a long time whenever we met his first question was likely to be, "Have you seen Mishima-san lately?" The two men, so different in almost every way, recognized each other's merits. I am sorry that they never became friends and discovered how much pleasure there was in each other's company.

*****

One more memorable acquaintance formed in the sixties must be mentioned—that of Abe Kōbō, who became my closest friend in the Japanese literary world after the death of Mishima and remained such until his death in 1993.

My first meeting with him was not auspicious. He had come to New York in the autumn of 1964 for a brief visit in connection with the publication of the English translation of *Woman in the Dunes.* He was accompanied by Teshigahara Hiroshi, the director of the film made from the novel, and by a young woman who was his interpreter. As a professor of Japanese, I was rather annoyed that anybody thought it was necessary to supply an interpreter, and I ignored the young woman. Not until years later did I learn that I had been ignoring Yoko Ono. This was not the most disappointing aspect of our first meeting. I was suffering from insomnia, the result of jet lag, and Abe, who has a degree in medicine, diagnosed me on the basis of my sleepiness as a drug addict.

In the spring of 1967 Ōe Kenzaburō, then a close friend of Abe, suggested that the three of us have a meal together. Abe refused, saying he was to attend a boxing match; but more likely, he had received such a dismal impression of me in New York he never wanted to see me again. Eventually his resistance broke down and we had a Chinese meal, along with a vast amount of *lau chiu.* From that day Abe and I became fast friends.

Abe was perhaps the most unusual man I have ever met. He possessed an astonishing range of knowledge in the sciences, linguistics, and, above all, literature. He seemed to have read everything that has ever been translated into Japanese. It would have been natural to suppose that a man of his gifts must be able to speak several foreign languages. I was present on several occasions when people insisted on talking English to him, refusing to admit the possibility that such an obviously intelligent man might not understand them. But Abe insisted (as a paradox, of course) that no Japanese can really master a foreign language, and he delightedly subscribed to theories that suggest it is physiologically exhausting for a Japanese to process foreign languages in an unfamiliar hemisphere of the brain.

In the West it is common to say of someone who possesses unusual talent in many fields that he is a "Renaissance man." Abe Kōbō more closely fitted that description than anyone else I have met. But he was not content with being proficient in many fields; he intended in whatever he did to stand in the forefront, not only in Japan but in the world. His experiments in the theater were perhaps the most striking example of this attitude. The plays performed by members of the Abe Kōbō Studio were the most memorable examples of modern theater I have seen in Japan, and when his company visited America, it enjoyed a triumphal success wherever it performed. Tickets were so hard to get for the last performance in New York that there were fistfights at the box office, and inside the theater people clambered over the lighting equipment to get a glimpse of the stage.

This triumph was the result of the infinite patience Abe had demonstrated day after day, from morning until night, guiding the members of the company. In his mind was an ideal of drama that went beyond words to the most basic forms of movement, heightened by an effective use of lighting and music. The actors were trained in calisthenics and modern dance, and drilled by Abe in voice production. The results were brilliantly successful, but the closer Abe and his troupe came to achieving his ideal of theater, the further they moved from his most precious talent, the mastery of words. Sometimes I regretted that he had abandoned the stage in favor of the novel, but surely it was the correct decision for someone with his rare novelistic skill.

This does not mean, however, that Abe concentrated solely on

With Abe Kōbō

the writing of novels. He won third prize in an international competition for the best new invention, his simple device for changing tires having impressed the judges more than machines costing vast sums of money. He was actively concerned with linguistic research, especially into the origins of the Japanese language. He was an expert photographer. He was devoted to the music of Bach and, among modern composers, Bartók. I could prolong this list, but it probably would make him seem less like an author than some composite being.

Abe's novels, no matter how far from reality they seem to

stray, are always based in a particular place in Japan. After completing *Woman in the Dunes* he is reputed to have said that the sand dunes of Sakata had now outlived their usefulness. That was an obvious example of how one place had inspired Abe's sense of fantasy, but unless one heard from Abe himself that a certain novel was written with Tsuruga or the outskirts of Odawara in mind, it would be difficult to guess it. Most novelists who take the trouble to travel to different parts of Japan to ensure accuracy in their portrayal of particular localities carefully incorporate in their descriptions exactly what they have observed, but Abe deliberately concealed the identity of the places he had in mind.

This was true not only of places but of personal experiences. Every writer must, in some sense anyway, depend on personal experiences as the basis of his writings, and in Japan the "I novel" has carried this practice to an extreme. But Abe seemed determined to keep his personal experiences from intruding into his works. Of course, it has often been argued that because he grew up in Manchuria he had a broadness of outlook not found in writers whose experiences have been confined to Japan, but it would be difficult to point to specific experiences of Abe that have been utilized in his novels or plays.

It is not because his life was absolutely free of dramatic incidents that Abe depended on invention rather than recollections. I can recall any number of personal experiences related by Abe that would make splendid stories. For example, he mentioned once in a lecture his extraordinary success in Manchuria with a soft drink he had invented. So much money rolled in that he had trouble finding hiding places for the banknotes, finally stuffing them into the shutter-boxes of his house. Or his return to Japan from Manchuria with many other refugees on a battered old American landing craft. Or the circumstances of the poverty of his early married life when he and his wife lived in a hut that he himself had fashioned out of loose timbers. Or his living in the house of a *yakuza* boss who wanted Abe to be his successor. Or his futile attempt to sell his first book, a collection of poetry, in Hokkaidō, where he had relatives. All of these (and many more incidents he has related) would have provided the typical "I novelist" with the materials for twenty novels, but (as far as I know) Abe never used them openly in his works, though these incidents sometimes appeared, heavily disguised.

Abe seemed like a most practical, down-to-earth man whose works are based on a fund of scientific information, but he possessed at the same time the mysterious qualities of the true artist. Though a writer of the most intense seriousness, he wrote with comic brilliance, both in his novels and in his plays. Above all, he was an absolutely honest writer. This makes his books difficult at times, and readers accustomed to a more conventionally beautiful style of Japanese sometimes complain that they miss something. But I cannot imagine him attempting to ingratiate himself with readers at the cost of his honesty.

Abe-san was an extraordinarily painstaking writer and seemed rather surprised that nobody ever praised his style. Surely this was because it is impossible to distinguish the style and the content. One can praise some writers without referring to the content of their books, but praising the content of Abe's works inevitably also involves praising the style.

If I did not know Abe-san I would suppose, on the basis of his writings, that he was a completely efficient man governed by the most rigorous logic and incapable of wasting time. This picture is not totally incorrect, but he was at the same time completely impractical and unworldly. He was the worst correspondent I know, even when purely business matters were concerned. I even sent him letters threatening to set the Mafia on his trail if he failed to reply, but obviously he preferred the risk of death to the trouble of writing a letter.

Some years ago he invited me to a carp dinner. He said the restaurant was somewhat out of the way, but promised we would eat early and return to his house that evening for drinks. The restaurant was seventy miles away and the road was terrible much of the distance. We did not return to his house until two in the morning, after almost twelve hours in the car. The carp dinner was excellent, but would anyone else in Japan have traveled that distance for one meal?

Though Abe-san spoke no foreign language, he was uniquely cosmopolitan. I think this quality must have come from his confidence in himself and his work. His was one of the rare houses in Tokyo where an international gathering was pleasurable. Usually if I am invited to a party in Tokyo and I see another foreigner, my heart sinks. I know I will have to talk to him as a fellow foreigner probably in English, though everyone else is speaking Japanese. And even if the other foreigner speaks Japanese, there is likely to be tension between us. But there was absolutely none of this in Abe-san's house, where everyone who appeared became in some way an aspect of Abe-san's personality. He need not have worried about learning any foreign language. Everyone who mattered to him surely spoke his language.

*****

In 1965 I was asked by the owner of Grove Press (the company which published my *Anthology of Japanese Literature*) if I would become a juror of the Formentor Prize. Two prizes had been established, one with the purpose of encouraging a new writer, the other (the international prize) in order to promote international recognition of a writer already well established in his own country. The seven juries were known by the nationality of the sponsoring publisher—English, French, German, etc.—but writers and critics were chosen as jurors irrespective of nationality. For example, the American jury that year included an Indian, and a Greek who had never even visited the United States. The international prize was second only to the Nobel Prize in monetary value and prestige, and since it was awarded by writers, rather than by an academy, it had special importance, at least in the eyes of the jurors.

From the moment I accepted the invitation I decided I would win the prize for Mishima Yukio. The meeting was held in the palace at Salzburg in Austria, and the jurors were treated lavishly by the publishers. This was the first meeting of its kind I had attended, and I was rather intimidated by the domineering personalities of some jurors. I was not the only one. The previous year an American critic had been so awestruck by the European celebrities assembled that when he stood up to speak he was totally unable to utter one word. At the session at Salzburg, even the redoubtable Mary McCarthy, a tigress among critics, was so overpowered that halfway through her speech she stopped and said like a little girl, "I can't go on!" I can still see the faintly mocking faces of some jurors as they listened to remarks made by persons outside their own circles.

From the first it was clear that Nathalie Sarraute was likely to win the international prize for her novel *Les Fruits d'or.* Indeed, the only other candidate seriously mentioned was Witold Gombrowicz, a Polish writer living in exile in France.

During the first session the cases for and against the different candidates were presented. As expected, many jurors spoke in favor of Sarraute's novel. Mary McCarthy (before she broke down) declared with her usual oracular certainty that some novels achieve the status of classics but others are classics from their birth; the latter was true of *Les Fruits d'or*. There were also jurors who, alluding perhaps to Sarraute's Russian origins, compared her novel to Dostoevsky. I requested permission to speak. When some jurors saw that an American was to speak they naturally supposed it would be in English and those who made it a point not to understand English stood up and started to leave. I was sure these were the jurors most committed to Sarraute, so I decided on the spot to speak in French.

At one time I could speak French almost as easily as English, but after a long period when I used French only rarely and spoke Japanese as my second language, my French had become quite unpredictable—sometimes fluent but sometimes halting. This time, miraculously, I spoke French better than ever before in my life. The jurors who had started to leave sat down and listened. I launched into a devastating attack on Sarraute's novel, directing all my sarcasm at its pretentiousness and essential triviality. When I finished I could tell I had made an impression on even these fearsome jurors. I felt exactly as if I had successfully performed as Tarōkaja.

Having attacked Sarraute somewhat intemperately, I had now to convince the jurors that Mishima was superior. There was opposition expressed to him because he was "insufficiently Japanese," a charge that no doubt would have infuriated Mishima-san. But these critics, though terrifyingly self-confident with respect to European literature, were unsure of themselves when it came to Japanese literature, and it proved unexpectedly easy to sway them. After I had spoken on Mishima's behalf I heard his name being pronounced in the corridors by jurors of different countries. Then, to my great surprise, a member of the French delegation, Roger Caillois (later of the Académie Française), told me he thought he could persuade the French to vote for Mishima rather than Sarraute. I also learned that political antagonism between some pro-Moscow and pro-Peking jurors might result in their voting for an author unconnected with either faction.

On the final day Caillois approached and shook my hand, saying, "We've done it!" He was sure there would be a three-way split of the juries and Mishima would win. I wanted to telephone Mishima-san at once, but prudently waited for the final vote. Unfortunately, the Spanish delegation, which had supported Gombrowicz all along, suddenly shifted to Sarraute, and Mishima lost. I realized I was still an amateur at literary politics.

Twice afterward I attended Formentor meetings and on both occasions Mishima almost won the prize, only to be defeated for some nonliterary reason. After the third failure a Swedish publisher said to console me, "Mishima will win a more important prize very soon."

The Formentor Prize was discontinued after 1967 as the result of dissension among the participating publishers. It is now almost forgotten and my own participation had almost no repercussions. But perhaps I at least called the attention of some European critics to the fact that modern literature was being created outside Europe and America. This obvious truth was made even more apparent the following year when the prize the Swedish publisher had mentioned was awarded to Kawabata Yasunari.

*****

My attempts to win the Formentor Prize for Mishima were not dictated solely by friendship for him, or even by the desire to have *some* Japanese win the prize; I honestly believed that he best deserved this recognition. I was happy to discover that I had allies not only in the American jury but in the French and other juries, reassuring me that my expressed admiration for Mishima's work was not simply the product of enthusiasm for everything Japanese. Of course, I could not foresee that Mishima's works would in the not too distant future attain the status of world classics, translated into many languages and treated in learned dissertations.

No doubt it was a disappointment to Mishima to have the prize elude him on three occasions, particularly the third time, in 1966, when the juries that awarded the prize met in Tunis. I had almost succeeded in my efforts to win the prize for Mishima, but at the last moment I failed. Mishima sent me a telegram to my hotel in Tunis: "I have learned of your wonderful speech, and I feel only gratitude. The question is not the result, but that you should have supported me with such friendship, and I am happy and satisfied."

Shortly after my return to New York from Tunis the introduction I had written for a collection of works by Mishima was published in Tokyo, and this became the occasion for another "clash" between us. Once again, the fault was mine. I had agreed to write this introduction because Mishima (who always professed to have a poor opinion of the works of Dazai Osamu) had generously praised the introduction I had written for a Dazai collection. He wrote, "I consider that this introduction is absolutely ideal. Japanese reviewers for the most part ignore the details when writing an introduction, and twist the work to yield a message of some kind. For this reason authors always feel bitterness in their hearts."

I suppose that this praise must have given me the courage to be unconventional in my choice of works by Mishima to be included in the volume. I also expressed frank criticism of some works I had not chosen. Mishima was clearly annoyed. He wrote, "What is known as a *kaisetsu* [introduction] in Japan is an act of *hommage* in which the criticism is wrapped. I have never con-

sented to write an introduction to the works of an author whom
I disliked."

The letter, six pages long, described in particular his dissatisfaction with my criticism of his short stories, which I had said
were overly ingenious and unconvincing. (Some years later
Kaikō Ken remarked to me that the only part of Mishima's
oeuvre he really envied was the short stories—evidence that my
feelings were not shared by a man who was himself a writer of
splendid short stories.)

Fortunately, Mishima's disappointment in what I had written
did not lead to a rupture in our relations. But something else in
the letter suggested he was passing through a difficult period
when criticism was likely to arouse irritation. He had been attending the Tokyo Olympics as a correspondent for three different newspapers. He wrote, "Needless to say, this sort of thing
has absolutely no literary significance. But the Olympics have
brought a marvelous discovery that has healed my wounds. Every time I go to the stadium, I have wished that there were something equally clear in the world of literature. For example, even
though I think of myself as being the champion, and of writer
A as being in second place, and writer B only in third place, the
world does not necessarily agree with me. I can't help feeling
irritated when people suppose I am in third place when I have
swum faster than anyone else."

I felt my share of guilt at having aroused such thoughts. Not
only had I failed to win the Formentor Prize for him, but I had
written an introduction that had brought him pain.

Fortunately, he was not downcast for long. The late sixties, in
fact, were years of remarkable creative activity. I recall especially
our trip together to the Ōmiwa Shrine in Sakurai, Nara prefec-

ture, in the summer of 1967, when he was doing research on the background of *Runaway Horses,* the second volume in his final tetralogy.

Mishima always felt it was necessary, as a professional writer, to see with his own eyes any place he described in his books. For example, before he started to write about Tametomo, the superhuman warrior of twelfth-century chronicles, he made a trip to Okinawa to observe the scene of Tametomo's last struggles, even though he was surely aware of the dubious nature of the legend that Tametomo had journeyed to that distant island and founded a dynasty there. Again, I recall that when I suggested, in view of Mishima's absorbing interest in the young officers of the 1930s who had staged coups against the government, that he write a full-length novel about them, Mishima said he couldn't without seeing Manchuria (then closed to foreign visitors), because of its importance as a seedbed of the young officers' revolt. When he wrote about Japan or other places he had visited, every detail was meticulously noted.

From the moment that our taxi arrived at the foot of the stone staircase leading up to the great torii of the Ōmiwa Shrine, Mishima had his notebook ready and busily took notes or made sketches of everything he saw. This was not his first visit to the shrine, but he wanted to be absolutely sure that whatever he described in his novel would be factually correct. We spent altogether three days at the Ōmiwa Shrine, walking over the grounds, even standing under a waterfall on the other side of the mountain that is worshipped as the sacred "body" of the shrine. Again and again Mishima would ask if a certain shrine building was there in 1932, the year of his novel; but knowing how the shrine looked at that time was not enough for him: he tried to put himself into the frame of mind of the young officers he would describe in his book. I noticed, for example, that the priests of the shrine walked briskly by the many little holy sights within the precincts, hardly more than nodding, but Mishima stopped before each one and bowed in the stiff manner appropriate to a young officer of the thirties.

I have often told friends about one memorable anecdote of our visit to the shrine, but they seldom believe me. Mishima asked questions about everything in sight, including each and every tree. When he asked an elderly gardener to identify a pine, the man could not believe any Japanese would be unfamiliar with that tree. He seems to have decided in the end that Mishima was asking about the particular variety of pine, and he answered, "Female pine." Mishima thought a moment, then asked, "Are they all female pines?" The gardener said yes, and Mishima, pursuing the matter, asked, "But if there are only female pines, how do little pines get born?" ("Female pine" is a familiar name for the Japanese red pine, as opposed to "male pine" for the black pine.)

That night, as we lay in adjacent rooms at the shrine, there was a sound from the distance. "What's that?" Mishima called to me. "Frogs," I said. A little while later a dog barked, and I informed Mishima that it was a dog. "That much I know!" he said with a laugh. Considering his marvelous ability to capture nature in his writings, Mishima showed a startling ignorance of even the most common plants and animals. He was a city person through and through.

*****

The 1970s began (at least in my memory) with an event that shocked and horrified me, the sensational death of Mishima Yukio. Just before midnight on November 24, 1970, New York time, I had a telephone call from a Japanese newspaper correspondent stationed in Washington. He briefly stated what had just happened in Japan—Mishima's speech at the Self-Defense Headquarters followed by his *seppuku*. He asked my impressions (*kansō*). I am often asked my impressions of events in Japan, and I generally respond assuredly enough, but this time I remained silent. The reporter, not realizing that Mishima was a close friend, thought something had gone wrong with the telephone connection, and even in my daze I was aware of his repeated *moshi moshi*. I finally managed to say something, though I did not really believe what I had been told. I telephoned Nagai Michio, who happened to be in New York, and he verified the news by calling Tokyo. That whole night, until seven the next morning, the telephone kept ringing, as one after another of the Japanese newspapers and wire services called to ask my impressions. In the end I found myself giving these impressions quite adroitly, rather as if I were delivering lines from a play. My very glibness seemed to me a betrayal of my dead friend.

The reporters all wanted to know whether or not I had suspected Mishima would kill himself in so sensational a way. No, I had not, but on recollection I realized that there had been many clues that I ignored or passed over without thinking of possible implications.

After my failure to obtain the Formentor Prize for Mishima, I was consoled by a Swedish publisher who assured me that he would receive an even better literary prize in the near future. This could only be the Nobel Prize. I was excited by this prospect, but I knew how unreliable such predictions were and did not mention this possibility to Mishima. If he could receive the Nobel Prize it would be like a gold medal in the Olympics, incontrovertible evidence that he was the best.

The announcement in 1968 that Kawabata Yasunari had won the prize dashed these hopes. I was happy that Kawabata-sensei had received a prize that he richly deserved, but I could imagine how disappointed Mishima would be. He, too, surely rejoiced that Kawabata, whom he revered as a mentor, had been chosen, but in view of the tendency of the Nobel Prize committee to make awards geographically, it would probably be at least twenty years before he or any other Japanese was honored.

Mishima's letters became much less frequent. One, dated February 27, 1970, said, "If you could come to Japan now, you would surely see a person who is not all his usual cheerful self. The excitement after the anti-treaty demonstrations in 1960 has died down, and there is no feeling of crisis at all. And that is why I feel so listless—my vitamins have been cut off."

Mishima frequently complained in his letters that nothing ever happened in Japan. Earlier in 1970 he wrote that as a juror for the Akutagawa Prize "as usual it was a series of yawns. There was not the slightest surprise." In April he wrote, "Of late novels have been so boring that I read nothing but comic strips." Even his pleasure in his work, clear from his brief mentions of the progress of *Spring Snow* and *Runaway Horses,* seems to have disappeared. "Until last year I had hoped for a little Götterdämmerung of my own, but I have now lost that hope. Everybody has chosen to go on living happily. There is nothing I can do about this, so from the end of last year until February this year I have concentrated like a madman on my work, and I have completed *The Temple of Dawn* (the third part of *The Sea of Fertility*). . . . I went again for a month beginning on the first of March to the Self-Defense Force on Fuji, and left the transitory world behind me. But the transitory world is gradually becoming noticeable even within the Self-Defense Force. Now where am I to escape to?"

These comments are followed by a nightmarish experience: "Recently, a high school student who was not known to me, stood for three hours in front of my gate. I met him in the hall, with the promise that I would give him five minutes, no more. The boy's eyes were clear. I said, 'I have no time, but you can ask me one question, whatever you like.'

"He did not say anything for a while, but looking me directly in the eyes asked, 'When are you going to kill yourself?' I was stunned to be asked this."

In June, on the very night when the Security Treaty with America was renewed, our taxi had passed by the Diet building. A cordon of police stood on guard, but nothing suggested a repetition of the demonstrations against the treaty that had taken place ten years earlier. Mishima said he was disappointed. I took this as a joke, remembering how alarmed he had been by the 1960 uprising, but it later occurred to me that when he founded his Tate no Kai (Shield Society) he may have expected to die that very night along with his tiny "army," defending the imperial palace from a hostile mob. It had freely been predicted that demonstrations on an even greater scale than in 1960 would occur, but the sight of the bored policemen standing around the Diet building made it clear to Mishima that he would have to invent a reason to die.

In August Mishima invited me to Shimoda, where he always spent the month with his family. He took me to a sushi restaurant the first night. Instead of ordering some of each of the different kinds of fish available, he ate nothing except *chū toro* (the most expensive cut of tuna), as if reluctant to waste his time on lesser varieties of sushi. The next night he invited me and a British journalist to a restaurant where they served lobster (out of season). He ordered five dinners for the three of us, and when they appeared, he ordered four more, resolved, it seemed, that we would eat our fill. I should have recognized in this curious extravagance symptoms of special tension, but I did not.

In the afternoon, while I swam in the hotel pool, Mishima sat on a beach chair displaying his muscles. Sitting by the pool, we talked about the approaching completion of his tetralogy, *The Sea of Fertility*. He said he had put into these books all that he had learned as a writer, and that when he finished the only thing left to do was to die. He laughed and I laughed. What could be more absurd?

*****

Looking back to those few days I spent with Mishima and his family in Shimoda, I wonder how I could have been so obtuse as not to realize something was amiss. Or perhaps I did, only to dismiss the possibility. During our conversation by the hotel pool, I know I sensed his tension. From our earliest acquaintance Mishima had made it clear that he didn't like "sticky" relationships, and I had never asked him about personal matters. But I distinctly recall saying to him by the pool, "I know you don't like to talk about yourself, but if there is something worrying you, why not tell me?" He averted his glance and did not reply. I now know that he had already made up his mind to die on the 25th of November, the same day that he delivered to the publishers the completed manuscript of his masterpiece.

The day before Mishima killed himself, his editor asked as a special favor that he deliver the final episode of the book a day earlier because of end-of-the-year difficulties with the printers. Mishima refused, saying that the manuscript was not ready. But three months earlier, in Shimoda, he had placed in my hands the final chapter of the book. He told me he had written it in one spurt. I could have read it if I had wished, but I thought I would not understand it, not having read the sections of the book preceding this chapter. A month later, in New York, I was writing an essay about Mishima, and I needed to know his reason for giving the title *The Sea of Fertility* to his tetralogy. His answer to my letter was unusually slow for so prompt a correspondent. His words sent a chill through me. He wrote that, despite the name of this sea of the moon, the "sea" is actually arid. This, I recognized, was his judgment on life.

When I left Haneda in September 1970 for New York, Mishima went to see me off. The practice of seeing off friends at the airport was at one time so much a part of Japanese life that I rather expected to see friends—even extremely busy people—when I left for New York, but I certainly did not expect to see Mishima. I knew that he worked from midnight until six in the morning, and this plane left about ten, leaving him virtually no time to sleep. He was unshaven and his eyes were bloodshot. He said nothing unusual, at least as far as I remember, but he knew this was the last time we would meet.

After my plane had taken off, Mishima joined several of my friends in having coffee in the airport restaurant. He startled them by saying suddenly that he did not wish to die a "stupid death." No doubt the friends quickly changed the subject. I obviously did not hear Mishima's comment, but I knew of his special interest in seppuku, the ritual disembowelment. I had heard from someone that he had a collection of pictures showing men performing this grisly act, and I also remember that he told me once he had been practicing *kaishaku,* the severing of the head of a man who has committed seppuku in order to spare him the agony of a slow death. When he told me, I couldn't take him seriously, but (in the manner in which people ask, "What school?" when one says one is studying Nō or Kyōgen or every other Japanese art) I asked facetiously, "What school?" He answered, without a trace of a smile, "Ogasawara school."

I had just one more letter, written just before he killed himself. It opened, "I am about to become Mishima Yukio {I had long ago used facetious characters pronounced the same as the real ones for his name, but meaning "a ghost who is not yet dead"]. Your reading of my name was academically accurate. I am sure that you understand the actions I am about to perform, so I will not say anything about them. I have long thought that I wanted to die not as an author but as a military man."

Early in our correspondence he had used the characters *ki-in* (devils' temple) for my name and "in revenge" I had given his name the characters he used in this last letter. The irony and the pain of my gesture still haunts me.

I had certainly been provided with ample clues that Mishima planned to commit seppuku, but I was commonsensical rather than sensitive, and guessed nothing. Mishima did not die a "stupid death." With his suicide he became, at least outside Japan, the most famous Japanese who ever lived.

CHAPTER SEVEN

*****

ON FAMILIAR
TERMS

I realize that my account has not touched on what, after all, was my main activity during those years, teaching at Columbia. By now my teaching had settled into a routine of three courses—a year-long survey of Japanese literature from the beginning to modern times, an introductory course on reading classical Japanese texts, and an advanced class that was devoted in alternation to the Nō plays, the poetry of Bashō, and the plays of Chikamatsu. The survey course attracted thirty or forty students each year, and since I did all the talking, I have forgotten the faces of most of the students who attended, but I think I remember everyone who read with me texts of Japanese literature. I taught only works for which I had the profoundest admiration, and my greatest pleasure was to feel that I had communicated my enthusiasm to the students. I had some extraordinary students during that decade, many of whom are now professors of Japanese. The book *Twenty Plays of the Nō Theatre,* which I published in 1970, contains translations made by some of them, a testimony to their level of accomplishment.

Probably it was because of the closeness I felt with the students that I was so shocked and pained by the student strike at Columbia in 1968. The strike was part of a worldwide movement of student dissatisfaction with the existing order, and was manifested in Japan and in various European countries as well as in America. I certainly did not feel committed to every existing institution; in fact, I sympathized with the students' idealistic grievances. But it was painful, all the same, when I saw the students directing attacks on those who felt they were closest to them, their teachers. I did not personally suffer in any way. When the strike finally ended, my only loss was the pages of manuscript that might have been written if I had not felt obliged to attend interminable faculty meetings at which the proper response to the students' demands was debated. And it came as a terrible shock to feel that students, with whom I had enjoyed warm relations, appeared to be hostile, not to me but to the kind of education to which I had dedicated my life.

Now that almost thirty years have passed, my relations with these same students are closer than before, and I realize that my fears of a polarization between students and faculty were exaggerated. Still, my memories of those days—in Japan as well as in America—are painful, and I cannot think of anything good that emerged as the result of the confrontation. The memory of the strike that lingers most vividly is of the faculty meeting at which the aged Professor Paul Kristeller, one of the great Renaissance scholars of the century, recalled with a trembling voice his experiences in Germany at the time when the Nazis seized power; he felt that we were facing a similar threat to human decency and the sanctity of learning. I was extremely moved by his words, but he, too, was mistaken: nothing terrible took place. Our ivory towers were knocked from under our feet, but it did not take very long to build them again.

The experience had the immediate result, however, of making me consider for the first time leaving the academic world. The justification I gave myself for abandoning my career as a teacher was that I found it increasingly difficult to write my history of Japanese literature while teaching full time. This was not self-deceit: it took days and sometimes even weeks to read enough of a given author for me to describe his works adequately. When I broached the matter with my colleague Ted de Bary, he urged me to consider teaching one semester each year. This would mean spending four months in New York, but I could pass the rest of my time in Japan if I so chose. I agreed, and the plan was eventually approved by the university.

The result of this compromise, though I did not foresee it, was an extremely agreeable life spent in two quite different environments. During my four months in New York I continued to do research, but I tried to give maximum attention to my students. I seldom gave lectures away from New York or engaged in the kind of popularization of Japanese culture that I had done earlier. The rest of the year was spent in Japan, living at first in the houses of friends who were away, but later in a place of my own in Tokyo. In Japan I of course continued my studies, but I also wrote for magazines, gave lectures widely, associated with members of the literary world, and even attracted some public notice. I felt rather as if I were leading two lives, and that two lives were better than one.

*****

The 1960s were especially important to my career as a scholar because this was when I first conceived the idea of writing a history of Japanese literature, the project that would occupy me for over twenty-five years. The only existing history in English had been published in 1899 by W. G. Aston. I had used this book as a student, often with irritation because of its old-fashioned judgments. Later, while I was in Cambridge, I read Aston's notebooks, on deposit in the university library, and I realized for the first time his immense achievement in learning Japanese well enough to write his history, at a time when there were no proper dictionaries or grammars, and when most of the texts in the books Aston had purchased were transcribed not in the clear print of a modern newpaper but in sōsho, the artistic, difficult to decipher "grass writing."

I felt new respect for Aston, but that still did not alter the need for a new history. For one thing—obviously—Aston's history had nothing to say about Japanese literature of the twentieth century, the second great period (after the Heian). It was time, in any case, to correct Aston's views on such subjects as the Nō dramas, about which he had written, "The Nō are not classical poems. They are too deficient in lucidity, method, coherence, and good taste to deserve this description. . . . As dramas the Nō have little value. There is no action to speak of, and dramatic propriety and effect are hardly thought of." Nor did I wish to leave unchallenged his comments on the great writer Ihara Saikaku: "He was a man of no learning. Bakin says that he had not a single Chinese character in his belly, and his books, most of which have very little story, are mainly descriptions of the manners and the customs of the great lupanars which then, as now, formed a prominent feature of the principal cities of Japan. The very titles of some of them are too gross for quotation." Aston's conclusion that the literature of the future—that is, of the twentieth century—would be markedly colored by Christian belief also needed modification.

I thought when, in 1964, I decided to write a history of Japanese literature that I would do more than correct Aston's rather narrow conception of literature. I would describe, as cogently as possible, why Japanese literature moved me so greatly. The best way, I thought, would be to set down on paper the kinds of information and opinions that I regularly transmitted in my lectures to students at Columbia. I supposed it would take perhaps two years to write the history, since most of what I wanted to say was already in my head.

I wrote quickly and soon had a manuscript of over 250 pages, covering the masterpieces of Japanese literature up through the thirteenth century. It was about this time that I took a trip around the world and visited the Soviet Union for the first time. I met the professor of Japanese at the University of Leningrad and in the course of our conversation (our mutual language was Japanese) mentioned that I was writing a history of Japanese literature. I said, with what I now realize must have seemed to be a supercilious tone, that my history would not be concerned with such dreary matters as dates but would be entirely personal. Dates, I said, could be found in other books. "What other books?" she asked, and I suddenly realized, with a sinking feeling, that there were no "other books," not in English at any rate. Like it or not, I would have to include not only dates but accounts of the careers of authors of no great importance—in short, I would have to write a real history, as opposed to the impressionistic guide to the masterpieces of Japanese literature I had first planned. The result of this decision was that, instead of taking two years to write the history, it took me twenty-seven.

I was faced with another decision at this point: should I start all over again from the beginning or take up where the earlier manuscript had left off, only in a more scholarly manner? It would have been better, I see now, to have gone back to the beginning, but it was psychologically difficult to take such a step, thereby admitting that I had as yet achieved no progress on my book. So I made up my mind to start writing in my new manner with the literature of the Tokugawa period (1600–1867), a decision that eventually hampered publication of the whole.

When, in the early seventies, I took the manuscript of the first volume I had completed to the prospective publisher, he noticed that it did not cover the early periods of Japanese literature. "Where's the first volume?" he not unreasonably asked. I explained that I would get around to it when I had finished the third and fourth volumes. He rejoined, "But how can we publish Volume Two of a history without Volume One?" This is where the matter stood for about three years until the publisher's successor had the brilliant idea of not calling the book Volume Two. That is how I was able to publish *World Within Walls: Japanese Literature of the Pre-Modern Era (1600–1867)* in 1976.

The response to the book, with a few heartwarming exceptions, was lukewarm or worse. Hardly a reviewer even made the conventional observation that it was good to have the first book in English on the subject. Instead, my history was generally attacked from the standpoint of the specialty of the reviewer. Although the literature of the Tokugawa period—especially the haiku poetry of Bashō and the dramas of Chikamatsu—was the part of Japanese literature in which I felt most confidence, it was perhaps inevitable also that I was not equally acquainted with all works of the period, and inevitable that a reviewer with special knowledge of one particular should have chosen to display this knowledge. Undoubtedly, too, it is easier to criticize than to praise: once one has said that a chapter is well written or that it reveals unusually wide reading, there may not be much else to say; but if one's aim is to criticize, there are likely be a fair number of points that can be treated with withering sarcasm. In any case, it takes a very brave or a very humble reviewer to admit that he has learned something.

There was never much danger that unfavorable reviews would induce me to give up my plan of writing a history of the entire literature, but the reviews may have been one reason why the publishers of the British edition decided not to bring out the rest of my history. This was a disappointment, but the much warmer response to the two volumes of *Dawn to the West,* the history of Japanese literature in the modern period, confirmed the validity of my resolution not to be discouraged by reviews. By the same token, I should not be encouraged by reviews either, but that would run counter to the basic human need for praise!

I confess that I sometimes have doubts about the history and, indeed, all of my writings. When I read contemporary criticism, much of it phrased in language that I do not understand, I fear that I may have fallen hopelessly behind the times. One reviewer of *Dawn to the West* listed all the contemporary critics I should have read before venturing to write my history. I had, in fact, looked at some of their writings, but found nothing I wanted to use in my history. If one recognizes that a history of literature is of value, something not every critic would do, it is obvious that the kind of criticism successfully applied to a single author or perhaps a single work may be inappropiate when one is attempting to provide what should be at once a reference book and a key to understanding the literary genius of a people.

But I should hate to give the impression that unfriendly reviews have soured me. No one knows better than I how fantastically lucky I was to write at a time when interest in Japan had enormously increased, and to have had far many more readers than I could otherwise have expected. The history was not the only book I was writing during the seventies and eighties, but it was my chief occupation and constant companion. When, in 1991, I handed over to the publishers the manuscript of *Seeds in the Heart,* the first (and final) volume of the history, I felt so at a loss to be without this companion that I fell into a state of depression that lasted nearly a month.

*****

In the spring of 1992 my retirement at Columbia was celebrated at a gathering that brought together many of my old students, most of them now professors in America or abroad. On the first day papers in the different fields of their specialization were presented. I confess that I had long since lost interest in hearing lectures by other people, unless they were genuinely funny, and I did not look forward to six or seven hours of papers on disparate subjects, but I have rarely been so moved as I was that day. It was not only because of the kind words about me with which many of them prefixed their talks, but because I was experiencing, in a way that was new to me, the joy of having been a teacher. These young (or not so young) scholars had gone beyond me in their fields, but I could not help but feel that I had somehow transmitted to them the love of my subject, Japanese literature.

There was also a testimonial dinner. What sounds less enticing than "testimonial dinner"? Yet this, too, was unforgettable, and I, who have wept very seldom in my whole life, was close to tears as I responded to the eloquence of old friends. Ted de Bary, my oldest and most loyal friend, of course spoke. Nagai Michio made the long trip from Japan just to be present on this occasion, as did Shiba Ryōtarō, an extraordinarily prolific and popular writer who had sacrificed precious time to be present. Shirley Hazzard, whom I had first come to know as a friend when both of us were mourning Ivan Morris, spoke beautifully. It was Mark Van Doren who first revealed to me that praising another is the most specifically human of actions. In a real sense it did not matter who was being praised—there was a warmth to this gathering that was surely felt by everyone present.

Three months later there was a similar gathering in Tokyo, though the occasion was different. In 1982 I had taken part in a symposium sponsored by the *Asahi Shimbun,* the most influential Japanese newspaper. Afterward, the participants and various people from the newspaper had gathered at a Japanese-style restaurant. Shiba Ryōtarō, whom I had first met in 1972, when we did a "dialogue" (*taidan*) together, and who had always been unusually kind and helpful, came up to my table from the opposite end of the room. Addressing the managing editor of the *Asahi,* who was seated at the same table, he said, "The *Asahi*'s no good." His voice suggested he had consumed a considerable quantity of saké. The managing editor looked at Shiba in surprise—this was evidently not a comment he was accustomed to hear. Shiba continued, "In the Meiji period the *Asahi* was also no good, but they hired Natsume Sōseki, and from then on it became a good newspaper. The only way to restore the *Asahi* now is to hire Donald Keene."

We all laughed. Natsume Sōseki, of course, was the most famous writer of modern Japan. The novels he serialized in the *Asahi* certainly improved its prestige, especially among intellectuals, but there was not much likelihood that hiring me would have any similar effect. A couple of weeks later, however, Nagai Michio, who had been an editor of the *Asahi* before becoming minister of education, invited me to dinner, during which he formally proposed that I join the *Asahi* as a guest editor. I was astonished, but before the evening was over I had agreed to the proposal, and not long afterward I was appointed.

I imagine that Shiba's reason for stating so forcefully that I was indispensable to the future welfare of the *Asahi,* though no one else would have thought so, was his belief that something had to be done to make the newspaper more international. As far as I knew, there was not a single foreign employee of the *Asahi,* at least in Japan. Although the newspaper prided itself on its international outlook, every single employee had a Japanese name and had received a Japanese education. He hoped that my presence in this sanctum of Japanese intellectual life would in some way change the outlook of the staff. He suggested that even if I did no more than eat in the employees' cafeteria, my face—if nothing else—would make the others realize that the newspaper was more than a Japanese club. As a matter of fact, I confess that I felt some tension when I first began to visit the newspaper offices, not only because I was the only non-Japanese but because I felt as if I were merely posing as a newspaperman.

Once I was officially a member of the organization, there was a discussion of what, exactly, I was supposed to do. I was told that I was welcome to attend the regular meetings of the editorial staff, but when I did, there was almost nothing I could contribute to the discussions, being ignorant of the newspaper business and reluctant to learn it at this stage of my life. It was finally decided that I would write serials of general interest. The first serial consisted of the twenty questions that I was most commonly asked by Japanese, together with my generally humorous responses. This serial went well and eventually was published as a book.

The next serial was considerably more ambitious. It was decided that I would write about my specialty, Japanese literature. But what aspect of Japanese literature would be of interest to the general public? At a meeting where this was discussed I heard a voice say, "How about diaries?" I have never discovered whose voice I heard, but hearing it was enough to decide me. For close to a year thereafter, five days a week, I wrote a column on Japanese diaries, beginning with the ninth century and continuing on to the nineteenth.

The pace was hectic for a scholar who was accustomed to verify his manuscripts and revise them without consideration of deadlines, but I managed to keep up with my task. I had written in Japanese the series on the questions Japanese ask me, but it took me more time to write Japanese than English, so I decided that the new series would have to be translated into Japanese. I was enormously helped by the translator, Kaneseki Hisao, whom I had known for thirty years and who had once taught my courses at Columbia while I was on sabbatical leave.

The title of the new series, *Hyakudai no Kakaku,* literally "travelers of a hundred generations," was taken from Bashō and meant to express the continuity of the diaries written over the centuries by Japanese, not only travelers (although many diaries did in fact describe travels) but people in many walks of life. The series was a success, and when the episodes were collected in book form, it sold surprisingly well. Later, while in New York, I had word that the book had won the prize for the best work of nonfiction of the year offered by the rival newspaper, the *Yomiuri Shimbun.* Later still, the book won the Shinchōsha Prize. I found it all but unbelievable that a book I had written in such haste and with so little agony should have been so honored, when the history, which has cost me so much effort, remained unsung.

A few years later I wrote another serial for the *Asahi,* a continuation of the earlier one, covering the period from 1860, the year that the Japanese sent their first mission to the United States, until about 1941, the year of the outbreak of the Pacific War. This volume seemed to me of even greater interest than the earlier one because the diaries, unlike the celebrated diaries I had treated before, were for the most part little known, and in a few cases had not previously been printed; but the sales were by no means as large, and the book was not a candidate for any literary prize. I clearly am not the best judge of my own writings.

The last *Asahi* serial, published in 1992, was devoted mainly to Japanese writers I had known. In 1964 I had served as one of the seven editors of the eighty-volume collection called *Nihon no Bungaku* (*The Literature of Japan*) published by Chūō Kōron Sha. I was the only survivor of the seven, who included Tanizaki Junichirō, Kawabata Yasunari, Ōoka Shōhei, and Mishima Yukio, and I thought that a time had come for me to write down my recollections. This serial was also a success. (Some of the present volume first appeared in the serial.)

But in June 1992 my retirement from the *Asahi* was celebrated. On this occasion, a counterpart of the one in New York, Nagai Michio and Shiba Ryōtarō again spoke with kindness and generosity about my work. Two such "recognition scenes" are surely an unusual phenomenon, made possible by my double life.

*****

Although my university career was officially at an end, I soon learned that I would be welcome to return on a part-time basis to supplement the teaching in Japanese literature. Indeed, if I so chose, I could go on leading exactly the same life as before retirement, but now that my history had been completed, I yearned to do something totally different. My first new book, published the year after I retired, was a translation of three plays by Abe Kōbō, whose death in January 1993 had been a great shock. I had planned to offer him this book as a token of my admiration for his work in the theater.

Most translators avoid plays. Dialogue always presents special problems, especially if the translator hopes to have his version performed. There may be difficulty also in finding a publisher, since plays rarely sell many copies. Only a translator like myself, fascinated by the theater since childhood, is likely to disregard these problems. I have had occasion, especially when a play I have translated was being considered for performance, to regret this devotion; but even the most frustrating experiences with theater people were not without interest.

My first venture, as I have described earlier, was in 1957 with Mishima's *Five Modern Nō Plays*. Hardly had my translation of the plays been published in New York than messages arrived from various producers expressing eagerness to stage the plays. Mishima was in New York at the time and remained about four months waiting for the plays to be staged. The producers he chose kept assuring him that they would unquestionably find the money, but the opening was delayed again and again. Mishima finally despaired of ever seeing his plays performed and left New York on New Year's Eve for Europe. I was unhappy to have been involved in a painful experience that would have been unimaginable for him in Japan. This first brush with the realities of the New York theater world would be typical of future contacts.

Two of Mishima's modern Nō plays were in fact eventually staged, though by different producers. The night of the opening there was a terrible snowstorm, and even though the review in *The New York Times* was favorable, the newspaper could not be delivered because of the snow, and almost no one knew the plays were being performed. Audiences were pitifully small.

Some years later, my translation of Mishima's *Madame de Sade* was scheduled for Broadway production with a well-known cast. I attended a reading of the parts at the house of the backer, a rich woman who enjoyed dabbling in the theatre. Arrangements were made for the costumes and even the wigs, but suddenly, for reasons that were never disclosed to me, the production was canceled.

I myself had an experience as a producer. In 1966, while writing a book on Nō, I met an actor of the Hōshō school named Homma Fusataka, who told me he was eager to perform Nō in America. He said that he and other young actors would travel on buses and sleep at the YMCA to save money. I was so impressed by his enthusiasm that I took his proposal to various producers in New York. They agreed that it would be impossible. One of them took me aside and, in avuncular tones, suggested that I meditate in my study until I perceived the folly of attempting to interest American audiences in a form of theater that even the Japanese found boring. But by this time I no longer believed anything a producer said, so I decided to arrange the tour myself. I wrote friends and friends of friends at various universities, about two hundred letters in all, and eventually secured agreements for thirty-six performances.

The tour of the Hōshō group was an unqualified success. Not only were the performances sold out but they were deeply appreciated, especially in the South, a part of the country foreign troupes rarely visited. The actors conscientiously performed a grueling schedule and, even though there were no contracts of any kind, every performance took place as scheduled and was paid for. Some members of the audience, it is true, walked out during the intermission, and the newspaper reviews were usually couched in the know-nothing tones of the barefoot boy from Manhattan who has never seen a Nō play and couldn't be expected to know what was going on. There were also, predictably, reviewers who could not resist making puns along the lines of "There's no business like Nō business"; but I remember even more the comment of a Dutch professor of Sanskrit who told me after the performance at Columbia that, having suffered as a prisoner of the Japanese in Java during the war, he had been reluctant to admit that anything Japanese could be worthy of praise, but he had changed his mind that night.

Such praise not only rewarded me for the trouble of arranging the tour but renewed my enthusiasm. It is for such recognition that not only playwrights and actors but even translators make the plunge into the crazy world of the theater.

In the years following these performances, American audiences from time to time had opportunities to see Nō. Perhaps the most memorable occasion was the series at the Metropolitan Museum of Art in the spring of 1993. The "theater," the space on three sides of the Temple of Dendur, was sold out, and the audience gazed at the stage with a rapt attention of a kind I have rarely seen even in Japan. The reviewer for the *Times,* no longer in the wise-cracking mood of his predecessors, concluded, "With the Kanze company in residence, time stands still and theater is transporting." It had taken twenty-seven years for this transformation in the American audiences and critics. I like to think that my efforts in 1966 had at last borne fruit.

In 1993, too, there were performances at the Brooklyn Academy of Music of Mishima's play *Madame de Sade* by a Swedish company directed by Ingmar Bergman. The play had had one matinee performance in New York at the Theatre de Lys, performed against a background of the scenery of the unrelated play that was to be performed the same night. The reviews were terrible, pointing to the implausibility of the dialogue Mishima had written and implying that such a play could not succeed with an American audience unless it actually presented the Marquis de Sade in pursuit of his notorious pleasures. The performances in Brooklyn, in large part because of an extraordinary review in *The New Yorker* of those in Stockholm, were completely sold out, and the effect of Mishima's play was little short of thrilling. Another transformation had occurred. I was glad that my translation of the play was made available through earphones for those who could not understand the Swedish spoken by the cast. And how happy Mishima would have been to receive the success he had hitherto been denied in New York!

These two theatrical events gave éclat to the New York season. At the same time, they suggested a great change had occurred in the appreciation of Japanese theater. The audiences and critics clearly felt that they were able to understand what was taking place on the stage, and they admitted that what they saw moved them as more familiar works did, by the beauty and strength of the texts and the performances. I felt not only pleased but gratified.

*****

In reviewing the events of the last twenty years of my life I detect a certain sameness. This does not mean that I have been bored or unhappy. I have been singularly fortunate in my friends and in the recognition that my work has been accorded. But I suppose that it is in the nature of things that when, for example, I visit Kyoto I do not feel the excitement or the compelling need I once experienced to tell others about this wonderful city. I recall, almost with disbelief, that ten years ago, when I visited Kyoto on the day of the Jidai Matsuri, a festival I always enjoy seeing, I was so far from eager to get a look at the procession of people dressed in the costumes of different centuries that I made a detour to avoid the crowds.

I wish more than anything else that I had kept a diary from the day of my first visit to Japan. It is ironic that now, thanks to the two serials I wrote for the *Asahi,* I am something of an expert on diaries but have none of my own. All I have by way of record are engagement books with the briefest of notations. I pick up one of these little books, the one for 1975. Most entries consist of nothing more than the name of someone I was to meet that day. Some of these people are dead now, others I have not heard from in twenty years. There are also the names of operas I saw in New York: *La Forza del Destino, Manon Lescaut, I Puritani.* These notations make me recall with pleasure that I have published in Japan three books of music criticism, though I am only an amateur music-lover.

The engagement book yields other information that I have almost forgotten. On May 13 Abe Kōbō arrived in New York. On the 15th I took him to see a writer he particularly admired, Philip Roth. I remember of the conversation only that both men revealed they had a photograph of Kafka on the wall of their study. On the 18th we attended a matinee of *Sizwe Banzi Is Dead,* the play about South Africa by Athol Fugard that moved us both. On the 21st we had dinner with Bernard Malamud, another American writer whom Abe admired. But what did we talk about? Was Abe satisfied with the meeting? Did he want to meet anyone else? Or, for that matter, what had brought Abe to New York in the first place? Diligent research might answer some of these questions, but how much of the last twenty years has disappeared forever!

It would not be difficult to fill pages with random recollections of Japanese writers or of travels in Japan and other countries. During the past few years I have become increasingly attracted to Italy, and I have lectured for a month at a time at the universities of Naples and Rome. I also remember with special pleasure the four lectures I gave in the autumn of 1990 at the Collège de France. These memories are precious to me, but unlikely to interest anyone else. There are also memories I do not wish to share, of experiences that are still too sad or too disagreeable or too happy for me to set down on paper; after all, I am not making a confession.

Perhaps the most notable feature of my last twenty years in Japan is that I feel that, in a real sense, I am now accepted. This may surprise people who have read the considerable body of writing in which the Japanese are portrayed as being suspicious of foreigners, reluctant to take them into their confidence, or difficult ever to know better than on first acquaintance.

The word *gaijin,* for foreigner (literally, "outsider"), is known even to people who know scarcely a dozen other words of Japanese because it encapsulates for them the gulf separating Japanese from all other nationalities. I do not wish to deny that the Japanese are acutely conscious of the differences between themselves and non-Japanese, but I cannot help mentioning that, although I am not a Japanese citizen, I was at one time a Japanese civil servant (*kokka kōmuin*), that I am now a member of as many scholarly and literary committees as I choose to join, and that I am a judge of one of the important literary prizes. I am frequently asked by magazines for manuscripts, more than I can possibly write, and I give lectures all over the country. Is this mere tokenism? Perhaps, but the process of "internationalization" must begin somewhere, at first with one individual, later (one hopes) with more. There are now several non-Japanese who are tenured professors of Japanese literature at Japanese universities, though this would have been inconceivable twenty years ago. I myself have taught Japanese literature to Japanese students, and they seemed ready and willing to consider and often to accept my views. I do not think I have ever "sold out" to the Japanese in the hopes of a reward or even merely of being liked; if I have made mistakes they were what my temperament dictated, not what I thought would bring me advantage.

This does not mean, of course, that passersby in the Tokyo streets recognize that I am, in a sense, one of them. Unless people are desperate—there being absolutely not one other person in sight—it would never occur to anyone to ask me for directions when once they have seen my face. Occasionally, even now, a child points me out to a friend and I hear the word *gaijin;* but compared to the past, when I was always an object of curiosity wherever I went, I seem to have succeeded by and large in fading into the Japanese landscape, and almost no one shows surprise or even awareness of my presence.

It used to be popular to compare the Japanese to other peoples. They were conservative like the British because they were also islanders; they were artistic like the French; they were methodical and efficient like the Germans; they were fond of gadgets like the Americans. It was less often considered in what ways they were most unlike these peoples. One respect in which they differ most conspicuously from Americans is their belief in the special nature of their culture. Americans tend to take it for granted that anyone in another country with even a modicum of education will speak English. They delight in discovering that American jazz or blue jeans or Kentucky Fried Chicken is popular abroad, taking it as evidence of the correctness of the view that sooner or later all other countries will become just like America (though they may deplore the readiness of foreigners to abandon their pretty native costumes). Many Japanese assume that foreigners will have absolutely no comprehension of their language. A foreigner who commands a hundred words of Japanese is likely to be told that he speaks the language better than a Japanese, a compliment that can hardly be meant seriously but indicates an appreciation of the foreigner's efforts. It is taken for granted that Japanese food is so special that foreigners are unable to eat it. (I am still regularly asked by taxi drivers in Tokyo if I eat sashimi.) And surely no Japanese believes that the whole world is likely one day to become just like Japan.

There are historical reasons for this divergency of attitudes. The American is heir to the conviction that Europeans all yearn to emigrate to America, and once in America desire nothing more than to be completely assimilated. The Japanese find it hard to believe that any foreigner will ever really settle in their country.

The changes have been enormous, but perhaps it is only natural that the non-Japanese should ask for even greater changes. They complain, for example, that they are so seldom invited to a Japanese home, blaming this on Japanese exclusiveness, and not taking into account that a foreigner in Paris is likely to be invited just as infrequently to a French home. They do not realize either how much less unusual it is now, than it was twenty or thirty years ago, for a Japanese to have close foreign friends. Tens of thousands of Japanese have studied abroad, and others have taken advantage of opportunities to make friends with people they meet in Japan or elsewhere. In some cases these friendships are stronger than those formed in Japan in childhood or at school, and some Japanese may even feel that their closest friends are not other Japanese but people who normally reside in distant parts of the world. For such Japanese the friends are not merely *gaijin* but have names and distinctive virtues and failings. They know that, despite the difference in nationality, these friends are worthy of affection, generosity, and respect.

Most Japanese, however, never develop such friendships. Some find the language barrier too great to surmount (and in this the foreigner in Japan is more to blame than the Japanese), others simply never have the opportunity to go beyond casual encounters. Many accept, at least unconsciously, that it is useless to try to make friends with foreigners; Japanese society as a whole tends to emphasize the ways in which foreigners and Japanese differ, rather than the possibilities of enriching one's life with friends from abroad, and novels depicting Japanese abroad almost always portray them as lonely and unable to penetrate the society in which they live.

Many Japanese assume that foreigners, even someone like me who has studied Japanese for fifty years, are unable to read their language. A few years ago I was a member of the jury which awarded a literary prize to the author of a work that described the effects on a group of schoolchildren of the explosion of the atomic bomb in Nagasaki. I later met the writer. First of all, she confessed that when she learned that I was a juror she thought her book had no chance of winning the prize. I inferred this meant that, as an American, I would have no sympathy with the victims of the bomb. This in itself was irritating, but she continued, "I suppose you read the book in translation." If she had thought a moment she would surely have realized that if every book that was a candidate for the prize had to be translated before I could read it, this would be a tremendous expense to the company offering the prize. But her ingrained belief in the inability of foreigners to learn Japanese blotted out the possibility that a particular foreigner might be different.

Recently, when I was interviewed by a Japanese news service in connection with my receiving a decoration, I mentioned this incident as an example of the paradox that I was honored for my study of Japanese literature going back half a century and at the same time had been treated as an illiterate by a highly intelligent woman. The article was printed in newspapers all over Japan, and perhaps it may help to shake some people into an awareness that even a foreigner can learn to read Japanese if he diligently applies himself to the task for fifty years.

But such minor irritations have never blinded me to my extraordinary good fortune in having devoted my life to the study of Japan. The study of the language itself was suited to my particular kind of mind, which delights in collecting obscure Chinese characters as once I delighted in collecting stamps. I have been happiest when I thought I had discovered some work not fully appreciated by the Japanese themselves, and as an enthusiast, I have not tried to keep my discovery to myself but to "publish" it. This trait was conducive to joining the academic profession, but also to establishing myself as a writer for the general public. I am glad that I had the chance to contribute to a basic understanding in the West of Japanese literature, and of Japanese culture in general, having begun my career as a Japanologist during the war, when Japanese culture was rejected in entirety or dismissed as mere imitation.

Sometimes I am asked, mainly by Japanese with masochistic leanings, whether anything in Japanese culture has contributed as much to the culture of the world as the plays of Shakespeare, the paintings of Rembrandt, the music of Beethoven, and so on. In one sense the answer is obviously no. Any fifteen-year-old in Japan would certainly be familiar with the three names I have given, but it would be a most unusual fifteen-year-old in any country of the West who could name even one Japanese writer, painter, or musician. But this is less a proof of the inferiority of the Japanese arts than of Western ignorance. I hope that my work has helped to dispel, even a little, this ignorance. I believe that it has, and I am grateful to the accidents of time, nationality, and natural inclinations that made this possible.

INDEX

Kawabata Yasunari, 141, 142–144, 144–
150, 197, 198–199, 244, 260–261,
277
Beauty and Sadness, 150
House of the Sleeping Beauties, The, 146
"Izu Dancer, The," 142
Lake, The, 146
Kawakami Tetsutarō, 227, 231, 232,
233–236
Keene, Donald
After the Banquet, 215–216, 239
Anthology of Japanese Literature, 139–
142, 150, 192–193, 252
Battles of Coxinga, The [*Kokusenya Kassen*], 86, 88, 106, 117, 122, 138
Blue-Eyed Tarōkaja, The [*Aoi Me no Tarōkaja*], 154, 181
at Cambridge University, 85, 95–97,
101–117, 121–125, 182–183, 186
Dawn to the West, 272
Essays in Idleness [*Tsurezuregusa*], 86,
189, 209, 239
Five Modern Nō Plays, 170–171, 201,
278
Friends [*Tomodachi*], 169, 239
in Kyoto, 131–139, 140, 150–152,
180–181, 183, 196–200, 210–213,
226, 281
in Navy Japanese Language School,
14–19
in postwar China, 57–68
in postwar Japan, 68–74
in Tokyo, 73, 74, 164–167, 226–228,
231
in World War II, 19–56
Japanese Discovery of Europe, The, 12, 83,
101, 117–118, 120, 122
*Japanese Literature: An Introduction for
Western Readers*, 126, 228, 229
Living Japan, 154
Madame de Sade, 201, 239, 278–279,
280–281
Seeds in the Heart, 272–273
Setting Sun, The [*Shayō*], 145–146, 189
Sources of Japanese Tradition, 125
student at Columbia University, 3–14,
79–87
teaching at Columbia University, 90,
182–183, 188–189, 191–192, 193,
208, 209–210, 266–268, 273–274

Twenty Plays of the Nō Theatre, 266
*World Within Walls: Japanese Literature of
the Pre-Modern Era (1600–1867)*,
268–271
writings for periodicals, 156–157, 172–
175, 189, 197, 231, 275–277
Kenkō, *Essays in Idleness* [*Tsurezuregusa*],
86, 125, 189, 209, 239
Kerouac, Jack, 194, 195
Kerr, George, 9
Kikuchi Kan Prize, 223–225
Kimura, Lieutenant, 48–49
Kinoshita Junji, 141, 165–166
Twilight Crane [*Yūzuru*], 165
Kipnis, Alexander, 112
Kissinger, Henry, 244
Kitano Temmangū, 162
Knopf, Inc., Alfred A., 170–171, 177,
188
Koe (magazine), 230–231
Kojiki, 116
Kokinshū, 103, 157
Konjaku Monogatari, 92
Kristeller, Paul, 267
Kutune Shirka, 115
Kyōgen, 151–152, 202, 211–212,
240–241
Kyoto, 131–136, 150–152, 156–162,
180–181, 183, 196–200, 210, 211–
213, 226, 281
Kyoto University, 136–139, 160

Lal, P., 219–220
Laughlin, James, 189
Lebanon, 220–221
Lehmann, Lotte, 112
Literature of Japan, The [*Nihon no Bungaku*],
277
los Angeles, Victoria de, 112

MacArthur, Douglas, 183
Madagascar, 241–242
Malamud, Bernard, 282
Mann, Thomas, 207
Manyōshū, 140
Matsukaze, 86
Matsuyama, 161
Mauritius, 242
McCarthy, Joseph, 182
McCarthy, Mary, 253–254